Your 24/7 Online Job Search Guide

LAMONT WOOD

John Wiley & Sons, Inc.

This book is printed on acid-free paper. ♾

Published by John Wiley & Sons, Inc., New York.
Published simultaneously in Canada.

Library of Congress Cataloging-in-Publication Data:

Wood, Lamont, 1953–
Your 24/7 online job search guide / Lamont Wood.
p. cm.
Includes index.
ISBN 0-471-12899-6 (pbk. : alk. paper)
1. Job hunting—Data processing. 2. Job hunting—Computer network resources.
3. Internet. I. Title: Twenty-four/seven job search guide. II. Title: Online job search guide.
III. Title.

HF5382.7 W656 2001
025.06'65014—dc21

2001046618

Printed in the United States of America.

10 9 8 7 6 5 4 3 2 1

To Louise

Contents

Introduction

Getting out and looking for a job used to be called "pounding the pavement."

Now, "pounding the keyboard" might be a more apt phrase. Using the Internet, you can magnify your job search efforts many times over, getting your name and resume in front of more people in an hour than you could have in a week using conventional paper-based methods. The difference between using the Internet and using paper is akin to the difference between driving a car and walking. Yes, you can still get to any destination on foot. But those who have adopted the new technology will get there before you.

When you, too, adopt the new job search technology, you'll find that hundreds of thousands of jobs are listed online at any one time. (Search results number as high as 3 million, but there is no way of knowing how much duplication is involved in such searches.) The numbers added daily are in the tens of thousands. Users report that job offers often begin arriving within a couple of days of starting their job searches.

And one other feature of online job searching may interest you: It's free. On almost all the myriads of Web sites devoted to connecting candidates with jobs, you can search for a job and post a resume for nothing. (Advertising a job opening may cost the employer something—but not always.) Of course, being online may cost something in terms of your hardware and Internet connection, but the incremental cost involved in searching for a job is exactly zero.

As for the people doing the hiring, current reliable figures are scarce, but ongoing trends indicate that the bulk of human resource (HR) departments today make extensive use of electronic recruitment techniques, usually involving the Internet and databanks of stored resumes. And the reason they have adopted this technology has nothing to do with its (undeniable) convenience for job seekers. Basically, they find that using the Internet is cheaper and faster.

Companies can spend $30,000 using a headhunter to fill a manager-level position or they can spend $4,000 advertising on various job sites. Their ads can appear on job sites in about the time it would take to line up a headhunter, not to mention the time the headhunter would take to launch a search. The turnaround time between posting a job and receiving resumes can be a matter of hours. Human resource departments that used to be happy if it took two weeks to present a list of prospects to a hiring manager now find themselves taking two days.

Advertising lower-level jobs through online job sites is reported to cost about 80 percent less than advertising in newspapers, and the reach is global. Posting jobs on Usenet (which also has a global reach) is free.

Because HR departments are increasingly online, you need to be online as well. The upshot is that searching for a job online is not science fiction. It's the norm in fields such as information technology and is widely accepted in other fields.

Of course, there is a downside:

- You'll hear from companies you would never have considered applying to. Sometimes, however, that means you'll get better job offers than you anticipated.
- You'll continue hearing from people for weeks after ending your job search (presumably after getting a job) because you have no way of telling all the people who looked at your resume that you are no longer available.
- You need to be careful about how much personal information you provide online.

If you can handle that, online job searching—and this book—may be for you. This book assumes a bare level of computer literacy—that you know a bit from a byte, a hard disk from a diskette, and so on. Beyond that, this book should provide enough information to get an Internet novice up and going. Nonbeginners may want to skip some of the exposition and can judge from the following outline:

- *Chapter 1: The Online Landscape.* This chapter looks at the features that make up the Internet—especially the Web, Usenet, mailing lists, and search engines—and how they can be used for job search purposes. It also looks at what hardware is needed. Internet veterans can probably skip this chapter.
- *Chapter 2: The Process.* This chapter examines the mechanics of the job search process as it is conducted online and shows how this book can help.
- *Chapter 3: The Danger of Identity Theft.* Everyone should read this chapter before beginning their job search; there are things worse than not getting a job.
- *Chapter 4: What Do You Want to Do?* Before beginning your job search—online or off-line—you need to answer some questions: What kind of job

do you want, what kind of job should you be looking for, and why? This chapter focuses on online methods of personal self-assessment.

- *Chapter 5: Writing Your Electronic Resume.* The whole concept of the resume has had to adapt and expand to meet the demands of the online world, and your personal resume will have to do likewise. This chapter shows you how.
- *Chapter 6: Leading Job Sites.* Specialized Web sites offer job-posting and resume-posting services (plus associated services, such as relocation). These sites are likely to be the foundation of the average online job search. This chapter examines the features of the leading examples.
- *Chapter 7: Sample Site.* Building on the previous chapters, this chapter leads you step by step through a specific site (Monster.com).
- *Chapter 8: Other Job Sites.* Many less well known job-related Web sites are devoted to specific industries or occupations. In addition, other sites list corporate "career-opportunity" sites. This chapter lists the leading examples.
- *Chapter 9: Using E-Mail.* Doing an online job search means that you'll be getting e-mail. The first part of this chapter lays out the mechanics of using e-mail; e-mail veterans can skip that part. The chapter then goes on to show how you can (in minutes) get your own private e-mail address that's safe from the boss's prying eyes.
- *Chapter 10: Using Usenet and Mailing Lists.* Closely related to e-mail are Usenet and mailing lists. This chapter shows how you can use these in your job search efforts—and perhaps more important, how you should not use them.
- *Chapter 11: Job-Related Newsgroups.* Usenet is a dauntingly huge landscape. This chapter points out places to start.
- *Chapter 12: Corporate-Information Sites.* With responses coming in from all over the Internet, you may want to check out a company before acting further. This chapter shows you how to start.
- *Chapter 13: What Comes Next?* Once you get the nibble, you have to go in for an interview with live people—and your online job search will have done nothing to prepare you for that. This chapter will try.

Finally, I've included a Glossary to help you wade through the torrent of technical terms.

Good luck, and good hunting.

CHAPTER 1

The Online Landscape

Everything that happens online is called "cyberspace." This chapter provides an overview of those parts of cyberspace that you can expect to use in the process of finding a job online. The components of the Internet that concern such a search include the following:

- The World Wide Web.
- E-mail.
- Usenet.
- Search engines.
- Mailing lists.

In addition, you will need certain things to make use of the Internet:

- *Requirements for getting online.* The computer, telecommunications connection, software, and so on.
- *Other things you will need.* Word-processor software, a printer, and so on.
- *Things you don't need.* Some high-tech toys are not necessary.
- *Overhyped nonsense.* Don't waste your money on this stuff.
- *Getting to know your browser.* It's your window to the Web and the thing you will be using most.
- *Under the hood.* You need a basic understanding of how your browser works.

As for computer literacy, you should know the difference between hardware and software, what a file and a processor is, and so on. If a term is unfamiliar to you, the Glossary may be of help.

This Internet Thing

It's the same with the Internet as with a car: You need to have a basic understanding of what is going on under the hood so you'll know that it's not magic, so you'll know what performance to reasonably expect, and so you won't be helpless in the face of the slightest problem.

The Internet is a vast network of computers that use the same networking protocol (i.e., method of accessing each other and exchanging files). The U.S. military developed this protocol, usually just called the Internet protocol (IP), to create networks that could continue operating in the face of random damage. With IP, transmitted files are broken into "packets," each of which may follow a different path to the recipient computer, which reassembles the packets into the original file.

It was discovered that such networks could continue to function in the face of random, unsupervised growth, a growth that is continuing at an astonishing clip. Today, the Internet consists of millions of interconnected computers, called hosts, mostly maintained by firms called Internet service providers (ISPs). The contents of those hosts—the files—are put there and maintained by the individuals and organizations who rent space on those hosts for their files. Some of these files are Web sites that offer lists of available jobs and help you circulate your resume, as explained in Chapter 6. Other hosts are maintained by corporations, universities, and even individuals who have connected their computer systems to the Internet.

As well as providing Internet presence, ISPs also typically offer Internet access via subscription arrangements, which is how home users typically access the Internet. The other organizations with Internet servers also typically arrange for their employees or members to have Internet access.

Once you have access to the Internet, it looks the same no matter how you got on, be it through an ISP or other organization. (Services like AOL offer content over and above what is on the Internet but still provide regular Internet access.)

The files residing on the servers are put there (through a process called uploading) through the Internet itself from the desktop computers of people who have Internet access. With proper password access, anyone with Internet access can load a file to any server. They can also retrieve a file from nearly any server (through a process called downloading). With modern software, no particular expertise is required to do this. When done abusively to alter files, the result is called "hacking." Physically, the servers usually remain in locked closets, untouched except for maintenance.

Residing on those servers are well over a billion files that anyone can access as long as they can get on the Internet. The exact number is unimportant—basically, it is growing faster than any one person can explore, making the Internet effectively infinite.

For job-finding purposes, only a subset (albeit a large subset) of the Internet is of interest. It's called the World Wide Web. (The rest, based on older software technology, is still largely accessible through World Wide Web software.)

The World Wide Web

The World Wide Web, or the Web, as it is commonly called, consists of Internet servers that use an addition to IP called HTTP (hypertext transport protocol) to send files to desktop computers. Those desktop computers need to be running special software called browsers. The original idea of the browser was to use "hypertext" to make Internet navigation easier: An Internet address would be linked to text, as if hidden in a layer under it, and invoking that text would cause the software to access the Internet address. Later, a graphical interface was added, so that one could invoke the text by clicking on it with the mouse cursor. With the arrival of a graphical interface, the addition of formatted text and graphics quickly followed.

Further developments will certainly occur, but the operation of the Web today consists of HTTP servers sending files to desktop computers running browser software, for display on the screens of those desktop computers. The files are sent primarily in hypertext markup language (HTML) format. What you see on the screen after going to a Web address is called a "Web page," such as the example shown in Figure 1.1. Each page consists of an HTML file, plus other files that are linked to the HTML file. Usually, the text you see on the page is part of the HTML file, and the graphics and other elements on the page come from separate files, whose transmission to the browser were triggered by commands embedded in the HTML file. (They do not have to be on the same server as the HTML file.)

A short explanation of how a Web page is created appears in the "Under the Hood" section later in this chapter. A big-picture overview of what the Web offers includes the following:

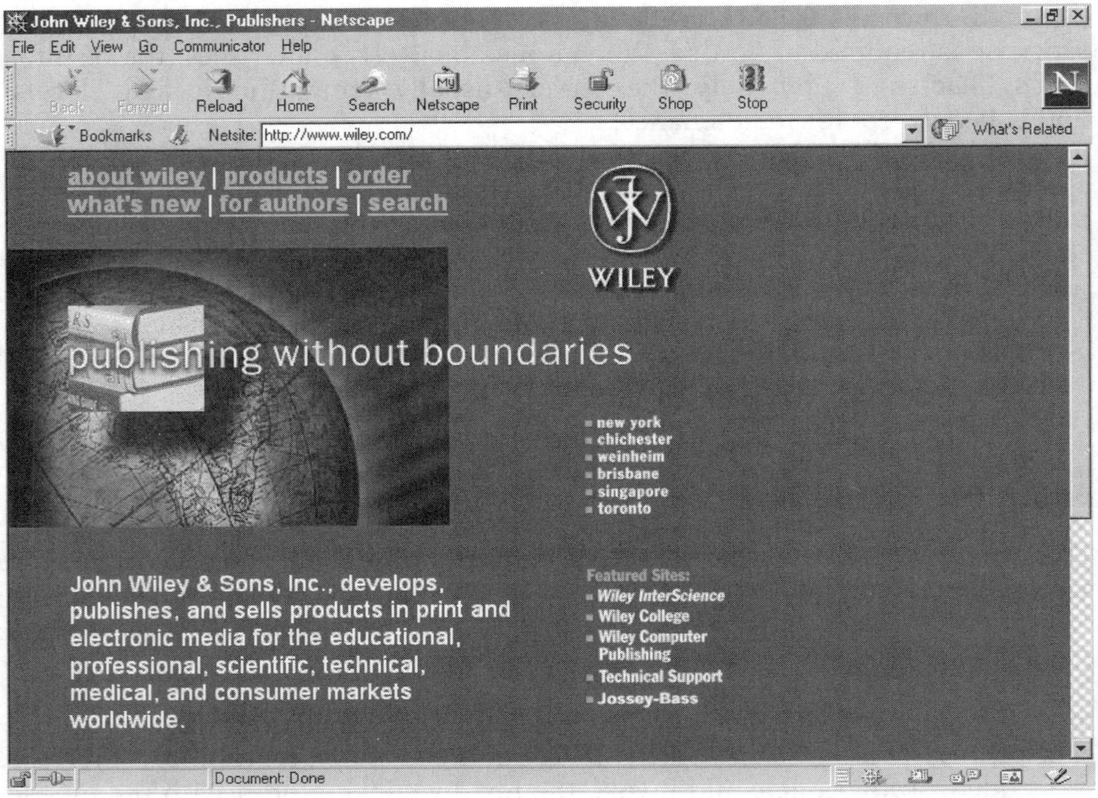

Figure 1.1 *Web page displayed by a browser, with a formatted combination of text and graphics. (Screenshot from John Wiley & Sons Inc.'s World Wide Web Site. Copyright © 2001 John Wiley & Sons, Inc. Reprinted with permission.)*

- *Formatted text.* The author can, within limits, control the on-screen positioning of the text, as well as its font, color, and face (i.e., regular, bold, or italic). HTML uses predefined "header" styles for titles and headlines. Alternatively, one can create these styles out of graphics. The author can place text within tables or can use the table feature to create multiple columns of text. Using the "frames" facility, one HTML file can display the contents of other HTML files within a framed section of the screen. This technique is often used to anchor an index along the top or side of the screen.
- *Graphics.* Pictures displayed as part of an HTML page typically exist as separate graphics files and are sent by the server in response to embedded commands in the HTML file. (Occasionally the pictures are embedded inside the HTML file itself.) Pictures can have "invisible colors" so that the

edges bleed seamlessly into the background of the page. The background of the page can be a solid color set by the HTML file or can be a special file loaded for that purpose.

- *Animations.* Little animations that repeat themselves over and over (often to the point of annoyance) are actually graphic files with multiple layers of material. The file is transmitted once, like any other graphics file, except that the browser sees the layers and displays one layer after another until it gets to the bottom. Optionally it then repeats forever. There is no sound.
- *Hyperlinks.* Any of the previous elements can be linked to another Web file so that the linked file is loaded when the hyperlinked element is invoked, usually by clicking on it with the mouse cursor. Hyperlinked material is usually highlighted—text with a colored underscore and graphics with a colored frame—but the author has the option to remove the highlights. Additionally, a graphic can contain areas with hyperlinks attached to it, as with regional material linked to a map. Hyperlinked portions of a map will only be evident as the cursor changes shape as it moves over the linked areas.
- *Input forms.* HTML lets you turn part of a page into an input form, with text windows, radio buttons, and list boxes. This feature is heavily used by job sites on the Web, as shown in Chapter 7.
- *Documents.* Sometimes you will find yourself linked to a file that turns out to be something other than an HTML file. The most popular alternative to HTML in the corporate world is the Adobe Acrobat format. (It is also called portable document format [PDF] after the file suffix it uses.) Acrobat is popular because it gives you a screen image that is basically identical to the printed page. Optionally, you can print it out. Software for reading Acrobat files is available free at www.adobe.com. Your browser may have the Acrobat reader already installed. Otherwise, you will need to save the Acrobat file to disk and then load and use the Acrobat reader program to view the file. Other common file formats include Microsoft Word and PowerPoint, as well as plain text.
- *Programs.* Small programs, called applets, can be attached to a Web page and are especially common on game sites. The program runs entirely on your computer but may access further data on the server.
- *Streaming media.* Audio and video files can be sent to your browser, which plays it as it comes in. (The alternative is to save the entire file and then play it later, but video files can be huge.) The browser may need to call up a separate program to play the file, such as RealPlayer or Windows Media Player.
- *Background sounds.* Short songs or sound effects are sometimes loaded with a Web page, to be played in the background while the page is on the screen.

- *Cookies.* A cookie is just a line in a special text file on your computer that the server tells the browser to put there when you visit a site, to in essence mark you. With a cookie, the server can know what you just did and therefore can offer you the next step in a process (such as moving from shopping to checkout on an e-commerce site). Some people object to this crack in their anonymity. The cookie process remains invisible to you unless you tell the browser to question them.

E-Mail

If you have Internet access, you can also have e-mail access. If you are using the Internet through an account with an ISP, the ISP should also be supplying you with an e-mail address. If you are using the Web from work, you will want to get a private e-mail account, as explained in Chapter 9. Any time you have Web access, you should be able to get to your e-mail, no matter where it is hosted, just as you should be able to get to the entire Web any time you are on the Web.

E-mail is a powerful tool: Messages that you write on your computer appear on the recipient's screen. Electronic documents, spreadsheets, presentations, and the like can be attached to an e-mail message and shared across vast distances.

But with power comes danger, and just because you can do something does not mean you should do it. Chapter 9 takes a closer look at e-mail and its use as a job search tool.

Usenet

Usenets are called bulletin boards, conferences, forums, or discussion groups. A useful analogy is the corkboard near the door of your local supermarket, where people pin up notes, offering things for sale. Imagine that the board is divided into sections, with each section devoted to a topic. Then, imagine that anyone who read a message could in turn post a reply on the board. Some sections of the board are used purely for posting comments, and comments on comments, finally resulting in a never-ending group conversation, carried out in text, outside of real time.

Many Web sites and services host their own separate set of discussion forums, but an umbrella system exists for the entire Internet, called Usenet.

Each topical section is called a newsgroup, and the number of newsgroups in circulation approaches a hundred thousand, in many different languages and character sets. Anything posted in a particular newsgroup on any server that carries that newsgroup will be propagated cross the Internet and be available to anyone on any server that carries that newsgroup.

Some newsgroups carry job postings (as well as corporate and industrial gossip). Depending on your field, and the region in which you live, Usenet can be an effective job search tool. Or it can be irrelevant, if your field has no significant online presence. Chapter 10 takes a closer look at Usenet and what you can do with it.

Search Engines

Although search engines are powerful tools, their use in a job search is limited. To understand their limitations, you have to understand how they work.

To use a search engine, you go to its Web site and input a word or phrase to search, as shown in Figure 1.2. It returns with a list of sites, as shown in Figure 1.3. Each entry of the list contains a hyperlink, on which you can click to go to that site. When you get there, you may find that it is exactly what you want. Or you may find it is something with no applicability at all, except that the words you input appear somewhere on the page. In fact, one search is rarely enough; typically, you need to keep refining your search terms until you receive a list of results that is both short and applicable.

There are two kinds of search engines: those with human beings who categorize the sites and those that rely on robots. For the first type, people actually look at each site. If a site is all about knives, they may file it under "cutlery" even though the word *cutlery* does not appear anywhere on the site. With the second type, the site automatically goes to every site on the Web that it can find, downloads the material that it finds there, and indexes the contents. Both approaches have problems.

With the human-controlled approach, the site typically has to be registered by someone and then categorized by someone else. Not every site gets registered, and not every categorization is correct. Once listed on the search engine site, the listing does not change until someone reregisters it. So what you get is not an index of the Web's contents but a catalog of Web sites, some of which is guaranteed to be obsolete.

With the robot sites, you might think you would have an index to the entire Web at your fingertips. But there is a practical limit to how often each Web site can be visited. A new file may take a month to show up. Material that is part of an on-screen graphic is invisible to the robot, which only sees text. Material that

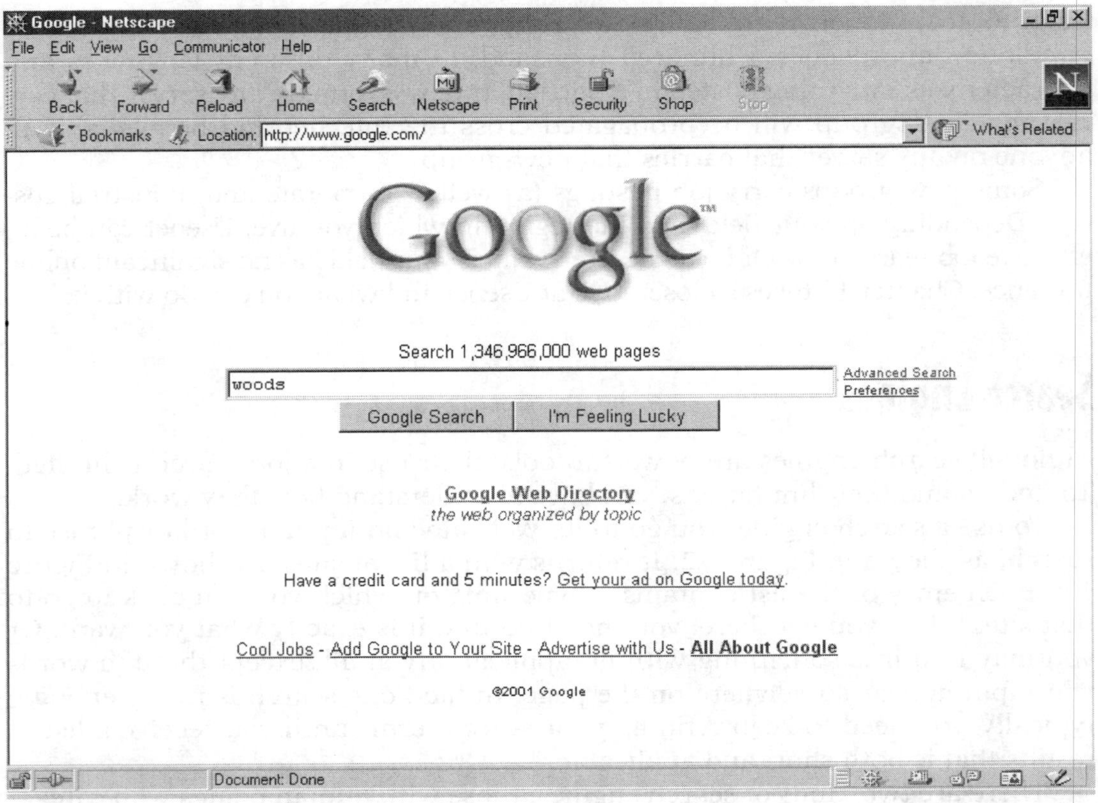

Figure 1.2 *Web page of a search engine, in this case, www.google.com. The user types one or more words to be searched for (*woods *in this case) into the input field and then presses the Enter key. (Reprinted from www.google.com, by permission of Google, Inc.)*

is part of a database file is also invisible. Material in other non-HTML formats may or may not be indexed. E-mail and Usenet are not searched.

But most especially, searches on robot sites can give results that are far off the mark. If you were to search for the word *woods,* you would get pages of results concerning lumber, forestry, hiking, mapping, shipbuilding, furniture making, whittling, people named Woods, and the Woods Hole Oceanographic Institution, not to mention William Woods University, as evident in Figure 1.3.

This problem can be addressed, with varying luck, by using advanced-search facilities, as shown in Figure 1.4. All the leading sites have advanced search facilities, although you may have to examine the fine print for them. They should allow you to search for phrases and perhaps exclude certain terms (e.g., "woods not forestry").

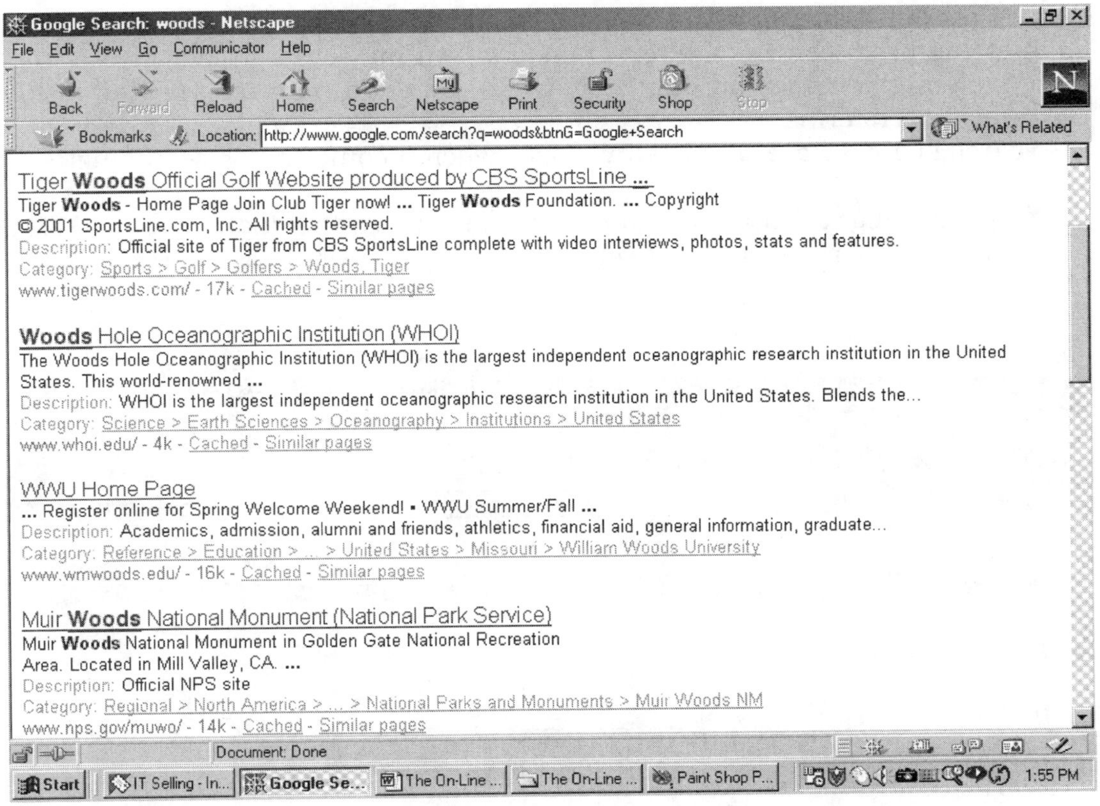

Figure 1.3 *First page of the results of the search depicted in Figure 1.2. The first line of each citation is underlined and hyperlinked to the actual Web page. Notice the wide range of topics. (The search produced more than three million hits.) (Reprinted from www.google.com, with permission of Google, Inc.)*

An advanced search may still give you a list of hits scores of pages long. To aid in your search, search engines use various rules to rank the lists by relevancy so that the hits at the top of the list will be the ones most likely to be useful to you. Of course, the search engine is still guessing, and you can only hope that the rules it uses are as good as the search engine's promoters say they are.

Search-engine rules, for example, consider whether the word is near the top of the site's page, how many times it is repeated (within reason), and how many other sites link to that page. In addition, HTML includes a "meta-tag" facility whereby Webmasters can embed key words in a Web page that will be read by the search engine but invisible to the person reading the page with a browser. A given search engine may or may not give any weight to the meta tags.

The result is that an identical search run on two different robot-based search engines can produce wildly different results. You may even get negative results with one search engine and immediately get what you want on a second, using the same search terms.

Search engines have serious drawbacks when it comes to job searching:

- Job postings are usually embodied in databases rather than separate HTML files and therefore are not likely to be found by a robot-based search engine.

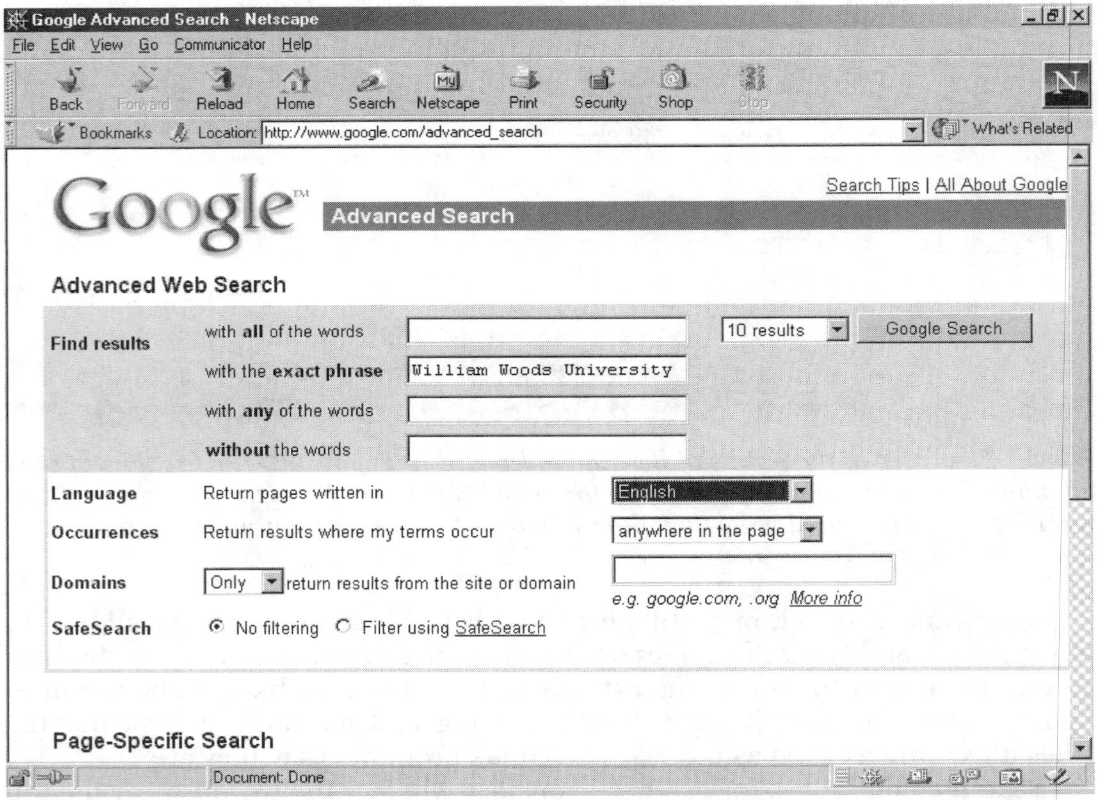

Figure 1.4 *Example of an advanced-search facility of a search engine. The user can use phrases instead of words, exclude words, exclude domains, and limit the languages of the pages to be searched, among other things. This search produced less than four thousand hits—an improvement over the search shown in Figure 1.2—but it still indicates a need for further search refinement. (Reprinted from www.google.com, by permission of Google, Inc.)*

- If a robot-based search engine did find a job posting, the information would probably be obsolete.
- The human-based search engines, meanwhile, do not contain that level of detail about the site contents.
- Search engines rarely include the contents of Usenet, which can be a rich vein of material.

The noncoverage of Usenet is an especially big problem. Searching for a job through Usenet is really not practical without the use of a search engine, as explained in Chapter 10.

Nonetheless, search engines can be astonishingly powerful for getting background material, for finding an address, phone number, the spelling of a name, and so on. The search-engine landscape undergoes constant change, but the following are the leading members at this writing:

http://www.yahoo.com

Yahoo! is the prime example of a human-based search engine. It does have a way to search for exact phrases, but only in the text of its database of site categorizations. If it finds nothing, it hands the search over to Google.com.

http://www.google.com

Google.com, a robot-based site, is reputed to have the largest index of any search engine. Its advanced-search facilities allow you to find phrases as well as words. It is also the only search engine left that attempts to do anything with Usenet, as described in Chapter 10.

http://www.alltheweb.com

The robot-based site Alltheweb.com is reputed to run a close second to Google.com in terms of breadth and speed. It, too, has advanced-search facilities to find phrases as well as words.

http://www.altavista.com

Formerly one of the leading search engines, Altavista.com, a robot-based site, has fallen behind Google.com and Alltheweb.com in popularity. The advanced-search feature allows "Boolean" commands, meaning you can use multiple keys separated by "and," "or," and "not."

http://www.northernlight.com

Northernlight.com specializes in indexing online publications. Its advanced-search feature lets you search by title, publication, topic, and source. It also searches the Web. It will try to categorize the hits by topic.

Mailing Lists

Mailing lists (also called mail lists or list serves) are a cross between e-mail and Usenet. As with Usenet, participants post statements and comments. However, everything takes place via e-mail. Instead of posting your comments on a newsgroup, you send them to a particular e-mail address, from which your contribution is remailed to everyone on the list. (In some cases, the contributions are aggregated and edited by a moderator.) Many professional groups use mailing lists to foster discussion. If there is one in your field, you should find out how to join. (Some professional lists may even have a coordinator, who will require you to present your credentials.) If you do join a mailing list, you do not have to contribute anything—you can just follow along and read what the hot topics of the day are and who is saying what about them.

If you have not heard of any mailing list in your field, the Internet has archives of lists that you can search, as discussed in Chapter 10.

Requirements for Getting Online

To make use of the Web, you need these basic things:

- A desktop computer suitable for the purpose.
- Telecommunications to get from your computer to the ISP.
- Browser software to run on that computer.
- An Internet access account with an ISP.

The following sections discuss these items in detail.

Suitable Computer

In the corporate world, the terms *desktop computer* and *PC* (personal computer) are synonymous. A PC is a machine using Microsoft Windows, running either an

Intel processor from the Pentium dynasty or a third-party clone processor. If you intend to communicate with the corporate world, that is what you should be running, too. Yes, they may have Macintoshes in the graphics departments, Linux machines running the intranet server, and Palms in the pockets of traveling sales reps that use the Palm operating system. You may also find Sun Solaris machines running the Web server and a Unix machine to store customer files. Each platform has its passionate proponents, and if you don't adopt their favorite they will act like you insulted their family.

But the PC is the tool of management, and management is what you want to deal with in your job search. If you use another platform, you run the risk of running into walls. You may get documents you can't immediately open. You may receive demo or presentation programs you can't run. You may need to access Web sites that require a browser version you don't have on hand. A guru for an alternate platform may be able to address every problem that arises, but you may not. And you have a job to do. So the most realistic advice is to get a PC (or have access to one).

Fortunately, it is difficult to go into a computer store these days and buy a PC that is not suitable for the Internet. Not only is the speed of off-the-shelf computers more than enough for Internet use, but pundits note that most office software has no use for the additional speed of anything that came after the 366 megahertz Pentium II. If, however, you plan to rely on something you found in a closet corner, you may need luck. If it has Windows 95 on it, you can probably get going, but you can't rely on getting software for earlier versions of Windows.

The other main variable is memory. Treat 32 megabytes of RAM (random access memory) as the bare minimum for a PC. As for the hard disk, you're probably fine with anything over a gigabyte of capacity, and these days companies don't sell less than 10 gigabytes. (There were days when *Fortune* 500 companies have been run with less than a gigabyte of computer storage.)

If you are using a Palm, do not count on it for your job searching; little or none of the material that you'll need to access will be in the format that these machines use.

Telecommunications

Your computer must be connected to the outside world. Fortunately, it is virtually impossible these days to buy a PC that does not come with the 56K modem (meaning 56,000 bits per second). That will suffice. All you then need is a phone cord with a "male" jack at both ends to connect the phone port on your computer to the wall phone jack. Such cords usually come with the computer, but you may want one longer than the six-foot cord typically included. Hardware stores sell them in nearly any length you want. (If your wall jack uses an older four-prong plug, you will need to get an adapter. Those, too, are sold in hardware stores.)

You will need to input certain software settings before you get going, including the phone number of the ISP, your user name, and your password. Your ISP should provide all the instructions you need. Once triggered, the software will dial the modem. You should be able to hear it happening. When the ISP answers, your modem and the ISP's modem will engage in "handshaking," which sounds like two harmonicas trying to get in tune. (They're determining what transmission speed works best.) Once handshaking is finished, silence falls, and you are online. Then you can load your browser (or flip over to it if it's already loaded). The browser will see that the computer is online, and you can immediately begin using it.

A 56K modem will never actually reach a transmission rate of 56,000 bits per second, that being a theoretical number. You should actually be happy if the rate gets above 40,000 bits per second. In any event, the data rate will vary during the course of an online session as the modem reacts to variations in line noise. You will have reliable information on the data rate only during long downloads.

On any but the worst days, a 56K modem should provide enough speed for job-finding purposes because you will be dealing with predominately text Web pages, rather than massive downloads. An older 28.8K modem may even be fast enough.

A bigger problem may be the annoyance of having the computer tying up your phone line. People who make serious use of computers from their homes or small offices often end up getting a second line for the computer. You won't want or need caller ID or call waiting or any other extras for the second (computer) line, making it surprisingly inexpensive. You also may not need any rewiring, if your house is wired with four-wire phone cord, because your phone only needs two of those wires. The other two are spares and can be used for the second phone line. You can get a new telephone wall jack at an electronics store with two ports in it. You connect one port to the red and green wires (the standard colors for phone lines). Use that one for the original phone line. Then you connect the second port to the other two lines (probably yellow and black) and use that one for the computer. (The phone company will still have to turn on the second line at your junction box.)

That said, if you can get broadband, you should, because it opens up a whole new world. Broadband usually refers to either DSL (digital subscriber line) or cable modems. (Both terms are described in the Glossary.) Typically, with broadband the phone company or the cable television company becomes your ISP. Transmission speeds from the Internet to your computer can be in the megabits. Pictures pop onto the screen instead of unrolling like cranky window blinds. Video becomes practical. Downloading a new version of your browser software, for instance, becomes a chore measured in minutes instead of an all-afternoon ordeal. The transmission rate from your computer to the Internet is slower than the reception rate, but the speed is still fast enough to make the sending of large e-mail attachments a trivial task.

The DSL or cable modem is a stand-alone device that is typically connected to your computer via an ethernet port. Ethernet is the de facto local networking standard for corporate offices, handling speeds of up to a hundred million bits per second and using "collision detection" to make the computers on the network take turns transmitting.

Computers sold to the consumer market usually lack ethernet ports. Fortunately, you can get ethernet cards in computer stores that cost less than most computer games. You will have to install the card in your computer by yourself; the hardest part may be getting the cover off the computer case—check the documentation. The cable, while not cripplingly expensive, may cost more than the card. The card should come with the necessary software, which you can configure in minutes.

Once you are running broadband, you are always online. Getting on the Web is a matter of flipping over to the browser. In a pinch, you should still be able to use your dial-up modem.

A Browser

A computer that is hooked to the phone line (or a broadband line) is still not on the Internet—you need a browser to display whatever comes in. Microsoft Windows comes with Internet Explorer, which will do everything you need. The major alternative is Netscape Navigator, which you can download free at www.netscape.com if it is not already on your computer. Rarely will you notice any difference in the results they give you.

Whichever browser you use, try to get the latest version. Certain features that are now in common use on the Web, such as frames, are not supported by early browser versions.

An ISP

You have probably been deluged with ads by firms offering Internet access. Pick one. Or look in the Yellow Pages. Just remember, you need only the minimum service for Internet access. You don't need a Web site, more e-mail addresses, static IP addresses, your own private domain name, or other extras.

For a dial-up ISP, you should be able to get set up with a phone call. The ISP will give you the instructions, and you give them your credit card number. For broadband, a technician may have to come out to install the service, especially for a cable modem.

Other Things You Will Need

To make full use of the Internet, you may need to have, or have access to, some peripheral items, including the following:

- Word processor.
- Computer printer.
- Fax machine.
- Phone.

Word Processor

You will need a word processor that can also generate text files. You will want the text files for e-mail purposes, and you will want the word processor to produce nicely formatted letters and resumes. You can output the latter on a printer or send them electronically as files attached to e-mail messages. You will also want it to have a spell checker; having misspelled words on your resume or letter can mean disaster. Fortunately, any word processor you encounter these days can handle those chores.

The difference between text files and word-processing files is extremely important. With a word processor, you can get the kind of formatting and layout shown in Figure 1.5. A generation ago, you would have needed a staff of typesetters and layout artists to get that result.

Text files consist only of the characters you can generate by pushing a single key on the keyboard. There is no facility for boldfacing, italicizing, underlining, or font changes. All you have left is what is shown in Figure 1.6. It includes no margin or tab settings—anything like that has to be done manually by inserting spaces. But the limitations of text offer a huge advantage—you can always find some software that will display it.

With a modern word processor, you can do almost anything you want to with the text. You can format your resume to look like a newspaper, a newsletter, a medieval illustrated manuscript, a ransom note, a magazine, a book, a brochure, or anything else that will fit on a page. Then you can print it out and admire it. If you dare, you can put your creation in an envelope and mail it to someone else. But if you want to send it electronically, your efforts are wasted unless the recipient has the same word-processing software as you do. (Often, however, "reader" software is available online that will let the recipient read the file without needing to own the whole word processor.)

In addition, Word Processor X may state that it can load the files of Word Processor Y, but you may find that it cuts corners when it comes to displaying the fancier formatting features. So even if the recipient's word processor can load the file you sent, you cannot be sure that what the recipient will see on the screen or on the printout will be absolutely true to the original. People run into problems even with different versions of the same word processor. The upshot is that spending a lot of effort into formatting your resume or cover letters may be a mistake because it can be wasted if you have to change media.

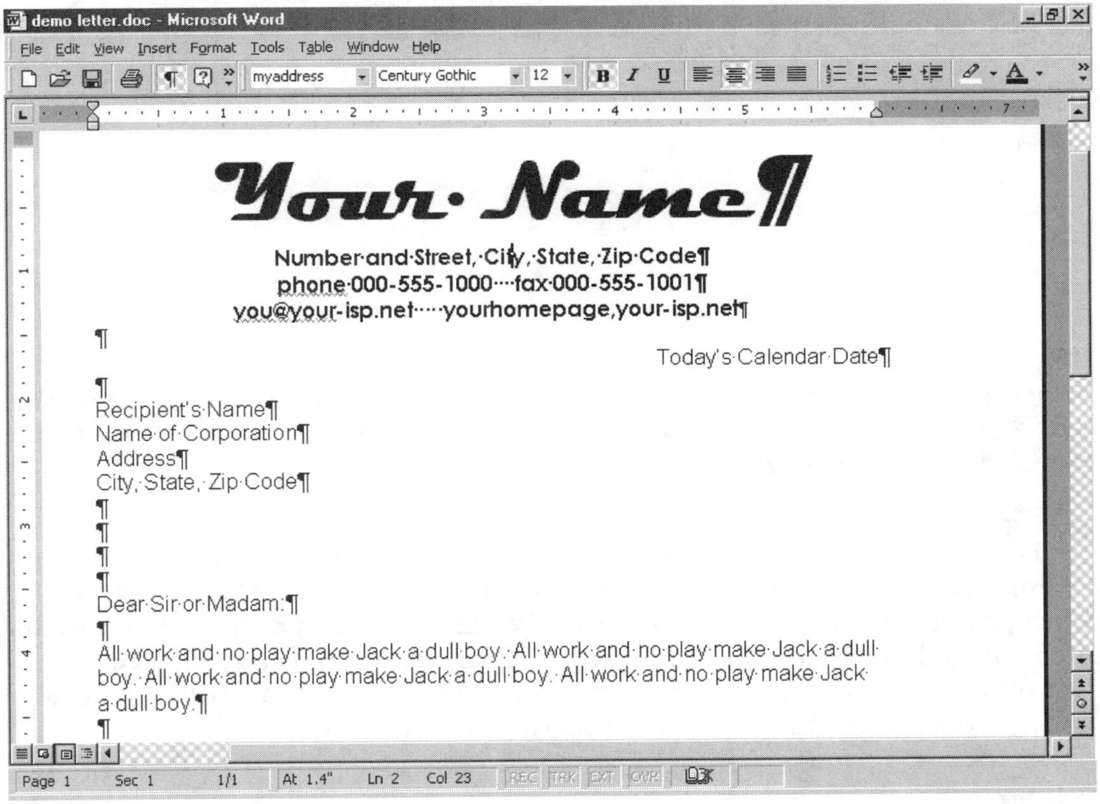

Figure 1.5 *With a modern word processor, you can create effects that you once would have needed to go to a print shop to get, such as your own letterhead. But such effects may not survive when the text is used to create an electronic document.*

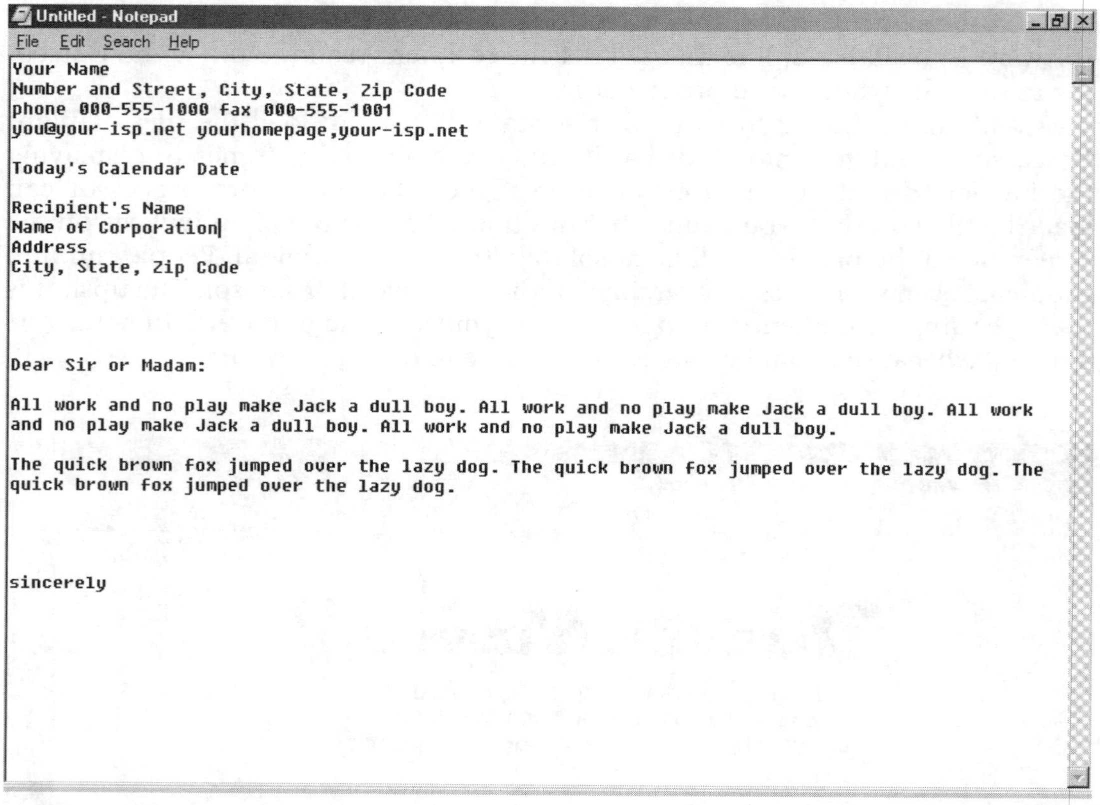

Figure 1.6 *When the material in Figure 1.5 is pasted into a simpler word processor, none of the special effects come with it. Something is likely to be lost any time you copy material from a word processor to another program.*

The standard word processor among corporations is Microsoft Word, whereas parts of the government have remained loyal to Corel WordPerfect. The word processor that is part of Microsoft Works (an office package often distributed with Windows) will read versions of both and also has a spell checker and will output material in the plain text format. The Windows WordPad accessory will also open Word files but does not have a spell checker.

Printer

Computerized as everyone is, situations will still arise when you need to put things on paper. If you do not already have access to a printer, you will be heartened to know that you can get good office printers for surprisingly little money. Some have scanners built in and can be used as fax machines and convenience copiers. Otherwise, they fall into two categories:

- *Ink-jet printers.* These printers squirt tiny drops of ink onto the page from a printhead that shuttles back and forth.
- *Laser printers.* A heated roller bakes fine dry powder (instead of ink) onto the page in a manner similar to that used in most photocopy machines. The laser illuminates (and thus electrostatically activates) those spots on the roller that need to pick up the ink—the laser itself does not actually touch the page.

Either type will do fine. A resolution of 200 dots per inch (dpi) is considered sufficient for correspondence that does not include graphics. Ink-jet printers typically have better than 300 dpi, and laser printers these days start at 600 dpi. So resolution is not a problem. Ink-jet printers are usually slower than laser printers and use more ink. But that will not be an issue unless you are churning out reams of material. Ink-jet printers offer color printing even at low price points, whereas you pay a hefty premium for color on a laser printer. But color (while nice to have at times) is hardly a requirement for business correspondence.

The latest printers use USB (universal serial bus) ports, which are superior to the parallel ports that used to be common for printer connections. But an older PC may not have a USB port.

Although printers are cheap, they still cost money that you may not have. Fortunately, most copy shops and mailbox outlets also offer printing services and will output your files for you. The price may be little different than that of photocopying. Also, they can bind documents for you, something you would have trouble doing at home. You can usually upload the files over the Internet. Find a shop convenient to you and see what they offer.

Fax Machine

As with printers, there will be situations in which you need a fax machine. Although e-mail has taken over some of the roles formerly filled by fax machines, faxing is still the preferred medium in some quarters, if only out of security concerns. (It is immune to viruses.) If you bought a printer-fax machine, you are in good shape. Get a two-port phone extension line, add it to the same line that you plugged the computer into, and you're in business.

Otherwise, you should find out what faxing services your local copy shop offers and keep their fax number handy. Whenever someone asks for your fax number, give out the copy shop's number. Don't worry; this won't brand you as a gypsy. Ask the copy shop to call you when your fax comes in, and also ask the sender to include a cover page with your name and phone number. Likewise, when you need to fax something, just take it over to the copy shop. Yes, they will charge by the page, but unless you are sending a book manuscript, it will still be cheaper than buying your own fax machine.

In addition, the modem in any of today's PCs includes fax circuitry, giving you the option of "printing" a file to a fax number. Although this is a neat trick, you may find yourself using the copy shop anyway. If you fax a piece of paper, you know what the fax is going to look like, whereas there is always nagging doubt when a faxing a file. More important, you can sign the piece of paper.

Of course, a true fanatic can scan in a signature and paste that into the document before faxing. But that leaves unsolved the problem of receiving faxes. You'll have to leave the PC on and its phone line free all day and night. Fortunately, you can still perform other tasks in the foreground.

Phone

Of course, you need a telephone. But you may not feel comfortable about the idea of taking calls about your job search at your current job, using your current employer's office phone. These days, you can handle the problem by getting a cell phone that fits in your pocket, and using its number for your job search process.

If you are worried about being overheard when talking on your cell phone, tell the caller that you will need to call him or her back. Then step away to a place where you won't be overheard, and continue with your conversation. (Your parked car can make a fine phone booth.)

Things You Don't Need

The Internet has a separate chat facility, called Internet relay chat (IRC). Anyone can have a text-based conversation with anyone else who is on IRC at the time and has joined the right "channel." There is no evidence that it has any place in the job search process.

Wireless modems are nice for e-mail for traveling salesmen but are too slow for intensive Web use. The so-called third-generation digital wireless technology may change that, when it does arrive. Meanwhile, if you are on the road, plan to get to your hotel room and plug into a landline before going Web surfing.

And that assumes the use of a laptop. As mentioned, Palms (and also WAP [wireless application protocol] phones) should not be relied on outside their own small subset of the Web, whether it's a wireless or a landline connection. In an emergency, you can use them to access a mainstream Web page to retrieve a phone number, if you are willing to wade through a lot of screen junk that the device cannot properly display. Otherwise, you should not depend on them for mainstream Web use.

Overhyped Nonsense

Doubtless you've seen people on television using their desktop PCs to carry out videoconferencing, chatting to another person while a smooth, fluid, live video of the person they are talking to is live on the screen, and their live video image is live on the other person's screen. It all looks very spiffy and futuristic—and also highly applicable to the job search process, allowing you to interview without having to travel. All you need is a relatively inexpensive, small video camera that hangs over the top of your computer monitor. Right?

Don't count on it. With a broadband connection, it is just barely possible to get acceptable results, with the screen window so small you'll think you're talking to a squirrel. With a dial-up modem, the results are not acceptable for any serious business purpose. You might use it to check to see if the baby-sitter is still awake, but don't count on making it part of your job search technology. Those videoconferencing sessions you see being used by businesses to let engineers in San Francisco and Hong Kong confer with each other are not comparable. Those hookups depend on multiple ISDN (integrated services digital networks) lines and are maintained by trained technicians.

Voice-over IP (VoIP) is easier to pull off. This technology lets you talk to another person over an Internet connection, using the microphone and speakers that usually come with today's PCs. Once connected, you can talk as if you were on the phone, with no long-distance charges. But the resulting sound is generally described as "Ham-radio quality." Again, this is a toy, not (yet) a serious business tool.

But . . .

There is, however, something called "Web conferencing" that is simple to pull off and could be as effective, in certain settings, as either of the two previous technologies. Basically, you phone someone who you know is sitting at a desk in front of an Internet-connected computer. You tell him or her go to the same Web page that you are looking at, and you talk about what you are looking at, confident that you are both looking at the exactly same thing.

Getting to Know Your Browser

Your browser is your window to the Web, so you need to understand how it works, first by examining the commands and then looking at what goes on under the hood. Figure 1.7 shows a sample screen using Inernet Explorer, and Figure 1.8 shows the screen using Netscape Communicator.

The standard window of both versions shows three levels of controls at the top of the screen. The top level is the standard menu of application commands. Everything of immediate interest is duplicated in the second level, called the *toolbar*. The third level is the address window. The following sections discuss things you can do with these controls and how to do them.

Go to a Web Address

A Web address is called a URL (uniform resource locator). If you know the address that you want to go to, you can just type it into the address window (called the "Netsite" window in Netscape) and press the Return key. The browser will try to predict what you are typing and fill in the rest of the address based on a list of places you have visited before. If it guesses correctly, you may only have to type the first few letters of the address.

Go to a Web Address You've Visited Recently

With both browsers, the right end of the address window contains a small screen button with a down arrow. Click on it, and you will see a list of sites you have visited recently. Click on its entry in the list, and you'll go there. Additionally:

- *Internet Explorer.* The "History" icon toolbar will trigger the display of sites you visited that day, that week, in the last two weeks, and in the last three weeks.
- *Netscape.* The "Go" entry in the command menu will display a list of sites visited during the current session.

Go Back to a Web Address That You Visited Earlier This Session

The "Back" icon in the toolbar in both browsers will cause you to return to the Web address that you were viewing prior to the current one. The "Forward" icon will reverse the action of the "Back" icon.

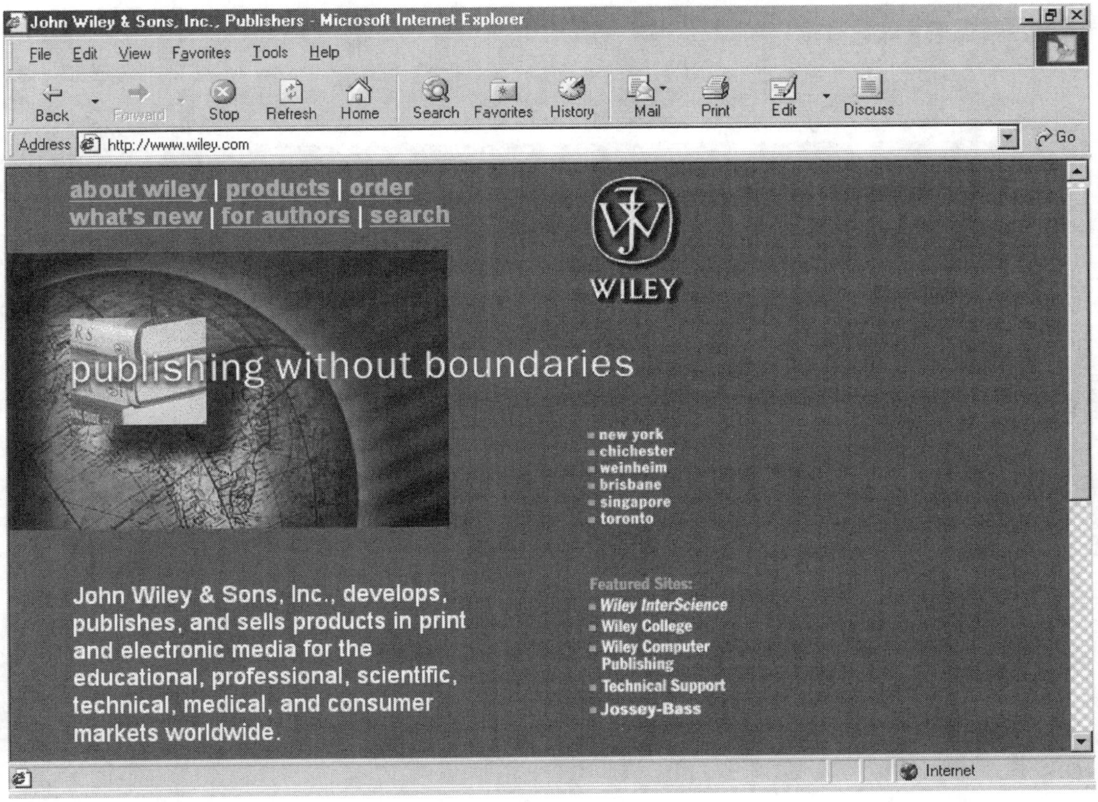

Figure 1.7 *Web page displayed by Microsoft Internet Explorer. Note the three levels of controls: the command menu at the top, the toolbar icons below it, and then the address window. (Screenshot from John Wiley & Sons Inc.'s World Wide Web Site. Copyright © 2001 John Wiley & Sons, Inc. Reprinted with permission.)*

Save the Address of Favorite Sites

Both browsers can save addresses of favorite sites, but they each use a different approach.

- *Internet Explorer.* Click the "Favorites" icon on the toolbar. A screen will appear with a list of Web sites. You can go to a site on the list by clicking it. Or you can add the current site to the list by clicking "Add." You can organize your list of sites by categories using the "Organize" button.
- *Netscape.* Click the "Bookmarks" entry to the left of the Netsite address window. A list of sites will appear. You can go to a site by clicking on it, or

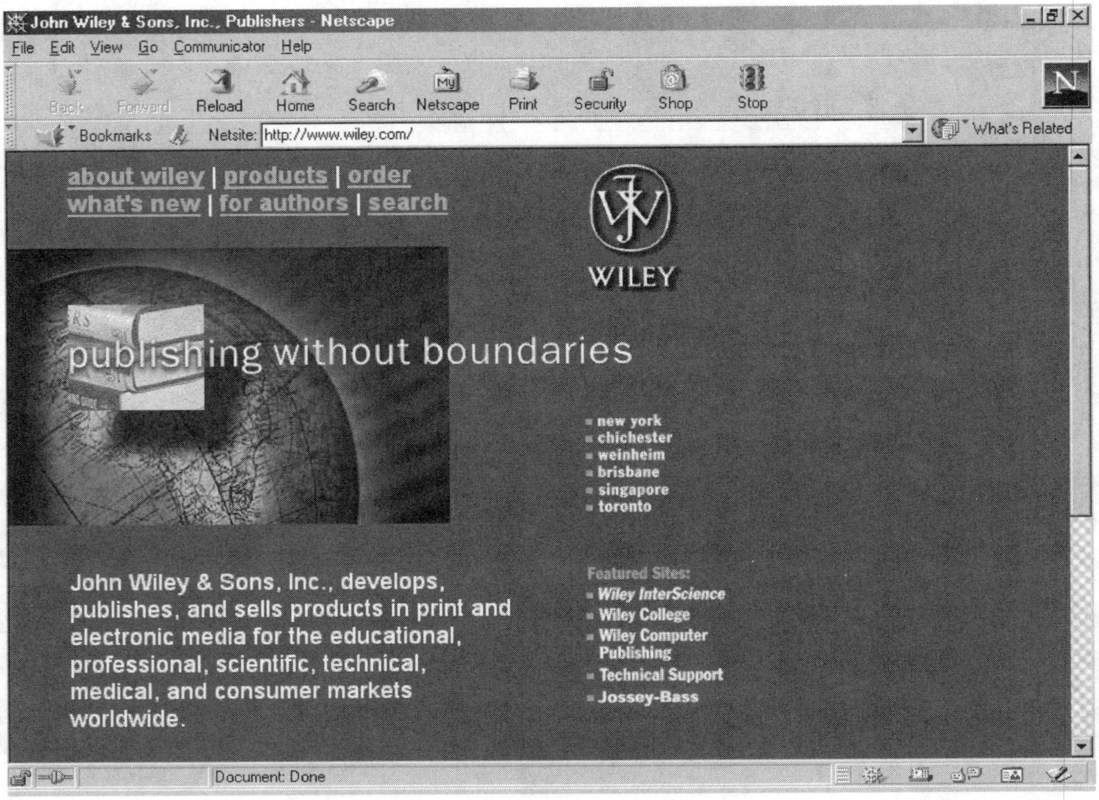

Figure 1.8 *The same page as in Figure 1.7, displayed by Netscape Communicator. Some functions are triggered through different commands, but otherwise there is little difference. (Screenshot from John Wiley & Sons Inc.'s World Wide Web Site. Copyright © 2001 John Wiley & Sons, Inc. Reprinted with permission.)*

you can add the current site to the list by clicking "Add Bookmark." You can organize your list by clicking "Edit Bookmarks."

Download a File

If you shift-click (press the Shift key while clicking the mouse button) on a hyperlink instead of just clicking, the browser will download the file to your computer instead of trying to display it. The browser will give you a Save As screen so you can control where it is saved and what name it is given. You'll want to do this with programs and with other files that you know are to be used outside the browser. If the browser at any time cannot figure out what else to do with a particular file, it will also give you the option of saving it.

Give Up

If a page is taking forever loading and you want to give up, click the "Stop" icon on the toolbar in both browsers. Then try clicking the "Refresh" button ("Reload" in Netscape) to reload the page. Servers can be swamped one moment and idle the next, so that aborting and reloading can be faster than waiting for a slow load—assuming, of course, that you have better luck with the server's workload when you hit it the second time.

Save Text from a Web Page

With either browser, the cursor will turn into a word-processor cursor (resembling an upright I-beam) when placed over text. At that point, you can highlight and copy the text, just as you would in a word processor. Then you can flip over to a word processor, or whatever text-based utility you are keeping notes in, and use the Paste command (under the "Edit" entry in the command menu) to input the text that you copied.

In both, you can also use the Save As command (under the "File" entry in the command menu) to save the HTML file of the current Web page to your hard disk. Additionally, Internet Explorer will save any graphics file that go with the page to a subdirectory it will create, using the same name it gives to the HTML file.

If you can't save the text, the text is likely part of a graphic, or was extracted for display from a database, and is not present in the HTML file.

Save Selected Pictures from a Web Page

Use the right mouse button (not the usual left button) and click on the image. In either browser, you will get a pop-up window with various options, one of which lets you save the image to a file on your computer.

Print a Page

Both browsers have a "Print" icon in the toolbar that will trigger the printing of the current page.

Alas, in some situations the printer is useless, such as when the page uses white text on a dark background. The browser will helpfully discard the background color, leaving you with white print on a white page. And in cases where there is more than one frame on a page, the browser may decide it is only supposed to print one of the frames, and it may not be the one whose contents interest you.

Netscape has a Print Preview command (under the "File" entry in the command menu) to let you gauge in advance what the printer is going to do. Internet Explorer has a facility in the Print command to control frame printing. If all else fails, you can always save the page as a file (as described previously) for later viewing, perhaps with a word processor that can process HTML.

If the page extends off the bottom (or side) of the screen, the extra material will also print out, using extra sheets if necessary.

Under the Hood

You don't need to understand how your browser works to use it, any more than you have to understand how your car works in order to drive it. But if you don't understand what the gasoline, oil, water, and air sold at the filling station are for, you will soon come to grief.

With that metaphor in mind, you need to understand under the hood of a browser the workings of Web addresses and formatting.

Web Addresses

As previously mentioned, the address of a Web file is called its URL. In the case of the example shown in Figures 1.7 and 1.8 the URL is http://www.wiley.com. To avoid TLAO (three-letter acronym overload), this book calls it a Web address. It can include the following elements.

The Prefix

When using the Web, the prefix is http://, meaning hypertext transport protocol. The "://" combination is used because that character combination has no other use and so confirms to the computer that this is a Web address. There are other possible prefixes for other things that the browser can do besides use the Web, such as "file://" for local file access.

The Domain Name

In the present example, wiley.com is the domain name. The www prefix, while part of the registered name, is optional and is not used by all Web sites. The .com suffix indicates that this is a commercial site. Other traditional suffixes include

.edu for educational entity, .mil for military unit, .gov for government agency, and .net for an ISP or other network entity. Other suffixes have been put forward, producing mostly controversy. (Despite its youth, the Internet community clings fiercely to tradition.)

The National Suffix

If a company is located outside the United States, its name may carry an additional suffix indicating its nationality, such as ca for Canada, de for Germany, uk for the United Kingdom, and so on. In the case of the present example, a British version of the site is called http://www.wiley.co.uk, and an Australian site is called http://www.johnwiley.com.au. (In case you were wondering, www.wiley.com.au belongs to a construction company in Australia. Which brings up another problem: Almost any name or word you could think of for a Web address is already in use.)

The File Name

The Web address used in the present example is enough if there is a file at that address named index.html (or index.htm if the server uses Windows software). That file is the "home page" of the site, and the server sends it to the browser automatically. If you want to go directly to another file in the site, you need to use its full address and name. For instance, if the Wiley site had a press release about the Harvard University library with the file name harvardunivlib.html, and it was located in the Corporate News subdirectory of the About directory, the full URL might look like this: http://www.wiley.com/about/corpnews/harvardunivlib.html.

Formatting

What you see on the screen after getting to a Web page may look like a picture of a page, but it is actually generated entirely inside your computer. The computer receives a string of text that makes up the HTML file. It arranges the material on your screen based on commands within the HTML file.

It is an efficient system, except that the person who writes the HTML file has no control over the size of the screen available on the recipient's computer or the available colors, fonts, or graphics resolution. Therefore, the kind of control you have with a modern word processor, where what you see on the screen is what you will get on the page, is not possible. Advancing standardization had eased this situation—until the arrival of Palms, and digital WAP phones with microbrowsers. They have tiny screens and limited graphics capabilities. These devices rely on a variant of HTML called WML (wireless markup language).

To give you an idea of what your browser is doing, the screen reproduced in Figure 1.9 shows part of the contents of the HTML file that underlies the browser example screen in Figures 1.7 and 1.8. If you look closely, you can pick out some of the text that appears on the screen. It is surrounded by what appear to be gibberish but are actually formatting tags used in the HTML language. These tags tell the browser how to display and position the text that is between the tags.

Notice that the screens in Figures 1.7 and 1.8 display several pictures, but the HTML file shows no evidence of them. Instead, other tags in the file (not visible in the example) carry the Web addresses of the graphic files to be used to create the pictures and carry instructions for placing the pictures on the page. A picture can be shown in its original size, or the HTML file can include a tag that tells the browser to scale it to a new size. The graphic files are usually in the same subdi-

```
www.wiley[1] - Notepad
File  Edit  Search  Help
<td colspan=2 width=370></td>
<td valign=top width=80>
<a href="about/" onMouseOver="imgAct('img1')" onMouseOut="imgInact('img1')"><img name="img1"
src="images/newyorkwhite.gif" alt="new york" align="top" width="67" height="13"
border="0"></a><br>
<a href="products/worldwide/europe/" onMouseOver="imgAct('img2')"
onMouseOut="imgInact('img2')"><img name="img2" src="images/chichesterwhite.gif" alt="chichester"
align="top" width="67" height="13" border="0"></a><br>
<a href="products/worldwide/europe/" onMouseOver="imgAct('img3')"
onMouseOut="imgInact('img3')"><img name="img3" src="images/weinheimwhite.gif" alt="weinheim"
align="top" width="67" height="13" border="0"></a><br>
<a href="products/worldwide/jacaranda/" onMouseOver="imgAct('img4')"
onMouseOut="imgInact('img4')"><img name="img4" src="images/brisbanewhite.gif" alt="brisbane"
align="top" width="67" height="13" border="0"></a><br>
<a href="products/worldwide/asia/" onMouseOver="imgAct('img5')"
onMouseOut="imgInact('img5')"><img name="img5" src="images/singaporewhite.gif" alt="singapore"
align="top" width="67" height="13" border="0"></a><br>
<a href="products/worldwide/canada/" onMouseOver="imgAct('img6')"
onMouseOut="imgInact('img6')"><img name="img6" src="images/torontowhite.gif" alt="toronto"
align="top" width="67" height="13" border="0"></a><br>
</td>
</tr>
<tr>
<td width=320 valign=top>
<p><br><br>
<font size="4" face="helvetica,arial">
John Wiley &amp; Sons, Inc., develops,
publishes, and sells products in print and electronic
media for the educational, professional, scientific,
technical, medical, and consumer markets worldwide.
</font>
<p>
<p>
<br>
<font face="helvetica,arial">
For better performance, visit the site closest to you:<br>
```

Figure 1.9 *Raw material from the HTML file that the browser used to create the Web page shown in Figures 1.7 and 1.8. Some of the text on the page is discernable amid a clutter of what appear to be gibberish but are actually formatting commands.*

rectory on the server as the Web page that called them but actually can be anywhere on the Web. (If the browser cannot find the picture, it replaces it with a broken file icon.)

Additionally, because the HTML file itself is pure text, it usually arrives quite quickly even on older dial-up modems. But any use of graphics on the page will slow down its completion. (Consider: Few HTML files are as large as ten thousand bytes long, but that's small for a graphics file.) Fortunately, you can usually read the page without waiting for all the graphics to arrive. (Background colors and font colors can be set with HTML tags and therefore do not require the use of graphics.)

Incidentally, once you have reached a Web page, and the material it contains is displayed on your screen, there is not necessarily any further interaction between your browser and the server that sent the Web page. By sitting there reading the page, you are not crowding some other users off the server. Likewise, hyperlinking is handled entirely by the browser, with no further involvement from the server; the browser determines the address being linked to, goes out on the Internet, and triggers the transmission of that page from whatever server carries it. The mapping of a hyperlinked portion of a picture is also handled by the browser. The exception is streaming audio or video, for which the server can handle only a set number of users.

The next chapter looks at the job search process and how you can use the Internet in that process.

CHAPTER 2

The Process

Whether conducted online or off-line, your job search process will involve a series of decisions and actions. Using the Internet will add only a couple of steps, but it can help greatly with the some of the other steps. The process of using the Internet should look something like this:

- Decide what do you want to do.
- Decide if you want to relocate.
- Decide how much you are worth.
- Decide if you need to be discrete.
- Line up references.
- Compose your resume.
- Select one or more job resources on the Web.
- Search for job openings.
- Research prospective employers.
- Apply.
- Keep records.
- React to responses.
- Disengage from your present job.
- Throughout the job search process, avoid parasites.
- Understand the new world of identity theft.

One more thing needs to be said before going on: You should not rely solely on the online process. You should also pursue an off-line search, through your network of friends and acquaintances in your field of work. People who already know you will be more receptive to you than total strangers to whom your name is just another string of text on a computer screen. The results may be slower but should not be neglected—after all, they may be disappointed that you didn't call them.

That said, this chapter looks at the job process, step by step, in the order just given, and discusses how it can be done online. And, of course how this book can help.

Decide What You Want to Do

Ultimately, only you can decide what you want to do, but increasing numbers of online sites are devoted to self-assessment. Chapter 4 explains where you can find them and what they can do for you.

Decide If You Want to Relocate

Deciding whether relocation is an option is usually simple for unattached youths but torture for entrenched couples. However, you must decide early on because it will affect the course and direction of your entire job search. If you cannot relocate, then your search is restricted to local job openings. If you are willing to move, then the world awaits. But even if in theory you are willing to move, in practice you may not be interested in moving to certain places. Chapter 4 discusses sites on the Internet that let you compare cities according to various parameters.

Decide How Much You Are Worth

Financially, some jobs are not worth having, depending on your situation. You must not waste your time (and risk embarrassment) applying for one of these. Inevitably, however, somewhere in the process of getting a job, the subject will turn to specific sums of money. And you should not put yourself in a position where the sums in question come as a complete surprise (pleasant or unpleasant) for you.

Instead, you need to establish, early in the job search process, what your market value is. Some Web sites specialize in that task, as detailed in Chapter 4.

Decide if You Need to Be Discrete

You may be in a job in which the act of looking for a new job is considered treason and responded to accordingly. If so, you must be discrete. But the Web offers ways to do that, perhaps more so than the off-line world.

If you have not noticed any beheadings recently, you should still probably not flaunt your efforts, lest you be thought of as "that person who's leaving."

Of course, interns, students, and those facing the downsizing ax are expected to be looking for a job, and your current employer may even offer outplacement services.

Keep the following in mind:

- Do not overtly use office resources. There are copy shops on every corner these days, so you don't need to risk getting caught using the office photocopier to churn out resumes.
- Get a free, throwaway e-mail account (covered in Chapter 9). That way, you will not have to use your office e-mail account, which links you to your current employer and whose privacy cannot be assured. For maximum security, you won't want to use your home e-mail address either because it may be easily linked to you.
- Prospective employers will want to call you during work hours. If you are not in a position to talk privately on the phone at your job, get a cellular phone and use that number for your job searches. When you get a call, excuse yourself, walk out to the lobby, or to your parked car, or somewhere private, and call back.
- Ask that prospective employers call you after hours only as a last resort. (They will probably understand, though.)
- Use vacation or sick days to go to interviews.
- If you are slipping out to an interview during office hours, and you want to dress more formally than usual, bring a change of clothes and change in the restroom when you get there.

Line Up References

Be ready to supply references. Unless you are going to be hired by your brother-in-law, you must realize that strangers are going to have to put their trust in you. Before they do that, they will want someone else to vouch for you. "References available on request" is fine for your resume, but when things get serious, prospective employers will actually ask for those references.

This is not a simple matter. You must consider several things:

- Whom to use?
- Where are these people?
- What are they going to say about you?

Whom to Use?

You need to be able to supply the names of people at your previous jobs who can confirm your employment, title, responsibilities and performance, and reason for separation. You should go back five to seven years. Don't worry about that job as a lifeguard you had in college.

The simplest answer is to provide the names of your former bosses. But especially for high-level positions, the person checking your background may end up finding and checking with whomever you reported to, regardless of whether you listed that person. So although giving out the name of your boss (if that person is well disposed toward you) is fine, giving out the names of former colleagues is also fine. Someone who worked for you can also be a reference. There is no hard and fast rule—just find people who can encapsulate your past for a prospective employer.

Where Are These People?

You must supply current contact information for your references. If the call is made and they find that the reference is long gone, then it's the same as if you had not supplied a reference. Your prospective employer's HR department is not going to track down your references for you. You must do that.

Nonetheless, the departed person has probably left a wide trail, so tracking down your reference should not involve any heroic detective work. Ask other former colleagues. Try searching the Internet. Make a few long-distance phone calls.

And do it before anyone asks for references, not as a hurried afterthought.

What Are They Going to Say?

When you do locate prospective references, ask politely if you can use them as a job reference.

If they say no, thank them. They've done you a big favor. They would probably have come across negatively when asked about you, but they removed themselves from the running. (Fear of litigation has led some people to have a policy of not talking, but a "no comment" can also sound damning.)

If they say yes, don't stop there. Go on and ask what they would tell the background checker. Keep in mind that the reference does not have to be adulatory—people don't expect that and get suspicious when they come across it. But assure yourself that your reference feels okay about you.

So far so good. Having located four or five references, you may be able to relax.

Or maybe not. Because in the end, you really don't know what the reference is going to say, even if you came away with the feeling that you were still buddies. You, after all, knew how to elicit good memories from the reference person. A random caller asking about you may hit a nerve.

And don't comfort yourself with a belief that laws protect you from being bad-mouthed by former employers, or that a prospective employer can only ask a reference about certain things. There may be some such laws in your jurisdiction, but things like that don't matter in private conversations between two individuals, where what is not said may drown out the few words that actually get spoken. Consider this exchange:

> *Background checker:* "Did the subject get along well with fellow employees?"
> *Reference:* Clears throat and lapses into uncomfortable silence. Finally, "Hmmm. Yeah. Fellow employees. Could we just go on to the next question?"

Nothing overtly negative was said. You can't say the reference maliciously gave false information designed to hurt your reputation because the reference really didn't say anything. But you're sunk. The background checker will come away with a negative impression.

If job offers mysteriously melt away, you may have to consider the possibility that you have been living in denial. The references that you thought were your friends may be saying negative things about you. Rather than feeling betrayed, however, you should approach the issue in a businesslike fashion—that is, by spending time and money on it. Services exist that, for a fee, will approach your references saying they are checking your background for a third party regarding the possibility of employment. The third party is you and the "possibility of employment" is your personal job search, but those details won't come up. These services include (as examples, without implying any endorsement) the following:

- *Allison & Taylor Reference Checking, Inc.* At this writing, fees start at $59 for one reference check wrapped up in a written report, with numerous extra-cost options. They can be reached at http://www. myreferences.com.
- *References-Etc.* Prices start at about $30 for one reference. They can be reached at http://www.references-etc.com.
- *Background References.* Prices start at about $50 per employment verification, which includes the asking of a list of background questions. They can be reached at http://www.backgroundprofiles.com.
- *Employment Reference Check Associates.* This firm charges about $35 for the first reference check and about $30 for each subsequent one. They can be reached at http://www.employment-reference.com.

Some career-counseling firms will also undertake reference checking for job candidates.

Compose Your Resume

Now that you have some references lined up, you can compose your resume. That will require cataloging your career and educational history, your achievements, and your goals and putting them in a coherent format. Chapter 5 covers the process in detail.

You will need several versions of your resume. An online job search especially requires a plain-text version for use in composing your resume at job sites on the Web and a plain-text version with line breaks for e-mail submission.

Actually, you should be prepared to compose a separate and distinct resume for each job you are seriously interested in. Fortunately, that's not a big deal when you use a word processor.

Meanwhile, be prepared to write a cover letter to accompany each resume.

Select One or More Job Resources on the Web

As you will see by flipping through this book, there is no shortage of online ways to look for a job. In order of likely usefulness, these consist of the following:

- Job sites on the Web, covered in Chapters 6 and 8, with a step-by-step example in Chapter 7.
- Usenet newsgroups, covered in Chapters 10 and 11.
- Mailing lists, covered in Chapter 10.

If there is a particular resource that is favored in your field, make use of that first. But do not stop there. You cannot count on any one site or resource to have everything you need. Rather, you should pick out some Web sites that look promising, start with one, learn it, and then use it until you are satisfied that you understand its potential. Then do the same with a second, third, and fourth site. Then examine the situation on Usenet and look for a suitable mailing list. Then start over again with our Web sites; by then, the list of job postings on each will have changed. Or, ideally, you'll have found a job.

Search for Job Openings

The method used to search online for a job is different for each Web site but will be explained at that site. Chapter 7 contains a step-by-step example.

Chapter 10 covers looking for a job on Usenet.

Research Prospective Employers

Some jobs are not worth having, and some companies are not worth working for. On the other hand, companies you may not have heard of could be up-and-coming players with exciting opportunities. Once you get a nibble, check out the company. Chapter 12 offers resources that will help. Do it even if you think you're familiar with the company in question because things change rapidly.

Apply

Each employer that you apply to, and each application method, will have different requirements. Job postings in any medium may list an address to which you are supposed to send your resume. They may want it in electronic or scannable form, as explained in Chapter 5. If you are using a job site, such as the Monster.com example in Chapter 7, you may be able to apply through the job site, which will automatically send your resume and cover letter to the right person. Some companies will direct you to a Web site that hosts their own online application process.

Keep Records

To keep from going in circles, keep track of what applications you have sent, and when, together with the time and nature of any responses. You may also want to keep a copy of the resume and cover letter sent to each company. You can keep a neatly organized computer database or toss hand-annotated printouts into a drawer—whatever suits you. The point is that you will have something to refer to when it comes time to decide where you stand and where to turn next.

React to Responses

Once you get a nibble, the realities of the off-line world kick in. You will have to go in for at least one interview—perhaps more. Suddenly, understanding how to use the Internet, its job sites, and Usenet newsgroups carries no weight. The Internet has done its job. Now it is all up to you and your social skills. Chapter 13 contains detailed advice on how to proceed.

Disengage from Your Present Job

Leaving your present job the wrong way can hurt your job search. It's not that the decision makers of corporate America have some kind of shared consciousness, and if you offend one of them you offend them all and you'll never get a good job again. Rather, you don't want to get the reputation of being a tantrum-throwing troublemaker who storms out of jobs and leaves your employer and coworkers in the lurch. Frankly, you don't want people saying bad things about you, ever. Because if they have a choice between talking about your years of dedicated service or that cloud under which you left, they'll talk about that cloud.

So please heed the following advice.

Read the Writing on the Wall

You don't want to wait to leave until you are crushed and defeated, so spiritually sapped that you can't imagine continuing with this or any job. Instead, you want to leave when you can see that if you stay, you will end up crushed, defeated, and spiritually sapped. Sometimes the job itself generates the bad times, and sometimes the company itself is having bad times. Danger signs include the following:

- All you can think about on the job are the other things that you would rather be doing.
- You are no longer giving the job serious effort.
- The job no longer seems like a good opportunity.
- You are continually impatient with everything about the job.
- Everyone seems to be quitting except you.
- Rumors of layoffs follow one another.
- You would secretly welcome a layoff.
- The company seems to be cutting corners instead of merely containing costs.
- Internal communication is dominated by bickering.
- Your performance reviews are not turning out as you would desire.

Be Discrete

The advice given in the "Decide If You Need to Be Discrete" section applies.

Give Notice in a Businesslike Fashion

It is best not to announce that you are quitting your present job until you have another job lined up. Beyond the issue of financial security, prospective employers will take you more seriously—it is obvious that you are employable because you have a job. In addition, the pace of your job search can be more relaxed.

When giving notice, it is standard to give your present employer two weeks' warning; in other words, you give notice that your last day is in two weeks and then you are leaving. This is simple courtesy, to give the company time to adjust to your departure. (It will also give you time to plan your transition.) But some employers won't see it that way and will have you pack up and leave immediately, perhaps escorted by a security guard. This scenario is more likely if you are exposed to sensitive information, such as the company's ongoing marketing plans. Because you are not being fired, you should still be paid for the remaining two weeks or be put on vacation. (Bring up this issue if no one else does.)

Therefore, if you would like to bring with you certain work samples, you need to secure them in the days before giving notice, taking them home in a way that does not attract attention. (You should probably make a habit of securing samples as you go along, knowing that you won't stay at that job forever.)

Also in the days before giving notice, you need to make sure that any personal property or equipment that you have in the office is clearly identified as yours, so that no one objects when you take it with you. Again, this should actually be an ongoing practice.

Your soon-to-be-former employer will want a statement from you in writing. President Nixon's consisted of one sentence, but presumably you're not leaving in the same fashion. State the day's date and that you are hereupon announcing your departure, and give the date of your last day. Then declare that you got a lot out of working here and that you'll miss your coworkers. You can also give your reasons for leaving, but you don't have to, and you don't want to make an issue out of them anyway—your focus is now on the future. Especially don't go into a description of the conditions that led to your decision to bail out and what might be done to fix them. Nor should you add your thoughts about certain people in the office. Remember, this letter may be kept on file, and a time may come when any negative emotions it expresses could sound rather petty, even to you. Anyway, if the new job bombs you might want to come back. So keep everything upbeat, or at least neutral, and you won't be burning any bridges. Finally, sign the letter.

Ask for a meeting with your supervisor and make your announcement. Make it short and direct, and give your supervisor the letter. Do not invite discussion about your plans or where you are going. You are an adult, and as such you have decided to quit this job. That's all that matters. As a friend and coworker, your supervisor might actually be delighted to hear the news of your good fortune and have tons of good advice, but that should come later.

Leave with Dignity

Spend the remaining days tying up loose ends, leaving instructions for your replacement, and so on. If the company asks you to train someone, do so, even if you don't feel like doing any favors. Tell the HR department where it can contact you after you are gone. Don't be surprised if your coworkers throw a good-bye lunch or party on your last day. Again, keep things upbeat or neutral, even if you are inwardly still seething. The coworkers, after all, want to have fun.

Meanwhile, you did not give notice in order to get your employer to offer you a pay raise, promotion, or something else that amounts to a counteroffer. (If you did, it's not a good idea—see Chapter 13.) If they do try to induce you to stay, take it as confirmation that the inducement was available for you all along. Ask yourself why it took the spectacle of your departure to move them to actually give it to you.

Do the Final Paperwork

Check with the HR department on continued health insurance coverage (if that is an issue) and the status of pension and investment plans. You may or may not get paid for unused vacation or sick days. All company perks should be settled or returned; don't make them have to come after you for that laptop.

Final Note

Don't be afraid to give up on a new job that turned out to be a poor fit. Having a misadventure on your resume will not condemn you as an unstable job-hopper.

Throughout the Job Search Process, Avoid Parasites

Communities attract parasites. There is always a body of people seeking work, creating an ongoing community with stable characteristics, yet whose membership is in constant turnover. For sustaining parasites, it's perfect. Meanwhile, "infection" can travel fast on the Internet.

When it comes to Internet job searching, there are three prominent forms of parasitism: that which feeds off people's desire to get rich quick, that which feeds off people's desire to get a guaranteed job, and that which feeds off people's desire to work at home.

Get Rich Quick

To be on the Internet is to be exposed to Ponzi schemes. They don't call themselves Ponzi schemes, of course, but they are. Many are chain letters that invite you to send money to the people who sent out the chain letter and then to send it on. Some letters have been circulating for years and can be spotted instantly.

Slightly more sophisticated are investment schemes promising huge returns. Of course, the original investors are paid from the money sent in by follow-on participants. Soon, the inverted pyramid collapses and the later participants lose their entire investment. (Often, they are bitter at the police for arresting the perpetrator, whose glowing promises they still believe.) In one sad case, the perpetrator actually tried to pay them all off—by investing his take in other Ponzi schemes.

Whatever wrinkle they employ, all insistently claim to be legal. They're not. Pyramid schemes, Ponzi schemes, and chain letters are illegal in most jurisdictions, and people have gone to jail for perpetrating them over the Internet.

Guaranteed Jobs

The U.S. government's Federal Trade Commission apparently spends a lot of time on complaints about job-placement agencies. Its recommendations:

- Be suspicious of any employment-service firm that promises to get you a job (as opposed to promising to try to get you a job).
- Be skeptical of any employment-service firm that charges up-front fees and guarantees refunds to dissatisfied customers.
- Don't give out your credit card or bank account information on the phone unless you are familiar with the company and are ready to pay for something.
- Get a copy of the firm's contract. Review it carefully—especially its refund policies — before you pay any money. If oral promises are made that don't show up in the contract, walk.
- Be aware that some listing services and "consultants" place ads that seem to offer jobs when, in fact, they are selling employment information.
- Follow up with the corporate offices of any company listed in an ad by an employment service, to find out if the company is really hiring.
- Be wary of firms promoting "previously undisclosed" U.S. government jobs. All such jobs are announced to the public.
- Check with your local consumer protection agency, state attorney general's office, and the Better Business Bureau to see if any complaints have been filed about a company with which you intend to do business.
- There have been cases of people calling a toll-free "jobs information" number and finding later that they were switched to a 900 number and that hefty service charges were attached to their phone bill. To make that switch without notice is against U.S. law.

Work at Home!

If you work in an industry where it is possible, you probably already know all about working at home. Telecommuting, meanwhile, is a common practice among office workers, involving staying home part of the work week and doing purely clerical tasks from a home-office computer.

You must seriously question anything you come across that goes beyond that—especially if someone is asking for money to train you for a work-at-home job or to look for one for you. Occasionally, legitimate work-at-home opportunities do arise. If you think you have run across one, get the names of work-at-home employees and talk to them in person, not over the phone. Alas, you are more likely to be on the receiving end of come-ons like the following:

- *MLM.* Remember those initials; they stand for multi-level marketing, and they have blighted many lives You buy a distributorship to sell a product but find that the real money is in selling distributorships. You get a cut of everything sold by the people you sell distributorships to—your "downline." But they are in the same situation and are selling mostly distributorships. Eventually, everyone runs out of gullible acquaintances to sell distributorships to, and few products ever get sold. It may sound like a pyramid scheme, and in situations in which there is no worthwhile product, it is indeed a pyramid scheme. Some MLMs are run like a cult, in which you are expected to surrender your free will to your "upline."
- *Medical billing services.* Pay thousands of dollars for software to set yourself up to address the "billing crisis" that the vendor assures you exists in the medical field. Your crisis will involve discovering that the field is already crowded with large, highly competitive firms.
- *Random high-tech gadgets.* It will sound intriguing—maybe television, over the Web, or kid-tracking Global Positioning System, or cable television peripherals. But if the vendor had a commercial, marketable product, the real money would be in the consumer-electronics channel, and there would be no reason to sell distributorships to random people outside the industry.
- *Become an Internet consultant!* Yes, take a free seminar for that purpose. Only you can't learn that skill from one seminar, and anyway the seminar turns out to be a high-pressure sales pitch to buy a bogus Internet-based "business opportunity."
- *Bulk e-mail.* Buy a distributorship for software that generates spam. Then spam millions of people with a pitch to buy the software. Then discover what your ISP does to people who send spam. With your account closed, you won't even be able to send an e-mail complaint to the people who sold you the spam software. How convenient for them.
- *Stuff envelopes!* You pay somebody to set you up as a work-at-home envelope stuffer. The only envelopes you'll stuff (should you decide to perpetuate the scheme) are your own pitch letters offering to set up the recipients as envelope stuffers. (Commercial envelope stuffing is done by machines and has been for generations.)

- *Craft/assembly work.* You buy a machine and material from the vendor. You assemble the material as directed and send it back. Somehow, however, your work never meets "quality standards," and the company never pays you.

Understand the New World of Identity Theft

Parasites are not the only dangers lurking in cyberspace. If you are not careful, cyberspace can expose you to a new breed of robber. The next chapter spells out the situation in detail, and you should read it before launching your online job search.

CHAPTER 3

The Danger of Identity Theft

When you search for a job online, your name will be getting around a lot on the Internet. Which means a lot of exposure. As public health authorities have been explaining for decades, through various media, wide exposure is not a good thing. Although they're concerned about another form of exposure, the Internet form can involve consequences that can be fully as painful: identity theft.

Basically, professional thieves have found stealing credit cards to be less and less profitable. The report of the theft can be in general circulation within hours, making the card dangerous to use. So, instead, they have learned to steal your identity. It can work in various ways:

- Using your name, birth date, and Social Security number, they open a credit card account in your name. They start buying things with the card and don't pay the bills. The delinquencies show up on your credit report (because it's your Social Security number), and the merchants may try to collect from you.
- They open a bank account in your name and write bad checks.
- They establish cellular phone service in your name that they then do not pay for.
- They figure out your bank account information and drain it with counterfeit checks.

- They take out a car loan in your name, drive the car off the lot, and are not seen again.
- They may drag out the charade by filing for bankruptcy protection under your name, to avoid paying the debts occurred in your name.
- They may pirate your existing credit card account by calling your credit card issuer and (pretending to be you) giving a change of address. They get your next bill—which contains the account number. They use it to run up mail-order purchases. It will take you at least a month to realize something is wrong—and by then the damage is done.
- They may give your name when arrested, giving you a criminal record.

If thieves were to rob you or embezzle from your bank account, the damage is limited to the money you have on hand. The horror of identity theft is that they can plunge you into an arbitrary amount of debt.

The credit card company may believe your protests, and the incident may pass like a bad dream. Or they may decide that you must have authorized the account and press for payment. They may turn the issue over to a collection agency that will calmly and professionally hound you at every turn. With the bad report on your credit record, you will have a hard time getting a job because credit checks are part of routine background checks. And you won't be able to get a mortgage or car loan or receive backing for a business. You will have trouble getting a new phone line. If you have to move, you will have trouble finding someone to rent to you, and if you do move in somewhere, the utility services won't want to give you an account.

Now that you are properly frightened, it's time to talk about ways to reduce exposure during your job search:

- Do not give out personal information through the Internet, especially your Social Security number, unless you know exactly who is getting it. Before giving it out, satisfy yourself that the site absolutely needs your Social Security number. (If a site seems to require it, contact the manager, who may surprise you by providing a "by-pass" number to type in, in place of your Social Security number.)
- On resumes that you post online, do not include your Social Security number or your birth date (or even your address beyond stating your city). Your name and phone number should suffice.
- If you want to include your e-mail address, use a free account that you have acquired specially for job search purposes (as explained in Chapter 9).
- There is rarely any reason to give your date of birth (as opposed to your age) except when filling out insurance forms after you have been hired.

Meanwhile, you can be taking certain precautions even if you never go online for any reason. Most identity thefts occur because of stolen mail, purloined trash that contained billing information, or because dishonest people (friends of friends of roommates, sleazy coworkers, bribed bank workers, etc.) got access to your information. Therefore, you should do the following:

- Memorize your Social Security number and leave the card in a safe place.
- Be aware of billing cycles so you will notice if a particular bill has not arrived.
- Before tossing those preapproved credit cards into the trash, cut them up.
- Get a paper shredder and use it on all financial documents (including credit card bills) that you are going to throw away.
- Secure your financial records.
- Use postal service drop boxes to mail checks (rather than leave them waiting in your mailbox for the letter carrier to come by), and remove incoming mail from your mailbox promptly.
- Do not write down your PINs (personal identification numbers) and passwords for financial accounts. Chose ones that are idiosyncratic and memorable to you, but which someone else would not immediately guess. (In other words, do not use birth dates and phone numbers.) If they ask for your mother's maiden name, give some other name that you'll remember.
- Cancel credit card accounts that you are not using.
- Do not have your Social Security number or birth date printed on your personalized checks.
- Carry no more identification on your person than you actually need.
- Get a copy of your credit report at regular intervals, perhaps yearly.

Credit-Reporting Services

Basically, credit has replaced money as the thing you need to safeguard. So instead of worrying about how solvent your bank is (although that issue does come up occasionally), you need to find out what the credit-reporting companies are saying about you.

These companies make their money by selling information about you, and they will sell it to you as well. Under the Fair Credit Reporting Act of 1971 (amended in 1997), they have to provide you a credit report about yourself at no charge if you can show that you have been subjected to adverse action due to a credit report within the last 60 days. (Several states—Colorado, Maryland,

Massachusetts, New Jersey, and Vermont—require free access to your own data once a year, and twice a year in Georgia.)

You can also obtain a free report if you are unemployed and state that you plan to look for a job within 60 days. You will have to provide some documentation, such as an unemployment relief card. You also qualify by being a welfare recipient, but this will, again, require documentation. You can also get a free report if you can state that you believe that you have been the victim of fraud. But you must approach each of the credit reporting firms (there are three main ones) separately.

(Note that the credit-reporting firms do not themselves extend or deny credit. They supply reports to subscribing merchants, who use or ignore the reports, according to their own established policies or whim.)

Equifax (http://www.equifax.com)

Equifax will sell you basic online access to your file for $8.50. (Some states require a lower fee.) For $12.95, you get to see the creditworthiness score that Equifax has figured for you, with a personalized explanation. For $39.95, the service will send you e-mail notification of any changes to your file, plus other extras, such as online dispute procedures. To report fraud, call 800-525-6285 and write P.O. Box 740241, Atlanta, Georgia, 30374-0241.

Experian (http://www.experian.com)

Formerly called TRW, Experian offers online access to your credit report for $8.50. (Some states require a lower fee.) To report fraud, call 888-397-3742 and write P.O. Box 9532, Allen, Texas, 75013.

Trans Union (http://www.tuc.com)

Trans Union will sell you online access to your credit report for $8.50. (Some states require a lower fee.) They also sell, through a sister firm called Intersections, Inc., a service called Identity Guard, for $8.99 per month. The service will notify you of changes to your file, provide quarterly updates of your credit report, and analyze your credit history with points on how to make it look better. To report fraud to Trans Union, call 800-680-7289 and write the Fraud Victim Assistance Division, P.O. Box 6790, Fullerton, California, 92634.

Fighting Back

If you suspect identity theft has occurred, you need to do certain things immediately. Your course will depend on the exact nature of the fraud, but the U.S. Federal Trade Commission lists three steps that are nearly always applicable.

First Step

Contact each of the credit-reporting firms listed in the previous section and have them put a "fraud alert" in your file. This will tell the credit card companies and other credit grantors to contact you before opening a new account or changing an existing account. At the same time, ask for a copy of your credit report. Now that you suspect fraud, you are entitled to a free report, although you will have to apply in writing. If you see "inquiries" on the report from the firms that opened the fraudulent accounts, ask that these be removed from the report. Get another report in a few months to see if the changes were made.

Second Step

Contact the creditors whose accounts were either opened fraudulently or tampered with. These are usually credit card companies but may also include phone companies, utilities, banks, and other lenders. Find someone in the fraud department to talk to and always follow up with a letter. Following up in writing is particularly important with credit card companies because laws exist that limit your liability for fraudulent changes on your card if you give prompt notice. Close all accounts that have been tampered with. If you open new ones, use new PINs and passwords.

Third Step

Call the police in the town where the identity theft took place. If that is not apparent, call your local police. Having reported the crime, you should then get a copy of the resulting police report. Frankly, the police may not be able to do much immediately, but you will have that police report to show to any defrauded creditors who are not convinced that you are telling the truth. (Always keep your copy of any and all documentation you acquire, and only submit copies of your copy.)

Further Steps

You may have to go through a dispute-resolution procedure with one or more credit-reporting firms. If, in the end, changes are made to your report, you can have a corrected copy sent to anyone who received a credit report about you for employment purposes within the previous two years and anyone at all who received it within the previous six months.

As for further steps, the Federal Trade Commission provides reams of advice at http://www.consumer.gov/idtheft. The Privacy Rights Clearinghouse also has an Identity Theft Resources Web page at http://www.privacyrights.org/identity.htm. There is also information at http://www.identitytheft.org and doubtless, other places.

Just keep in mind that the Internet (like the off-line world) is a jungle and that some of its denizens are predators.

That understood, some big questions (as mentioned in Chapter 2) need to be answered before you begin your job search. The next chapter looks at these questions and how to answer them.

CHAPTER 4

What Do You Want to Do?

Before you go out and start looking for a job, you have to answer the first three questions posed in Chapter 2, involving self-assessment, relocation, and salary expectations. To paraphrase:

- What do you want to do?
- Do you want to relocate?
- How much are you worth?

Only you can answer the first and second questions, although this chapter looks at resources that can help you arrive at a working answer. As for the third question, you can't answer it: The market determines how much you are worth, just as it determines (to use a gritty example) how much a used car is worth. True, every used car is different. But it is not enough that you feel that what you have to offer is more akin to a mint-condition Silver Shadow than an Edsel that has been used as a chicken coop for 30 years. You still have to know what Silver Shadows are going for before you can start thinking about what price to put on yours. And there are places online where you can do that (determine salary levels, that is, although you can also price cars).

The following sections will help you look for online answers to these questions.

What Do You Want to Do?

The pundits say that you should work at the thing that represents your bliss, the thing that is so absorbing that hours pass without notice—that thing that you can't wait to tackle anew each morning.

But unless you've already had that job, you may not know what that thing would be. And, it is not practical to sample one career after another until you find the one that fits, like shoes in a shoe store. True, like the shoe store, you can tell at a glance that there are some careers that you just don't want, others that obviously don't fit, and some that are sold out. But an impractically large selection may still be left. Meanwhile, trying one on (i.e., getting a job) means changing your life completely. So it would be nice to select one with some assurance of a good fit.

There are places online that can help you do that. But keep in mind that no software in the world is smart enough to tell you what you should do, just like there is no person smart enough to tell you that. You have to make the decision for yourself, and the decision has to come from deep within because for 40 hours a week, you are your job. If the decision is a painful one, then your search-and-decision process needs to be broad ranging. The online tools listed in this section should be merely one aspect—quick, convenient steps in a longer process. Other parts of the process that pundits suggest include looking seriously at yourself, looking seriously at the world outside you, and possibly talking to professional counselors. So before going online, look first at these three steps.

Looking at Yourself

The thrust of most of the Web sites listed later in this chapter is to help you identify your areas of genuine interest. Besides taking the tests they offer, you might also do the following:

- Look at what you do with your leisure time, and ask yourself what that says about you.
- Look at your academic and work achievements. What did you excel in, and what did you have trouble with?
- Write an autobiography and look for themes.
- Write a mission statement covering what you want to be, what you want to accomplish, and what values will guide you in the process. (For instance, do you want family stability? Or are you willing to accept the disruptions that ambition can generate?)

- Talk about your life with a friend or family member who is a good listener. (You do the talking.)

Looking at the World

Once you have identified a job or career that you might be interested in, the trick is not to rush out and start making job applications. Instead, find people who actually have such a job and talk to them. The results may be superior to all the government labor statistics or career handbooks on Earth. Those other sources won't come out and tell you that people in the field typically burn out in eight years, or that there is not a coherent path of advancement, or that advancement is controlled by a small clique or is snarled in licensing requirements, or that this job is really just a resume stuffer for advancement in a parallel field. But you want to know things like that. In addition, you can't turn to a career handbook and ask certain questions that have been nagging you, such as these:

- How did you get started?
- What do you like/dislike about your job?
- What preparation, previous experience, stepping-stone jobs, or other prerequisites are there?
- What do you do in a typical day or week?
- What skills and abilities does this job demand?
- What will this job be like in five years?
- What are the possibilities of advancement?
- Any advice?
- Who else can I talk to?

You can pose these questions over the phone, but try for a face-to-face meeting in order to experience the general atmosphere. Basically, just locate someone who has the job and ask for a few minutes of his or her time. Start by asking around through your usual network of friends and acquaintances, and almost always someone will know someone who will know someone. That's good enough. Call that person and ask for a meeting.

Some pundits say that you should write a polite note asking for a meeting. And if you had wanted to get in to see Charles Dickens 125 years ago, that would have been the way to do it. Today, business is conducted by phone tag, and the person you have targeted won't want to change methods just for you. Call. If you get a receptionist, explain straight out what you want to do. You may then be put through to the person. Start over and explain yourself again. However, you will probably end up in voice mail. Leave a clear, businesslike message. Explain what you want, and ask for an "informational interview." The person will understand what you are doing.

Don't be surprised if the return call is from the receptionist, giving you possible times. Show up promptly, alert, and well groomed. Have prepared questions, but let things digress. Be ready to leave when your time is up, but be prepared to stay if your contact keeps talking. You will find that people love to talk about themselves, and you may have more trouble getting out of the interview than getting in.

After you get home, break the phone-tag rule and write a thank-you note. Mention something about the interview so the person will remember you specifically. Include your name and contact information. Congratulations—you've begun networking in your new career field.

Except that you may decide that this field is not for you. Be prepared for that eventuality, and don't be daunted by it. Better to turn back now than to head down a path that you suspect you'll hate.

Consulting the Pros

Career counseling is actually a profession. Career counselors hold a graduate degree in counseling with a specialization in career counseling, and the services they offer vary according to what you feel you want and what each individual counselor is qualified to perform. But they do not make any decisions for you; they help you make your own decision and perhaps help you make and execute plans that stem from that decision. They will know more about personal-assessment tests, job-hunting tips and career outlooks than you can ever hope to know. And they will charge money.

The National Career Development Association of Tulsa, Oklahoma, states that a career counselor can be expected to offer some or all of the following services:

- Conduct counseling sessions to help you clarify your career goals.
- Administer and interpret tests to assess your abilities and interests, thus identifying career options.
- Encourage exploratory activities through various kinds of homework.
- Use various resources to help you understand the "world of work."
- Reinforce your decision-making skills.
- Help you write a career plan.
- Teach job hunting and resume writing.
- Help resolve personal conflicts on the job.
- Help with job-related stress or the stress of losing a job.

According to the association, you should look for someone who is a "National Certified Career Counselor." To get that certification, a person has to have a degree in the field, three years experience, and passed a certification test.

Beyond credentials, the association recommends that you ask for a detailed explanation of services and fees, the time involved, and assurances of confidentiality. Make certain that you can terminate the services at any time, paying only for services rendered. If they imply a promise that they can get you a bigger salary or a better job, or fix your career, or get immediate results with a job search, walk. Counselors counsel; they don't go behind some curtain and pull strings.

To look for a career counselor, probably the best place to start is in the Yellow Pages. But the National Board for Certified Counselors will also send you a list of people in your area who are National Certified Career Counselors if you send them a request. Check their Web page at http://www.nbcc.org/find/nccc.htm.

The Yahoo! search engine lists career-counseling centers—just run a search on "career counseling." Some are just advertising on the Web, while others operate over the Web, mailing out personality and aptitude tests for you to take, then sending back bound reports based on the results, with consultation over the phone. Prices start at several hundred dollars. You might be better off doing it face to face, but time and geographical constraints may make the Web/phone option a reasonable alternative.

Web Self-Assessment Resources

The following are Web-based personality tests that should help your self-assessment efforts. Although these sites appear to be the main examples at present, you should treat the list as representative of what's out there. (Many either use the Holland model or link to the Keirsey site, both of which are covered here.) As always, a site's inclusion on the list should not be taken as an endorsement.

http://www.self-directed-search.com

The Self-Directed Search test site, at www.self-directed-search.com, offered by Psychological Assessment Resources, Inc. (PAR), of Lutz, Florida, offers an online test based on the six personality types determined by Dr. John Holland. For $8.95, you get an 8- to 12-page report.

Originally developed for the U.S. Army, the Holland personality types are based on the idea that people work best around people like themselves. Holland identified six different personality types and six different job environments in which those personalities would be comfortable. The personality types and the job environments have the same names:

- *Realistic.* Practical people who like to work with tools, machines, mechanical drawings, or animals and would be comfortable as farmers, pilots, police officers, and so on. They would be compatible in the Conventional or Investigative environment but not in a Social environment.
- *Investigative.* Precise, scientific intellectuals who would be comfortable as architects, dentists, doctors, medical technicians, and so on. They would be compatible in the Artistic and Realist environment but not the Enterprising environment.
- *Artistic.* Expressive, original, and independent people who would be comfortable as actors, musicians, editors, and so on, as well as doctors. The Investigative and Social environments are compatible, but not the Conventional one.
- *Social.* Helpful, friendly people who would be good as teachers, dental hygienists, librarians, and even parole officers. They would be comfortable with Artistic and Enterprising types but not the Realistic type.
- *Enterprising.* Energetic, ambitious, social people who would be good as sales reps, lawyers, real estate agents—you know the type. They would be comfortable in Social and Conventional environments but not Investigative environments.
- *Conventional.* Orderly, systematic people who would be comfortable as secretaries, bookkeepers, postal workers, and so on. They would be comfortable in Realistic and Enterprising environments but not Artistic environments.

Of course, most people are a combination of types, and therefore, as the site stresses, a candidate should investigate more than one approach.

http://www.ncsu.edu/careerkey

The site at www.ncsu.edu/careerkey contains a 20-minute "Career Key"—an interest "inventory" (i.e., test) to pinpoint what you like to do and point you to an appropriate career, based on which of six Holland personality types you fall into. The results are scored instantly, and you are then linked to the online version of the government's Occupational Outlook Handbook. It is free, and the site boasts that more than a hundred thousand people a month visited it in the year 2000. The Career Key's server is hosted at North Carolina State University, where the author (Lawrence K. Jones) is a professor in the College of Education. It is aimed mostly at students trying to pick a major or career, as well as adults thinking about changing careers. For them, the site provides potentially valuable material on how to make decisions.

The four-step decision-making process that the site promotes (drawn from the work of Irving L. Janis and Leon Mann) is called ACIP (as in "a sip"), for alternatives, consequences, information, and plans. Here is the breakdown:

- *Alternatives.* Look at all your choices and ask yourself, "Are there any other ways I can solve this problem that I have not thought of?"
- *Consequences.* Having arrived at a list of acceptable alternatives, weigh the pros and cons of each.
- *Information.* Get further information about each alternative that remains under consideration.
- *Plans.* Make detailed plans on how to implement your decision and how to respond to any negative consequences that you encounter.

http://Keirsey.com/frame.html

The temperament types defined by David Keirsey are the subject of two different online tests (one is twice as long as the other) that you can take at Keirsey.com/frame.html. (Keirsey differentiates between temperament and character, asserting that temperament is apparently inborn, while your character can change over time.)

The tests decide if you have one of four types of temperament: Guardian, Artisan, Idealist, or Rational. The site estimates that the U.S. population is 40 to 45 percent Guardians, 35 to 40 percent Artisan, 5 to 10 percent Idealist, and 5 to 10 percent Rational. (However, Idealists and Guardians are generally more interested in taking the test.)

To each type is added four additional characteristics: (1) extroversion versus introversion, (2) intuition versus "sensing," (3) thinking versus feeling, and (4) judgment versus perception. That gives 16 total types, ranging from Performer (an Artisan who is extroverted, sensing, feeling, and judgmental) to a Field Marshal (a Rational who is extroverted, intuitive, thinking, and judgmental).

Interestingly, the site suggests that you never accept the results of a personality test without checking them out by watching the person in action. What people habitually do and what answers they habitually give may be two different things, but you can spot the difference by watching them. How you spot the difference in yourself is another question, but the site suggests that such tests will at least give you a place to start looking for an accurate self-portrait. You may begin to know yourself better, if only through a process of elimination.

Having taken the test online at the site for free, you are told which of the four basic groups you fall into. To get the full report and a further breakdown of where you fall in the subtypes, you have to pay $9.95.

http://www.myfuture.com/career/interest.html

The site at www.myfuture.com/career/interest.html also contains a test, called the "Work Interest Quiz," based on Holland's six personality types.

It also provides a link to the site's "Personality Test," which actually jumps you to the Keirsey site previously described. In addition, this site contains a list of careers that are supposed to be good fits for each of the 16 subtypes. A Teacher makes a good writer or psychologist, while a Supervisor makes a good government employee. Field Marshals make good lawyers, but they also may be happy as chemical engineers or investment bankers. And so on.

http://www.utne.com/azEQ.tmpl

What's your "emotional IQ?" The Web site www.utne.com/azEQ.tmpl defines E-IQ as the ability to know your feelings and emotions and use them to your best advantage, rather than be held hostage to them. It gives you a short test to determine your E-IQ. The thing may smack of a parlor game, but reading the computer-generated discussion of your answers could give you food for thought. The *Utne Reader*, a literary magazine, maintains the site.

http://www.acareertest.com

The American Career Test Services of McKinney, Texas offers the American Career Test at www.acareertest.com. Reportedly, it only requires 10 minutes to take online. The computer-generated reports come in four sizes, ranging from $7.95 for an 8-pager on your work style to $59.95 for a 15-page report that goes over how others in the same field did, how you'll do as a manager, and "career optimization" tips.

The test is based on seven personality (or motivational) traits and four work styles. Here are the personality traits:

- *Observer.* The tendency to see beyond the surface and put things in logical order.
- *Performer.* The aptitude toward fixing and building things.
- *Philosopher.* The ability and desire to process facts and communicate them.

- *Inspirer.* The tendency to encourage, motivate, or just exhort others.
- *Contributor.* The tendency to perform when motivated.
- *Leader.* The possession of vision to see broadly and to lead and organize.
- *Supporter.* The tendency to help others.

The four work styles are as follows:

- *Action.* Oriented toward fact problem solving
- *Conceptual.* Oriented toward new and creative methods.
- *Facilitating.* Focused on solutions through group consensus and cooperation.
- *Process.* Oriented toward processing and monitoring methods and procedures.

The site indicates that everyone is a mix of these traits and styles, exhibiting a detectable pattern. Figure 4.1 shows sample test results with one candidate's pattern. An individual's personality and work patterns remain stable over time, the site contends, as do the patterns reflected by a career field. But within one's pattern, Observer traits are most evident in people under 30 and over 40, according to the site. (Do people shut their eyes in midlife?) The Leader trait is the opposite, strongest in the 30s. The Performer trait is most strongly expressed by people under 40, and the Philosopher trait by people over 40. The Inspirer trait is seen most strongly in people under 30. It slumps and levels off after that, the site maintains. The Contributor trait increases with age, and the Supporter trait usually remains stable.

The Conceptual work style peaks before 30 and then fades rapidly, possibly explaining a phenomenon often commented on by young workers behind the backs of old bosses. The Process style rises after age 40, after you have figured out what to pay attention to.

Men and women in the same field usually experience similar test results, However, men tend to exhibit more of the Philosopher trait, and women more of the Supporter trait. Men test higher in the Action work style, and women higher in the Conceptual and Facilitating styles.

http://www.CareerPerfect.com/CareerPerfect/careerplan.htm

CareerDesign is actually a set of four tests (plus decision-making advice) offered by www.careerperfect.com, the online service of Career Services Group, Inc., in Newman Lake, Washington. You can take it online or off-line (via downloaded software) for $49.95. The tests include a career-interest inventory, a personality

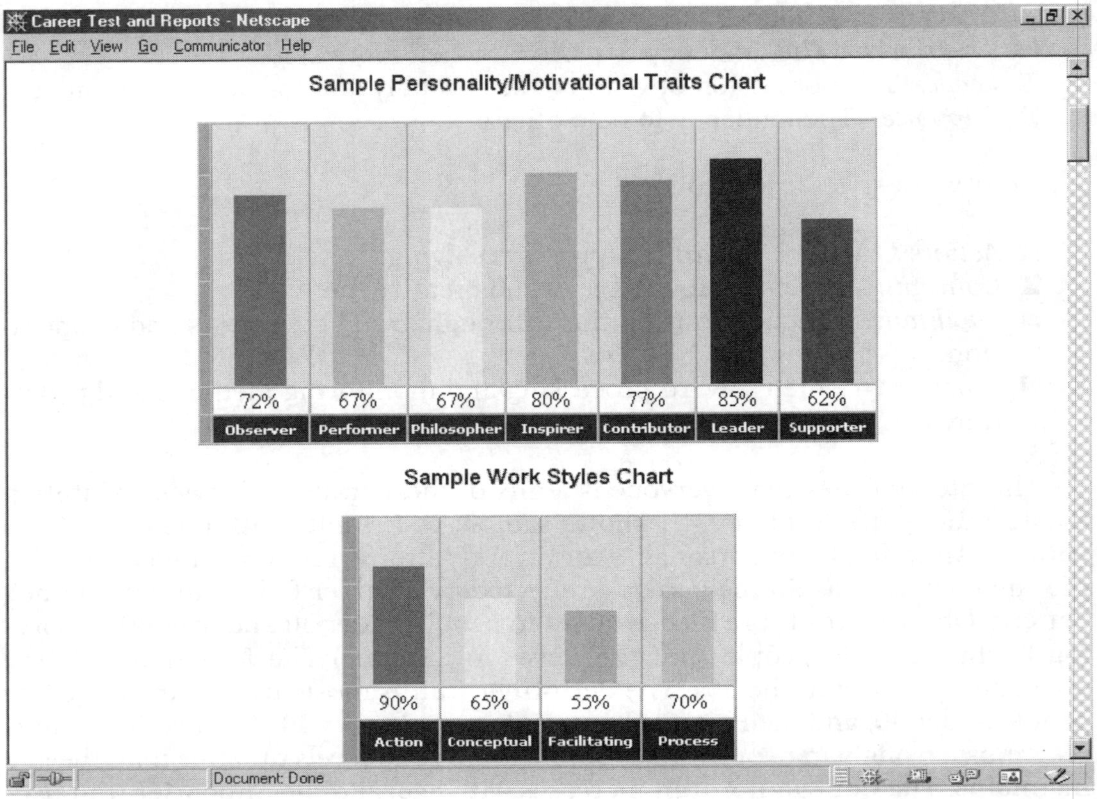

Figure 4.1 *Sample pattern of personal and work patterns that the American Career Test examines. (Reprinted from www.acareertest.com, by permission of American Career Test Services.)*

inventory, a value inventory, and a skills inventory. The site does not name tests or describe the theories behind them, but it does indicate that the results of the tests are delivered with extensive reports. The decision-making tools include links to salary and job-outlook sites.

http://www.jvis.com

The Jackson Vocational Interest Survey (JVIS) is offered through www.jvis.com by its developer, Sigma Assessment Systems, Inc., of Port Huron, Michigan. You can take the test free, online or off, but getting a report of your results costs $14.95. The online version is said to be available the instant you submit payment. The test covers more than five hundred questions and is said to take about forty-five minutes. The off-line version can be printed out, taken at leisure, and mailed back. The site boasts that the test places equal emphasis on the measurement of interests of women and men, using factors that do not take into account traditional male and female occupations.

http://careeradvantage.com

Bridges.com, a career counseling software firm in Kelowna, British Columbia, Canada, offers a career test at careeradvantage.com. Most of its products are aimed at students, but it also offers the "Career Advantage" package for $24.95. The package includes a test, career-planning training, and a library of career material.

The package's "Career Finder" test appears to build on the Holland system, charting your results in terms of Realistic, Investigative, Artistic, Social, Enterprising, and Conventional traits. It also rates your creative, interpersonal, organizational, leadership, math, physical, literary, and technical skills. It suggests possible career paths and plots your score against the requirements of that career.

http://www.careervectors.com

Federation Employment and Guidance Service's (FEGS) Career Vectors System in New York City offers an online test at www.careervectors.com for $69.95. But the time investment may be more off-putting than the price—reputedly, it takes about three hours to finish. But if you want something in-depth, that's the level of effort it will take.

Designed for people in the white-collar professions, the Career Vectors System reports that it will analyze your data and recommend "career clusters" that match your interest. It then provides specific job descriptions, as well as links to Web sites of possible interest, including job banks and resume services.

http://6steps.monster.com/step1/careerconverter

The branch of Monster.com at 6steps.monster.com/step1/careerconverter is a "Major to Career Converter." If you are a recent or pending graduate, you enter your major from a list. The site then returns a list of careers applicable to that major. You can then immediately search the Monster.com database for jobs in that career.

You've presumably inquired into the jobs that your major would lead to long before graduation, so the information should not be a revelation. But here you can keep running tabs on what the demand is like and adjust your expectations accordingly. (When you scroll down and see the words "Try A Different Major," don't be alarmed. That's not heartfelt career advice from Monster.com. Instead, it's giving you the option of running another search.)

http://asp.studentcenter.com/doctor/doctor.asp

The "Career Doctor" site at Monster.com, asp.studentcenter.com/doctor/doctor.asp, is aimed at students who are not sure what direction to go, in terms of a major or a career. The pages ask you to select either a college major from a list or the activity that interests you. (The latter list ranges widely, from accounting to "protecting property rights" to spelling to "applying history to contemporary problems.") If you input a major, the site then presents pages that describe the college major itself, the marketable skills that major should give you, and the careers it could lead to. If you input an activity that interests you, it presents college majors that emphasize that activity. "Applying history to contemporary problems," for example, points to anthropology and history.

http://6steps.monster.com/step1/teamplayer/

Team player is a big buzzword these days, and the page 6steps.monster.com/step1/teamplayer/, part of Monster.com, contains a questionnaire intended to determine whether you are a team player. If you score low, remember that people working in isolation can be very productive and additionally, don't have to attend meetings.

http://careerx.careerbuilder.com

The branch of www.careerbuilder.com at careerx.careerbuilder.com offers testing, counseling, and coaching. Testing includes CareerXpress, an entry-level test that takes about fifteen minutes to complete and will generate a report of 20 likely professions that fit your likes and dislikes. Taking it costs $17.50. For more in-depth results, there's the CareeRx Interest Test, which includes 316 questions and takes about forty minutes to complete. (It's based on a widely used test called the Strong Interest Inventory.) Taking it online costs nothing, or you can take the paper version for $15. Getting it scored and generating a report, however, costs $79. Having it interpreted for you by a professional staff member costs $189 (including scoring).

The site also offers counseling, via phone or online chatting. (The first session must be via phone.) The charge is $125 per 45-minute session.

Coaching costs the same. Coaching, the site explains, is aimed at specific career challenges (like looking for a job), whereas the intent of counseling is to improve your decision-making process by helping you know yourself better.

http://www.assessment.com

The Web site www.assessment.com is maintained by the International Assessment Network (IAN) of Minneapolis, Minnesota. The company sells the 40-year-old MAPP (Motivational Appraisal of Personal Potential), an assessment tool said to measure an individual's motivation toward specific work areas. The site offers an online version that you can take free of charge.

The MAPP consist of 71 questions that list three jobs or activities (e.g., operate a machine, teach a class, plan a vacation) and asks you to rate which you would prefer the most and which the least. (You leave the one you're lukewarm about blank.) It then generates a lengthy prose report, referring to you by first name as it describes your likes and dislikes before listing vocational recommendations (as shown in Figure 4.2).

Having read the assessment, you can then pick three jobs from a list and see how good a match they make with your assessment. (The site also gives a description of each job and a link to its entry in the online Occupational Outlook Handbook of the Department of Labor.)

Of course, the company also sells things. Instead of being limited to testing three jobs to see if they fit with your MAPP profile, for $9.95 you get 30-day access to the system. For $29.95, the Student Career Appraisal gives 30-day access to the MAPP matching system, plus a more extended analysis. The Career Appraisal gives 60-day access for $39.95, and the Personal Appraisal gives unlimited access for $129.95.

http://www.headhunter.net/JobSeeker/PsychTest/SalesInfo.asp

The section of www.headhunter.net at www.headhunter.net/JobSeeker/PsychTest/SalesInfo.asp offers, in partnership with the Computer Psychologist, what it calls a job-oriented personality profile, costing $40. Instead of asking if you'd rather be a salesperson than a pilot, it asks how you are with problem solving (pragmatic or conceptual, etc.), emotional patterns (unsure versus confident, emotional versus even keeled, etc.), and interpersonal skills (passive versus controlling, etc.). The report ends with a list of potential assets and liabilities. (The former might include, "He possesses well-developed listening skills." The latter might include, "His value system is in the process of development.") Finally, there is a "developmental recommendation." This might be something like, "She

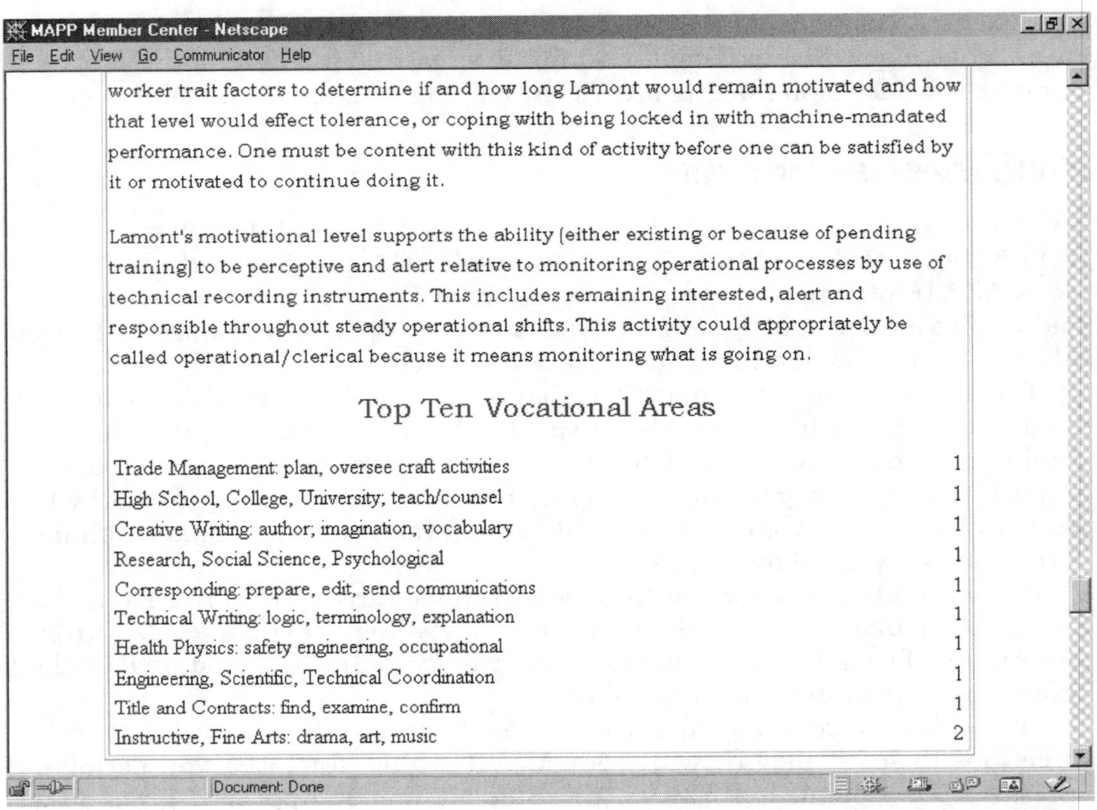
MAPP Member Center - Netscape

File Edit View Go Communicator Help

worker trait factors to determine if and how long Lamont would remain motivated and how that level would effect tolerance, or coping with being locked in with machine-mandated performance. One must be content with this kind of activity before one can be satisfied by it or motivated to continue doing it.

Lamont's motivational level supports the ability (either existing or because of pending training) to be perceptive and alert relative to monitoring operational processes by use of technical recording instruments. This includes remaining interested, alert and responsible throughout steady operational shifts. This activity could appropriately be called operational/clerical because it means monitoring what is going on.

Top Ten Vocational Areas

Trade Management: plan, oversee craft activities	1
High School, College, University; teach/counsel	1
Creative Writing: author; imagination, vocabulary	1
Research, Social Science, Psychological	1
Corresponding: prepare, edit, send communications	1
Technical Writing: logic, terminology, explanation	1
Health Physics: safety engineering, occupational	1
Engineering, Scientific, Technical Coordination	1
Title and Contracts: find, examine, confirm	1
Instructive, Fine Arts: drama, art, music	2

Document: Done

Figure 4.2 *Results of a MAPP assessment, showing suggested vocations. (Reprrinted from www.assessment.com, by permission of International Assessment Network.)*

will benefit from having extra time in learning new and complex material." Only the person who took the test can access the results.

http://www.adm.uwaterloo.ca/infocecs/CRC/manual-home.html

The Career Services site of the University of Waterloo in Waterloo, Ontario, Canada, www.adm.uwaterloo.ca/infocecs/CRC/manual-home.html, offers a six-step approach to career planning: self-assessment, occupational research, decision making, employment contacts, actually getting and working at a job, and reassessment.

The self-assessment step includes a worksheet to identify your own strengths, weaknesses, personality traits, and preferences; and to catalog your skills, experience, achievements, personal values, vocational interests, and your aptitude for entrepreneurism. You don't take a scored test and get an assessment; the act of doing the exercises is meant to provide the insight you need to decide what kind of job you want.

But if you already know what you want to do, you still have to decide if you are willing to relocate. And there are online tools to help even with that.

Where Do You Want to Live?

The job you want, or realistically expect to get, may not exist in your hometown. Or the job you want may exist in almost any town, and you anticipate offers from more than one. But a princely salary in Albuquerque, New Mexico, may condemn you to poverty in New York City. If you're dazzled by the lights of the big city, you may not care. But what if you get an offer from Fargo, North Dakota? The salary may sound fine, but what's the cost of living there?

Perhaps you would be perfectly happy to head off anywhere, as an adventure. But adventures are harder to justify if you are not single; in that case, you will want to see if the city in question has employment and cultural opportunities for your significant other. If you have children, then you want to see in advance what the schools are like. Crime, air pollution, and simple climate data will also help you make a calm decision.

Fortunately, you are not the first person to ever ask these questions, and there are sites on the Web poised to answer them. Some examples are listed in the following sections. Use more than one source, and arrive at a consensus. And as ever, inclusion on the list does not constitute endorsement.

http://verticals.yahoo.com/cities/

The real estate section of the Yahoo! search engine, verticals.yahoo.com/cities/, gives you two side-by-side lists of U.S. cities. You select one from each column and receive a comparison of the two cities on 25 different data points, including size, population density, crime rate, income, auto insurance, average commute time, and the number of days it rains or is sunny.

At the bottom of the page is a cost-of-living calculator, where you input a salary and see how it compares. Inputting $50,000, you are told, for example, that a $50,000 Albuquerque lifestyle will require $221,951.22 to maintain in New York City, whereas a $50,000 New York lifestyle would only put you back $11,263.74 in Albuquerque.

You are not limited to comparing two cities. On the opening page, you can list all the cities in the database (about eight hundred) by one data item, such as average rainfall or the percentage of the adult population that holds bachelor's degrees. Perhaps you feel you'd be more comfortable among educated people and check the latter. Chevy Chase, Maryland, comes in first, with 80 percent. Dead last is Crosby, Texas, with 4 percent.

Clicking on any data item in a report for a city will get you a sorted list of all the cities—for example, clicking on rainfall gets you a list from the wettest to the driest city. Clicking on a city name in a list results in a report on that city. (Average one-way commute times, incidentally, range from 36 minutes in Bridgeport, Massachusetts, to 11.4 minutes in Bismarck, North Dakota. The cost of a 2,000-square-foot home runs from $900,000 in Atherton, California, down to $100,000 in Sierra Vista, Arizona. The average monthly cost of electricity for that home ranges from $138 in Hilo, Hawaii, to $30 in Seattle, Washington. The cost-of-living index ranges from 364 in New York City to 49 in Anniston, Alabama, 100 being average. Crimes per 100,000 persons ranged from 26,714 in Atlantic City, New Jersey, down to 648 in Calabasas, California, although more than a hundred fifty cities made no report.

http://www.homefair.com/calc/salcalc.html

The "Salary Calculator" appears at www.homefair.com/calc/salcalc.html, maintained by Homestore.com, which operates a family of sites related to real estate and renting, headquartered in Westlake Village, California.

On the calculator form, you input your state of origin and the state you want to move to. The site then gives you a second screen where you can select cities or metropolitan areas in those cities, the salary in question, and whether you will be renting or owning your home. You will then see that to make the equivalent of a $50,000 salary in Albuquerque as a renter, you will need to make $109,996 in Manhattan. In Fargo, you will only need $43,518.

The site's cost-of-living data is provided by the Center for Mobility Resources in Scottsdale, Arizona, and assumes that the cost of living is 33 percent housing, 8 percent utilities, 16 percent consumables, 10 percent transportation, and 33 percent services.

The site also has a calculator for Canadian cities and a calculator in Spanish.

You can also get a report on the school districts of the city you are interested in, from National School Reporting Services, Inc., charting things like school-age population, average teacher-student ratio, average first-grade class size and high school math-class sizes, use of computers in elementary schools, SAT scores, percentage of students going on to college, and any awards or recognition earned by the district.

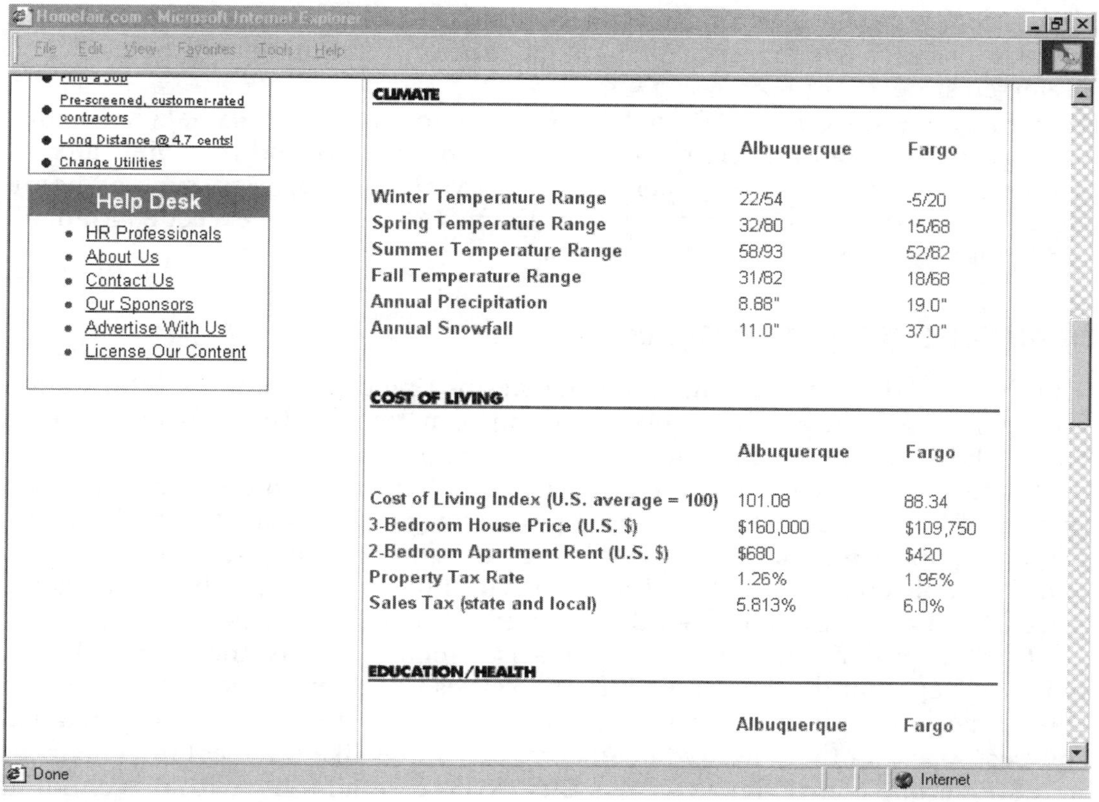

Homefair.com - Microsoft Internet Explorer

File Edit View Favorites Tools Help

- Pre-screened, customer-rated contractors
- Long Distance @ 4.7 cents!
- Change Utilities

Help Desk

- HR Professionals
- About Us
- Contact Us
- Our Sponsors
- Advertise With Us
- License Our Content

CLIMATE

	Albuquerque	Fargo
Winter Temperature Range	22/54	-5/20
Spring Temperature Range	32/80	15/68
Summer Temperature Range	58/93	52/82
Fall Temperature Range	31/82	18/68
Annual Precipitation	8.88"	19.0"
Annual Snowfall	11.0"	37.0"

COST OF LIVING

	Albuquerque	Fargo
Cost of Living Index (U.S. average = 100)	101.08	88.34
3-Bedroom House Price (U.S. $)	$160,000	$109,750
2-Bedroom Apartment Rent (U.S. $)	$680	$420
Property Tax Rate	1.26%	1.95%
Sales Tax (state and local)	5.813%	6.0%

EDUCATION/HEALTH

	Albuquerque	Fargo

Done | Internet

Figure 4.3 *Part of a city report comparing Albuquerque, New Mexico, with Fargo, North Dakota. (Reprinted from www.homefair.com. © 1999–2001 Homestore.com, Inc. All rights reserved.)*

You can also request a "city report" listing data on an origin city and two destination cities. But first you have to fill out a form with information that would be of interest to firms that want to advertise relocation services. That done, you get a side-by-side comparison of information about the origin city and a destination city on each report. Items include demographics, median income, climate, cost of living, number of hospitals and doctors, expenditures per pupil, names of local colleges and universities, and major local employers. At last check, the cost of a three-bedroom house, in case you were wondering, was $160,000 in Albuquerque, $800,000 in Manhattan, and $109,750 in Fargo, as partially shown in Figure 4.3.

The site also offers a "Lifestyle Optimizer," a sort of calculator that lists the best 10 cities for you to live in based on your answers to a questionnaire. Questions include your preferences on city size, crime rate, unemployment rate, housing prices, average income, tax rate, temperature, rainfall and snowfall, and preferred state, if any.

Finally, the site offers a "Relocation Crime Lab," similar to its Salary Calculator. Again, you input an origin city and a destination city and then view a chart comparing the rate of crimes per 100,000 in various categories, such as homicides, rapes, robberies, assaults, and car thefts. (Albuquerque exceeded Manhattan in all categories except robbery.)

http://www.monstermoving.com

This branch of Monster.com, www.monstermoving.com, contains information about moving, hiring movers, buying a house, and so on. In terms of picking a city, it also lets you generate city reports and compare two cities.

On the opening page, click the "Find a Place" option, and then find the Tools section of the page menu. It includes options for generating a city profile, a city-profile comparison chart, a cost-of-living calculator, a salary-comparison tool, and a school-report generator. (It also provides tools for researching real estate prices. Similar tools can be found on numerous real estate sites.)

The city report and the city comparison chart display the same 24 data points, except that the latter does it for two cities. Monster.com's note on the data states that you should rely on it at your own risk, without providing detailed sources. As with other sites, you can compare things like the local income taxes in Albuquerque (zero) and New York City ($1,342 for a family with two children and an income of $50,000). Additionally, this site gives the prices of a 2,000-square-foot home in New York City as $820,000, versus $180,000 in Albuquerque, with property taxes as $15,580 versus $1,980, and the cost of electricity as $116 versus $66. Education information consists of the percentage of the population with diplomas.

The cost-of-living tool asks not only where you live and where you want to live but where you work and where you want to work, assuming the two are separate. After asking for details such as salary, spouse's salary, dependents, amount of car insurance, yearly electricity bill, whether you will own or rent, how much rent you pay now, and how much living space you hope to inhabit after you move, it generates a five-part report. A single person making $50,000, paying $1,100 rent in Albuquerque, and hoping to inhabit 2,000 square feet in New York City will find life more expensive by the tune of $25,167. One would need an increase of $44,741 in gross salary to break even on this move. And the site is kind enough to point out that that $25,167 per year that you would be missing would, if invested at 6 percent, yield almost a million dollars in 25 years. (If you were moving to cheaper digs in Fargo, the calculator says you would have $2,792 more in your pocket at the end of the year, that the move effectively gives you a raise of 9.1 percent, and that you would have about $100,000 after 20 years if you invest it at 6 percent.)

The Salary Calculator applies cost-of-living adjustments to your salary, showing that a $50,000 salary will get you a lifestyle in New York equivalent to what $11,264 will get you in Albuquerque. If you make $50,000 in Albuquerque, you will need $221,951 to live the same way in New York.

The School Report gives you a chart about the school districts in that city or county, from National School Reporting Services, Inc., similar to the report generated by http://www.homefair.com.

http://www.wetfeet.com

The Web site www.wetfeet.com includes city guides on the 30 fastest-growing cities in terms of jobs. (That includes Frankfurt, Hong Kong, London, and Tokyo, as well as the usual suspects among U.S. cities.) View the list by clicking the "Locations" option in the Do Research heading. It also has a salary calculator and school reports similar to the sites already examined.

Other Sites

Several sites detailed in the next section also compare salaries by city.

Having decided what you want to do, and where you want to do it, you will want an idea of what you can expect to make in that job in that city. Again, there are Web sources to help.

What Are You Worth?

You must assure yourself that the job you are shooting for is worth your while. If it is not, then you should flip back to this chapter's first section to find some other line of work. (Otherwise, you'll be doing something you don't believe in, and it will show.) If you are convinced it is worth your while, then visions of the glittering purchasing power it will give you will provide all the motivation you need to carry you through the job search process.

But there is more to it than that. Once you do target a job in what you think is the right career, in the right city, apply for it, and make the cut, then you will be called in for an interview. At some point (preferably after the interview), you will be asked how much money you want. What comes out of your mouth next could pave the way to a fulfilling new job or could prevent you from ever feeling good about the job even if you get it. If you ask for grossly more than the going rate, they may drop you from consideration. If you ask for moderately too much, you may be in for some haggling, which is okay if it is confined to the HR department but potentially uncomfortable if future supervisors or coworkers are involved. If you ask for too little, you may get only what you asked for and miss out on the money that was available—and you will probably not remain blissfully ignorant of that fact after you start the job. Either way, you will start out on the wrong foot—feeling embarrassed that you did not know such a basic piece of information.

Of course, you should begin your research into salary information with your circle of friends and coworkers, branching out to whatever professional associations are available, plus whatever online (Usenet, etc.) contacts you have. Then you should go on and confirm your impressions with the sources of information detailed here. You should not rely on any single source.

Having derived some figures, however, do not treat them as if they were carved in stone. Remember the used car analogy: Each one is different. Some have better paint jobs, and some have radios that don't work. Hopefully, your self-assessment has given you enough confidence that you feel that you know where you are positioned within a range when you see it.

For purposes of comparison, each source in the following sections was asked for the salary range of an entry-level bank teller in Hartford, Connecticut. These sites, of course, should only be taken as a representative sample of what's out there, and their inclusion does not constitute an endorsement. Good luck—and don't be slipping in any extra zeros.

http://salarycenter.monster.com

The data at the Salary Center at Monster.Com, salarycenter.monster.com, is based on job searches, negotiations, and placements conducted by Robert Half International. The fields it covers are accounting and finance (auditing, banking, bookkeepers, brokers, etc.), creative (mostly advertising and public relations), financial consulting (project-related positions), legal (attorneys and staff), office support (receptionists, word processing, switchboard, etc.), and technology (database administration, groupware, security, e-commerce, etc.). It breaks down each job classification by position, and you then pick the desired city and state. But the site does not cover sales, construction, transportation, government, education, or entertainment.

There was also no mention of bank tellers in the banking category under accounting and finance. It did have information on entry-level commercial lenders, which pay $55,200 to $74,462.

http://www.salary.com

Salary.com provides compensation information to recruiters and employers but also offers a free service, its Salary Wizard that gives average salary by job and location. You'll find Salary Wizard on the site's opening page.

Salary Wizard lets you select from a list of about seventy job categories, ranging from accounting to warehousing. Then you input the metropolitan area (or the ZIP code) you are interested in and click Search. (Getting membership at the site is not necessary.)

Choosing Banking in the Hartford area brought up a list of banking positions, from accountant I to loan officer. (There was nothing that looked like a management position probably because those salaries are negotiated one-on-one.) Selecting "teller" then brought up a full-screen salary report, charting the low ($16,705), medium ($20,524), and high ($25,191) range, shown charted in Figure 4.4. Keep in mind that the range covers the percentile between 25 and 70 percent. Therefore, a quarter of the tellers were making above the high range, and (sadly) another quarter were making below the low range. The report also included a job description.

The page also lets you check the cash compensation (including incentives and bonuses) that could be expected with the job. (It made no significant difference in this case, but it would with certain sales and management jobs.) You can also compare the pay for that job in Hartford to other cities, as well as the national average, plotted on a new graph. (For instance, Hartford was slightly below San Francisco and slightly above the national average.) You can also compare the pay to that of other jobs in the same industry, again plotted on a graph. (A credit analyst I, whatever that is, gets paid nearly twice as much.)

Salary.com also includes a link to a list of Web sites of related trade associations, government data, and trade publications.

Salary.com derives its salary data figures from employer-reported data and does not use reports from individuals about what they make or data from placement agencies or job postings. It claims to have reviewed data covering 1.3 million jobs from more than five thousand employers and that more than 90 percent of the pay levels in the Salary Wizard are based on data from more than a hundred salaries. Moreover, it only reports on a market if there are multiple sources reporting reasonably consistent data.

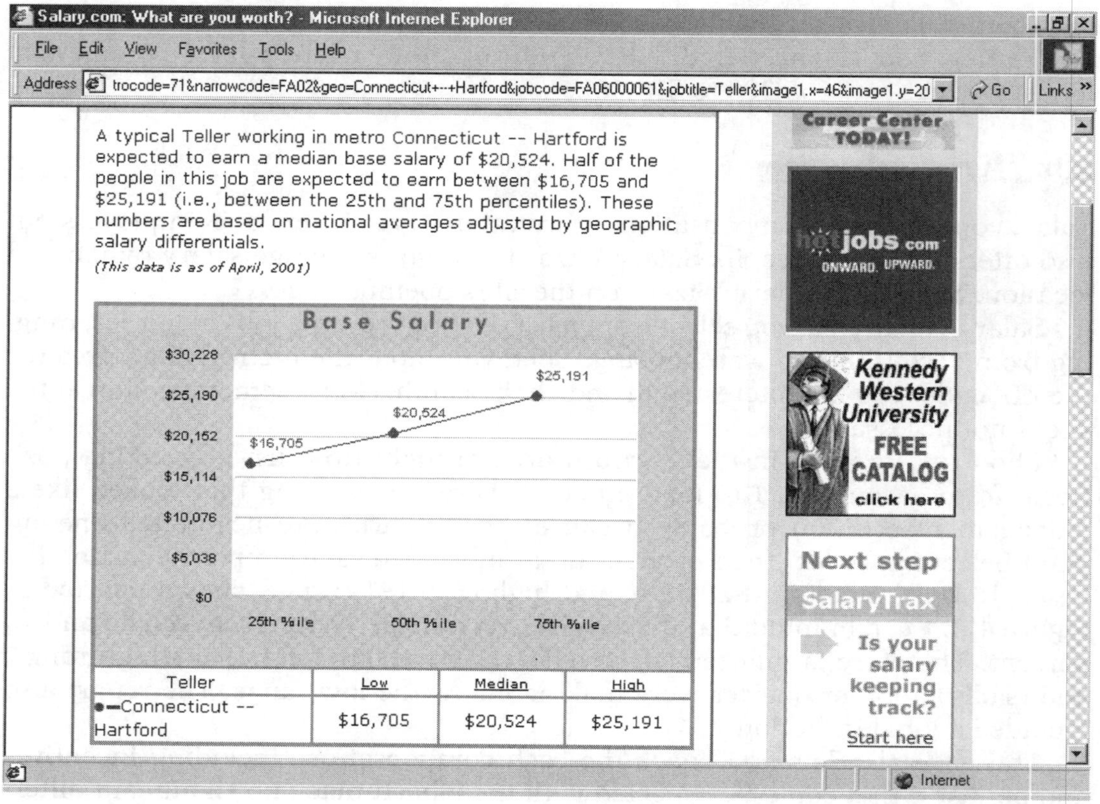

Fig. 4.4 *Salary range for a bank teller in Hartford, Connecticut, as charted by Salary.com. (Reprinted from www.salary.com, by permission of Salary.com.)*

The site also includes a service called SalaryTrax, which lets you plot your salary, bonuses, and compensation against your peers. It also links you to hotjobs.com so you can view job offerings that match your current one (or match criteria that you set).

http://jobsmart.org/tools/salary/sal-prof.htm

The salary information center at jobsmart.org/tools/salary/sal-prof.htm of JobStar, formerly JobSmart, is a job search site set up with a federal grant by the Bay Area Library & Information System, serving northern California (which includes Silicon Valley). The salary center is actually a collection of links to about three hundred other sites that include salary information concerning the job, career, or industry in question. The information and the organization and classification of that information is idiosyncratic to each site.

The site lists more than fifty profession-related survey links, from accounting to "wood and paper." For information on bank tellers, clicking on Banking gives four possible links, for investment banking, commercial banking, an industry report, and a report on information technology salaries in banking. Clicking the commercial banking survey brings up the salary-information page of http://www.careers-in-finance.com. This site does not go as low as teller, starting instead with credit analyst trainees, who get $27,000. It provides no geographic breakdown.

http://stats.bls.gov/ocohome.htm

The Web site of the online version of the Occupational Outlook Handbook, stats.bls.sov/ocohome.htm, is produced every other year by the Department of Labor Statistics of the U.S. Department of Labor.

The top of the page presents a search field. Searching for *teller* brought, among others, a long page about bank tellers, exhaustively covering the nature of the work, working conditions, employment statistics, training, qualifications, job outlook, earnings, related occupations, and other sources of information. About five hundred thousand people work as bank tellers, it notes, but demand for them is decreasing due to cost cutting and automation. The median salary was $17,200 in 1998. The site provides no geographic breakdown.

http://www.wageweb.com

Wageweb.com is a salary survey site set up by an HR consulting firm called Human Resources Programs Development and Improvement in Richmond, Virginia. It covers salaries in HR, administrative services, information management, engineering, health care, sales and marketing, and manufacturing.

Banking was not specifically covered, but the finance section listed 19 positions, from bookkeeper to chief financial officer, with averages as of June 1, 2000. For bookkeepers, the average annual salary was $27,901, based on 1,673 employees at 690 responding companies. It provides no geographic breakdown.

http://www.erieri.com/cgi-bin/benchsal.cgi

Forget what your job makes today: What will it make in 15 years? You can get that question answered at www.erieri.com/cgi-bin/benchsal.cgi, a promotional effort by the Economic Research Institute, a compensation-and-benefits research firm in Redmond, Washington. It lists more than four thousand jobs and shows that bank tellers should average $28,350 in 2015. It gives no geographic breakdown, but the user can specify Canada, where the job should pay $26,142 in Canadian dollars.

http://www.erieri.com/cgi-bin/alsurvey.cgi

Put together by the previously mentioned Economic Research Institute of Redmond, Washington, www.erieri.com/cgi-bin/alsurvey.cgi lists links to more than 750 online salary and compensation surveys, compiled by organizations large and small, local, national and international, from the Assisted Living Salary and Benefits Report of the Hospital & Healthcare Compensation Service to the Wyoming Compensation and Personnel Practices survey of the Mountain States Employers' Council, Inc. It takes up 300K, but you can download it and search it with your browser's Find command. The list may have just what you need, or it may be a waste of time—it's a matter of pure luck.

http://www.salaryexpert.com

Baker, Thomsen Associates Insurance Services, Inc., a privately held compensation-and-benefits consulting firm in Newport Beach, California, offers www. salaryexpert.com. Using a form on the opening page, you can select from 826 different jobs and then from a list of metropolitan areas in the United States and Canada. Or, you can input a ZIP code.

The site not only includes figures for bank tellers in Hartford, Connecticut, but can adjust the figure based on the cost of living in that area. The average teller there makes $19,543, plus benefits amounting to another 17.1 percent, giving an average total compensation of $22,885. However, that amount gives the teller "buying power" of only $18,339.

The site emphasizes that the cost of living and the salary levels in an area do not correlate and that to gauge the attractiveness of an offer you need to compare it with the cost of living in that area—hence, the addition of a "buying power" figure. The Salaryexpert.com model makes its comparison based on the differing costs of living that would be encountered by a family of four in a state with average state taxes (3 percent state income tax), two cars worth $20,000 driven 30,000 miles yearly, renting 1,240 square feet of living space, and covered by a health maintenance organization.

There's also a downloadable version of SalaryExpert that runs on Windows, offering about thirty thousand different job descriptions, starting at ATM Specialist and Abattoir Supervisor to Luge Coach, to Zyglo Tester. (What's a "wrinkle chaser" or "wrong address clerk"? This software may be your only chance to find out.) The metropolitan areas cover about two hundred countries or territories, from Aachen and Zweibrucken, Germany, to places like Gisenyi, Rwanda, Kathmandu, Nepal, and Outer Island, Kiribati. Alternately, you can restrict it to the United States and Canada. (There's also a version of the software for the Palm Pilot operating system.)

The off-line data for a bank teller (shown in Figure 4.5) was the same as the online data. (For some reason, however, the site distinguishes between a "bank teller" and a lower-paid "banking teller." The previously quoted figures were for the latter.) It also charts a comparison with the national average and gives exten-

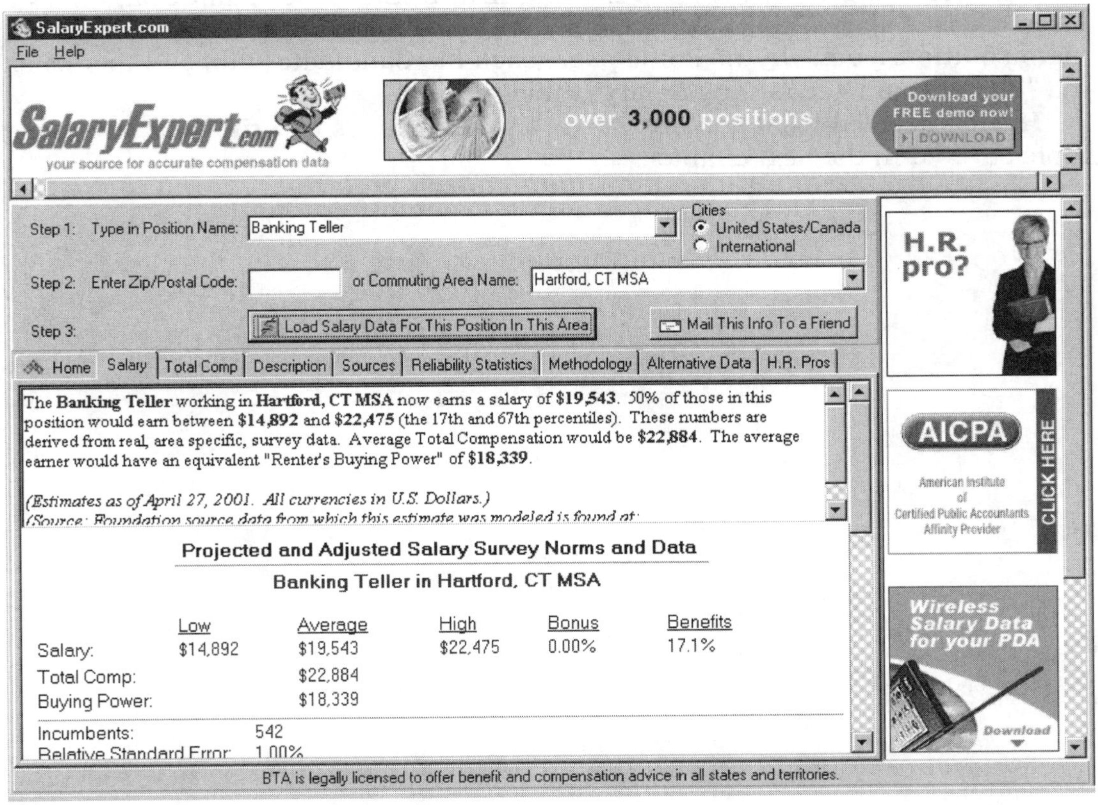

Figure 4.5 *Salary range for a "banking teller" in Hartford, Connecticut, using SalaryExpert.com's off-line version.(Reprinted by permission of Baker, Thomsen Associates Insurance Services.)*

sive data on the job description and data methodology. (You will want the latter if you are ever involved in deep compensation disagreements, the kind that end up in court.)

In case you were wondering, a banking teller in Aachen averages 77,721 deutsch marks, one in Zweibrucken has to get by on 76,126 deutsch marks, one in Gisenyi makes 3,115,863 Rwandan francs, one in Kathmandu makes 671,701 Nepalese rupees, and on the Outer Island they make 15,706 Australian dollars, with the caveat that there may not actually be any banking tellers there.

Data is provided by Economic Research Institute of Redmond, Washington.

http://www.mgmtsolutions.com

Management Solutions, Inc., a recruiting firm in San Jose, California, offers a "West Coast Salary Guide for Finance and Accounting Professionals" at www.mgmtsolutions.com. On the home page, click the Candidates tab, and then click the "Finance and Accounting Salary Guide" option.

Having decided what you are worth, the next step is to write your resume, a topic covered in the next chapter.

CHAPTER 5

Writing Your Electronic Resume

Whether you call it a resume, résumé, curriculum vitae, or CV, things have changed. Yes, the resume is still a document that summarizes your life. It still must sell you to total strangers and convince them to give you an interview. You still want it handsomely formatted and printed so that it commands respect.

But these days, the printed resume is not what does the trick. You still want to have one to pass around, but you also need electronic versions of the same information for various purposes. Notice that "versions" is plural; you may need several electronic formats before you're through:

- *Keyword:* Your resume with a keyword listing, to make it stand out in a database.
- *Scannable:* Your resume printed in such a way that it can be scanned into a corporate HR database.
- *ASCII:* Your resume in plain ASCII text, to submit via e-mail (often in place of a scannable resume).
- *Web form:* Your resume broken down into data entries on a Web page form. You can usually cut and paste it from the ASCII version.
- *Web page:* Your resume published on the Internet as a Web site.
- *The cover letter.* Your resume isn't complete without it.

In this chapter, you'll learn how to assault the battlements of the Paperwork Empire using these new weapons.

But slow down. Dealing with the formats is the easy part. First, you have to write your resume.

You and Your Resume

A large amount of literature out there covers resume writing. For now, just keep in mind that the people who write the paychecks and have created the position you are trying to get are not really interested in hiring anyone. Instead, they want to solve a problem. The job in question exists because they have decided to hire a person to solve that problem. So your resume needs to demonstrate that you are the kind of person who could solve the problem that's troubling them because you have done so in the past.

Therefore, your resume must focus on your past accomplishments. You can't say, "I was a schoolteacher." You have to turn yourself into a verb and see your job as a series of accomplishments: "I managed the educational attainments and molded the behavior of 20 fourth graders, successfully meeting state-mandated curriculum goals." Surely, anyone who did that can run General Motors.

On the other hand, if they are truly looking for a schoolteacher rather than a chief executive officer, then your verbal packaging will go right over their heads. In that case, they want to know that you have the necessary credentials and experience. The problem they are trying to solve is that they have an opening that has to be filled, and whomever they hire to fill it must meet specific requirements.

The trick is to know what the company is after. That involves knowing what problem they are trying to solve and what buzzwords they use to describe the problem. Being in the profession yourself, you are probably already familiar with its buzzwords. You can get additional guidance from the job posting itself.

Here is some more specific advice:

- *Be concise.* Two pages are all they are likely to read. If you think a little more exposition is required, put it in the cover letter. (But longer resumes are common in highly technical fields because you'll have to describe the projects you worked on.)
- *Quantify.* You saved X amount of money for your employer. You managed X number of people. And so on. Little details show that you were paying attention. A lot of people seem to think that they are supposed to be vague. Don't be one of them.

- *Don't bore.* Many people also seem to think that resumes are supposed to be dull as dishwater. Don't be one of them, either.
- *Tailor it.* Revamp your resume for every job you go after. Word processors make it easy.
- *Polish it.* Make each resume a finished product. Word processors make that easy, too—rent one at a copy shop if you have to. Use a letter-quality printer and white, letter-sized paper.
- *Update it.* This week, you may not need your resume. Next week, things could be different.
- *Don't inflate it.* Using strategically enhanced action verbs is not the same as making up a new past. Once they find one little inoperative statement, they'll think the whole thing is a lie.
- *Don't decorate it.* Go easy on the fancier word-processing features. Whoever gets the resume is supposed to read it for its information, not stand in awe of its intricate, decorative, multicolumn layout.
- *Observe the unwritten rules.* Don't use the first person (I, me). These days, you're not supposed to include your photo or marital status because of the affirmative action implications. You are assumed to have references, so you don't need to say "references on request" (although some think that saying it will reassure the reader). Just don't actually include the references. Don't state your salary requirements. Don't go on about what you did in high school. And to be really fashionable you need to omit anything that labels your document as a resume because that is supposed to be self-evident. Some insist that the word *resume* should not appear in your resume. Doubtless the fashion will eventually swing the other way.
- *Show you have a life.* Do you know languages? Have you ever coached a Little League team? Do you have any hobbies? Do you belong to any notable organizations? Have you won any awards? Those are the things that make you an individual. Mention them, and you may find that they carry a lot of weight.

Parts of the Resume

Any resume should include the following:

- *Contact information.* Although you need to include your name and contact information, you should leave out marital status, health, and age. Do not include your Social Security number, for reasons given in Chapter 3.

- *Objective.* You are drawn by your abilities and background to a career path whose next step happens to be the job in question. However, don't be so specific that you put yourself out of contention for related jobs. (But if you are in a field without established career paths, you can usually skip the objective.)
- *Summary.* State your qualifications for this job, without getting into details.
- *Employment history:* What jobs have you held and what have you accomplished in those jobs? State the job title, employer, and dates and then artfully summarize your responsibilities and accomplishments using action verbs. You can break it down into "Professional Experience" and "Other Work Experience" if you've had jobs in a different field.
- *Education.* State what academic degrees you have and where and when you got them, starting at the highest and then working backward. Omit high school.
- *Your life.* That stuff about hobbies and honors should be included, usually in a section labeled "Additional Information."

Certain fields or life situations call for additional sections, such as the following:

- *Skills.* What other training have you picked up along the way?
- *Credentials and certifications.* For jobs that require that you have certain pieces of paper, you need to state unequivocally that you have them, down to the serial numbers.
- *Research.* In some fields, listing your research publications is a life-or-death issue, even if it takes 50 pages. Papers that have been accepted but not published yet are listed as being "in press."
- *Extracurricular activities.* Graduating students need to demonstrate that they were not hiding in their rooms during their college careers. But established professionals needn't revisit those years.
- *Military experience.* Mention if you were in military service, highlighting your accomplishments with action verbs just like you would with any other job.
- *Keywords.* In some cases, you will want to have a keyword section so that your resume will show up on a database. Think of it as a summary section intended to be read by a computer (although human beings are also free to read it.) The use of keywords is explained in a separate section later in this chapter.

Organizing Your Resume

If you have cataloged your life and your aims and are ready to commit the results to paper, the next step is to decide how to arrange it all on the page. There are three schools of thought when it comes to organizing the resume: the chronological style, the functional style, and the combination style. All have their place, and you may consider trying all three versions.

Chronological Resumes

With a chronological resume, you step through your life, moving in reverse order from your current situation back to the dawn of your career (putting in the contact information, objective, summary, and so on, first).

Use a chronological resume when the position you are seeking is the logical successor to your previous jobs. Those jobs presumably show that your responsibilities have increased as your experience has deepened. They also, you hope, indicate a solid job history rather than the kind of turnover that hints at marginal employability.

Figure 5.1 illustrates the idea. Another advantage of chronological resumes is that they are easy to do—all you have to do is think backward.

The chronological resume is probably the most common type of resume, and the job sites with online resume composition systems generally produce chronological resumes.

Functional Resumes

Also called the skills resume, the functional resume is best used when you are changing careers and the progression of your previous jobs does not exactly culminate with the job you want. However, many of the skills you have picked up would be applicable to the job in question (you hope). You may also want to use the functional resume if the companies you have worked for are obscure, you were self-employed, your work record embodies a lot of turnover, or there is no apparent theme in your job record because of career changes. You still give your job history, but briefly, in a separate section, as shown in Figure 5.2.

(There is also the analytical resume, where you analyze the skills and experience needed for the job that you are seeking and then catalog your career to demonstrate that you have those prerequisites, while detailing where you got them. The problem is that the person doing the hiring may not agree with your analysis.)

Combination Resume

The combination resume uses elements of both the chronological resume and the functional resume. The combined form is best when you have a long work

AMADEUS LAZLO "Lenny" JOBSEEKER
1234 Main Street, South Metropolis, Megastate 00001
Phone: (101) 555-1234 Fax: (101) 555-5678
E-mail: lazlo@whatever.com

OBJECTIVE

To become Accounting Manager at a large public firm where I can both fully use and extend my strong accounting, business, and social skills.

SUMMARY

My skills and background, plus my proven ability to perform under pressure, make me uniquely qualified for a financial position in the current unsettled economic conditions of the Megastate region.

PROFESSIONAL EXPERIENCE

<u>12/98–Present: Accounting Manager, The Wet Cement Group, Metropolis, Megastate.</u>
Manage the financials of a medium-sized ($50 million) construction firm. Responsibilities include budgeting and material requirements planning. Reduced the firm's cost of material 15 percent across the board by renegotiating contracts with suppliers, while the accounting staff was reduced from seven to three.

<u>2/95–11/98: Accounting Manager, AAA Bail Bond Corp., Sumburg, Mesostate.</u>
Managed and directed joint accounting/financial control and operations of a bail bond business. Prepared operating plans and budgets for presentation to senior management. Instituted controls that doubled the firm's return on invested capital, reduced operating expenses by 73 percent by firing the owner's nephew, and brought the firm to sustained profitability by helping corner a fugitive in a warehouse.

<u>10/87–12/94: Controller, Elemeno Corp., Atro City, Minorstate.</u>
Began as data entry clerk and rose to manage 21-person accounting staff. Prepared and analyzed financial statements, assisted the development of annual business plans, and audited operations to ensure internal accuracy. Was able (through swift adoption of the latest information technology) to respond to the rapidly shifting reporting needs of management and later the receivers as sales shrank from $400 million to zero and the firm was liquidated.

EDUCATION

1987, Bachelor of Business Administration
Tristate University, Metropolis, Megastate.

ADDITIONAL INFORMATION

Was a Little League coach until forced to retire by injuries. Hobbies include whaling reenactments, steam locomotive restoration, and collecting antique podiatry instruments.

Figure 5.1 *A chronological resume, with the professional experience listed as a series of jobs in reverse chronological order, beginning with the present.*

AMADEUS LAZLO "Lenny" JOBSEEKER
1234 Main Street, South Metropolis, Megastate 00000
Phone: (101) 555-1234 Fax: (101) 555-5678
E-mail: lazlo@whatever.com

OBJECTIVE
To become Business Manager at a large public firm where I can both fully use and extend my strong accounting, business, and social skills.

SUMMARY
My skills and background, plus my proven ability to perform under pressure, make me uniquely qualified for a financial position in the current unsettled economic conditions of the Megastate region.

PROFESSIONAL SKILLS
Accounting
- Handled budget and material requirements planning.
- Reduced supply costs by 15 percent through contract renegotiation.
- Instituted capital management.
- Introduced information technology.

Management
- Oversaw staff reductions.
- Prepared financial statement and business plans.
- Handled major bankruptcy.
- Eliminated nepotism and corruption.
- Pursued fugitives.

JOB HISTORY
12/98–Present: Accounting Manager, The Wet Cement Group, Metropolis, Megastate.
2/95–11/98: Accounting Manager, AAA Bail Bond Corp., Sumburg, Mesostate.
10/87–12/94: Controller, Elemeno Corp., Atro City, Minorstate.

EDUCATION
1987, Bachelor of Business Administration
Tristate University, Metropolis, Megastate.

ADDITIONAL INFORMATION
Was a Little League coach until forced to retire by injuries. Hobbies include whaling reenactments, steam locomotive restoration, and collecting antique podiatry instruments.

Figure 5.2 *Example of a functional resume, repackaging the same information that appeared in Figure 5.1, but with an emphasis on skills and what the candidate accomplished with those skills. Job history is put in a separate, skeletal section.*

history and you've picked up a lot of skills in various places. You list the skills while summarizing the work history, as illustrated in Figure 5.3. Additionally, if your skills seem to be a perfect fit for the desired job, the combination resume lets you highlight the fact.

Now Slow Down

The rest of this chapter covers how to put your resume into various computer formats that will be of use during an online job search. But realize that generating these formats is the easy part. Don't assume that getting your resume into a computerized format means that you have accomplished some wonderful feat and now belong to an elite club—and that being a member of that club makes the content of your resume secondary.

The content of the resume is primary. Get it the way you want it—in several versions. Revamp it for every job you apply for. Only then does the rest of the chapter come into play.

Keyword Resumes

The resume you have been working on up to now is referred to as your "visual" resume. It is intended to be handed out to people, who will read it the usual way. Of course, the act of reading involves analysis, and analysis leads to comprehension. For instance, someone reading the previous examples will comprehend that the job candidate has experience in the fields of accounting and business management.

The resumes that make up the rest of this chapter are intended for computer consumption. They will be put in a database and searched rather than read. Alas—searching does not involve comprehension.

For instance, in the previous resume examples, it is clear that the candidate has been working for a construction company. But the functional and combination versions of the resume do not explicitly say that. If someone were searching the resume database for a candidate with accounting experience in the construction field, those examples would not come up.

The problem is not limited to these examples. In fact, it's one of the major drawbacks of information technology. Remember, you may be the biggest seller of kitchen knives around, but no computer will find you if it has been told to look

AMADEUS LAZLO "Lenny" JOBSEEKER
1234 Main Street, South Metropolis, Megastate 00001
Phone: (101) 555-1234 Fax: (101) 555-5678
E-mail: lazlo@whatever.com

OBJECTIVE
To become Accounting Manager at a large public firm where I can both fully use and extend my strong accounting, business, and social skills.

SUMMARY
My skills and background, plus my proven ability to perform under pressure, make me uniquely qualified for a financial position in the current unsettled economic conditions of the Megastate region.

PROFESSIONAL EXPERIENCE
<u>Accounting Manager</u>
12/98–Present: Accounting Manager, The Wet Cement Group, Metropolis, Megastate.
2/95–11/98: AAA Bail Bond Corp., Sumburg, Mesostate.

- Handled budget and MRP (at Wet Cement).
- Oversaw staff reduction (at Wet Cement).
- Reduced materials costs by 15 percent through contract negotiation (at Wet Cement).
- Instituted capital management (at AAA)
- Eliminated nepotism and corruption (at AAA).

<u>Controller</u>
10/87–12/94: Elemeno Corp., Atro City, Minorstate.

- Introduced latest information technology.
- Prepared financial statement and business plans.
- Met all management and regulatory requirements through bankruptcy and into liquidation.
- Rose from data entry clerk to manage 21-person staff.

EDUCATION
1987, Bachelor of Business Administration
Tristate University, Metropolis, Megastate.

ADDITIONAL INFORMATION
Was a Little League coach until forced to retire by injuries. Hobbies include whaling reenactments, steam locomotive restoration, and collecting antique podiatry instruments.

Figure 5.3 *Example of a combination resume, in which the candidate's lists of skills also serve to summarize the candidate's work history.*

for "cutlery." If you sell cars, you may be in trouble if the computer is looking for automobiles.

The answer—to the extent there is one—is to help the search engine along by inserting into your resume a section that contains nothing but keywords that someone might use if they were to look for you. Anyone reading the resume will know from the header that the keyword section will be a nonsyntactical mish-mash and can skip over it. People do glance over them, however, so do not be afraid to repeat yourself in the keyword section, using words and phrases that appear in the body of the resume. (This would be pointless if the resume was to be used solely in a database because one occurrence of a word is enough to generate a hit.)

You need to come up with a list of descriptors that another person might use if they were looking for someone like you. A familiarity with the buzzwords used in your field is indispensable. But there is no science to the process of coming up with keywords—the decision is entirely subjective. Yes, there is a certain amount of luck involved because you must foresee the thought processes of a person you've never met. There is one main rule of thumb:

Use nouns and phrases as keywords.

People typically do not use verbs as the basis of searches because the tenses confuse the spelling. Anyway, you've already used verbs to get the attention of the human reader so that if someone does search for verbs, your words will be there.

Figure 5.4 shows the results with the present example. The keyword section has been added near the top of the resume, replacing the summary. It can be added to any of the formats already discussed.

Keyword sections are best used in situations where you are fairly sure your resume will be scanned into a database or if you are in a field (like information technology) awash with jargon and buzzwords. Someone who is looking for specific jargon or buzzword—"Does the candidate know Visual C++?"—can go straight to the keyword section on your paper resume, regardless of whether scanning took place.

Scannable Resumes

Keyword resumes embody the assumption that your resume is going to be converted into an electronic format so that it can be put in a database and searched.

AMADEUS LAZLO "Lenny" JOBSEEKER
1234 Main Street, South Metropolis, Megastate 00001
Phone: (101) 555-1234 Fax: (101) 555-5678
E-mail: lazlo@whatever.com

OBJECTIVE
To become Accounting Manager at a large public firm where I can both fully use and extend my strong accounting, business, and social skills.

KEYWORD SUMMARY
Accounting Manager. Controller. Business Manager. Budgets. MRP. Material Requirements Planning. Business Plans. Financial Statements. Construction. Bail Bonds. Anti-Corruption. Anti-Nepotism. Regulatory Compliance. Bankruptcy. Cost Reduction. Staff Reduction. Fugitive Surveillance. Contract Renegotiation. Capital Management.

PROFESSIONAL EXPERIENCE
12/98–Present: Accounting Manager, The Wet Cement Group, Metropolis, Megastate.
Manage the financials of a medium-sized ($50 million) construction firm. Responsibilities include budgeting and material requirements planning. Reduced the firm's cost of material 15 percent across the board by renegotiating contracts with suppliers, while the accounting staff was reduced from seven to three.

2/95–11/98: Accounting Manager, AAA Bail Bond Corp., Sumburg, Mesostate.
Managed and directed joint accounting/financial control and operations of a bail bond business. Prepared operating plans and budgets for presentation to senior management. Instituted controls that doubled the firm's return on invested capital, reduced operating expenses by 73 percent by firing the owner's nephew, and brought the firm to sustained profitability by helping corner a fugitive in a warehouse.

10/87–12/94: Controller, Elemeno Corp., Atro City, Minorstate.
Began as data entry clerk and rose to manage 21-person accounting staff. Prepared and analyzed financial statements, assisted the development of annual business plans, and audited operations to ensure internal accuracy. Was able (through swift adoption of the latest information technology) to respond to the rapidly shifting reporting needs of management and later the receivers as sales shrank from $400 million to zero and the firm was liquidated.

EDUCATION
1987, Bachelor of Business Administration
Tristate University, Metropolis, Megastate.

ADDITIONAL INFORMATION
Was a Little League coach until forced to retire by injuries. Hobbies include whaling reenactments, steam locomotive restoration, and collecting antique podiatry instruments.

Figure 5.4 *Keyword document, in this case Figure 5.1 with a keyword section added. Notice the use of capitalization and periods to tidy up what is otherwise just an ungrammatical string of words.*

The way many firms handle this chore is to take the resumes they receive daily and feed them into a scanner. The scanner performs optical character recognition (OCR) on each page, converting the image of the text into actual computer text. The text is then stored in a database. (Fancier systems also store the original image of the page.)

Scanner vendors brag about the accuracy of their OCR software, but the technology is hardly perfect. (For instance, you've probably never been confused by the similarity between *8* and *B* because those characters are used in different contexts. The scanner doesn't have your advantage.) You want your resume to get into the database without being cluttered with junk characters and bizarre misspellings. Therefore, you want to produce a scannable resume designed to minimize the shortcomings of OCR technology. Things you can do include the following:

- Use a sans serif font (like Arial) in the 10-point to 14-point size range. Stick to it for the whole document.
- Don't use boldfacing, italics, underlining, font-size changes, colored or highlighted text, and so on.
- Don't use columns. (Some OCR software can handle columns, with operator intervention, but don't count on it.)
- Don't put separate elements (such as name and address) on the same line.
- Don't use lines, borders, shading, or graphics of any kind.
- Avoid bullets. (You can replace them with asterisks if you can't live without them.)
- Abandon formatting involving tabs, indents, or centering because they will probably not come through.
- Don't fold or staple the pages. Mail them in a brochure-sized envelope, rather than a letter-sized envelope, to avoid folding.
- Send original printouts rather than photocopies.
- Use a letter-quality printer (never use a dot-matrix printer) and white letter-sized paper printed on one side only.
- Avoid parentheses and brackets because they often generate junk characters. (Dashes may come through as minus signs, but that is usually not a problem.)
- Using the desktop publishing features of your word processor, it is often possible to use a compressed or narrow version of your font to cram more material onto a particular line, in order to avoid forcing a new page break. Do not do that with scannable material.
- When detailing your job history, just give the last year of the job, rather than the range of years you were there. Using both dates can confuse the search results.

If some of these rules give you the idea that you need to give up most of the desktop publishing features of your word processor and revert to the days of typewriters—yes, that's correct. The result may look something like the example in Figure 5.5, which is the keyword resume formatted as a scannable resume.

If it pains you to give up your beautifully laid out desktop publishing resume, then take heart—you don't have to. Just send both versions. Take your original (i.e., handsomely formatted) version, staple it, and put a Post-It note on it with the words "Visual Version." Under it, put the unstapled scannable version, with a note saying "Scannable Version," or "Scan This," or something similar.

ASCII Resumes

The previous section covered the scanning process:

- You compose text in your computer.
- You print it out.
- You mail it to someone.
- That person scans it into his or her computer.
- You pray that the resulting text in the recipient's computer resembles the original text in your computer.

The process may strike you as slightly ridiculous when you realize that the text could be sent directly from your computer to the recipient's computer, skipping the risk and bother involved in the scanning process. That's what e-mail amounts to.

Basically, you should send in a scannable resume only after you have assured yourself that there is no way to submit your resume by e-mail. There will be no risk that the name "Brown" will be rendered as "8rovvr."

By using ASCII (or plain text, as it is also called), you avoid the problem detailed in Chapter 9, concerning e-mail attachments. With plain ASCII, you can just add the text of your resume to the body of your e-mail message. Plain text is compatible with essentially any other computer system, so it can be added to a database or put into another word-processing format with little fuss.

The downside is that plain text is just that—plain. The results will be less adorned than your scannable resume. Also, because you have no idea what font or window width the reader will be using, you have no control over how it will look to the recipient. But remember, your ASCII resume is going to be fed into a database, and the computer doesn't care.

AMADEUS LAZLO "Lenny" JOBSEEKER
1234 Main Street, South Metropolis, Megastate 00001
Phone: (101) 555-1234
Fax: (101) 555-5678
E-mail: lazlo@whatever.com

OBJECTIVE: To become Accounting Manager at a large public firm where I can both fully use and extend my strong accounting, business, and social skills.

KEYWORD SUMMARY: Accounting Manager. Controller. Business Manager. Budgets. MRP. Material Requirements Planning. Business Plans. Financial Statements. Construction. Bail Bonds. Anti-Corruption. Anti-Nepotism. Regulatory Compliance. Bankruptcy. Cost Reduction. Staff Reduction. Fugitive Surveillance. Contract Renegotiation. Capital Management.

PROFESSIONAL EXPERIENCE:
Present: Accounting Manager, The Wet Cement Group, Metropolis, Megastate.
Manage the financials of a medium-sized ($50 million) construction firm. Responsibilities include budgeting and material requirements planning. Reduced the firm's cost of material 15 percent across the board by renegotiating contracts with suppliers, while the accounting staff was reduced from seven to three.

1998: Accounting Manager, AAA Bail Bond Corp., Sumburg, Mesostate.
Managed and directed joint accounting/financial control and operations of a bail bond business. Prepared operating plans and budgets for presentation to senior management. Instituted controls that doubled the firm's return on invested capital, reduced operating expenses by 73 percent by firing the owner's nephew, and brought the firm to sustained profitability by helping corner a fugitive in a warehouse.

1994: Controller, Elemeno Corp., Atro City, Minorstate.
Began as data entry clerk and rose to manage 21-person accounting staff. Prepared and analyzed financial statements, assisted the development of annual business plans, and audited operations to ensure internal accuracy. Was able (through swift adoption of the latest information technology) to respond to the rapidly shifting reporting needs of management and later the receivers as sales shrank from $400 million to zero and the firm was liquidated.

EDUCATION: 1987, Bachelor of Business Administration, Tristate University, Metropolis, Megastate.

ADDITIONAL INFORMATION: Was a Little League coach until forced to retire by injuries. Hobbies include whaling reenactments, steam locomotive restoration, and collecting antique podiatry instruments.

Figure 5.5 *Scannable resume. All fancy formatting has been removed, including centering, boldfacing, and underlining, and a single sans serif font has been used throughout. The phone and fax numbers have been separated, but most of the headers have been put on the same line as the section text to make it clear what they are referring to. The date style has also been changed.*

Of course, a human being may glance at your resume in the process, and you want it to be legible at that moment. Your best bet is to assume the worst and to format it with the clunkiest nonproportional (typewriter-like) font you have. That's probably Courier or Courier New. A line length of 65 characters appears to be the accepted standard. You can create your ASCII resume using the following steps:

- Start with your scannable resume, which should already be shorn of any fancy desktop publishing features.
- Set the text to a nonproportional font (like Courier) with a 12-point size.
- Set the margins so that the line length is 6.5 inches. (This does not mean that the right margin is at 6.5 inches. It means that the difference between the left and right margins is 6.5 inches.) With a 12-point font, the line length will be 65 characters.
- Use the Save As command (not the Save) command to save the document. Not only will this let you give it a new name, but with most software you should be able to set a "file type" option. You should set this option to "Text only, with line breaks." (Doing it without line breaks is explained later in this section.)
- Note where the file was saved in your file directories.
- Close your word processor.
- Call up your system's plain-text editor, such as the Windows Notepad application, and use that to open the file you just saved.
- Adjust any line breaks that have gone astray and replace any non-ASCII characters that survived (such as can happen if your original resume included bullets).

The results may look something like that shown in Figure 5.6. The lines have a maximum length of 65 characters. You can safely copy and paste the text of your resume into an e-mail composition window (as detailed in Chapter 9). First, insert a cover letter. Then leave a few blank lines and insert your resume.

The Big Deal about Line Length

The problem with ASCII is that there is no separate end-of-line and end-of-paragraph character. Every line is a separate paragraph as far as ASCII is concerned. If one of those one-line paragraphs is too long for the text display window, the leftover text will be put on a new line. And that line will be rather short, since the end-of-line character at the end of the original line remains in effect. The results can be almost unreadable, as seen in Figure 5.7.

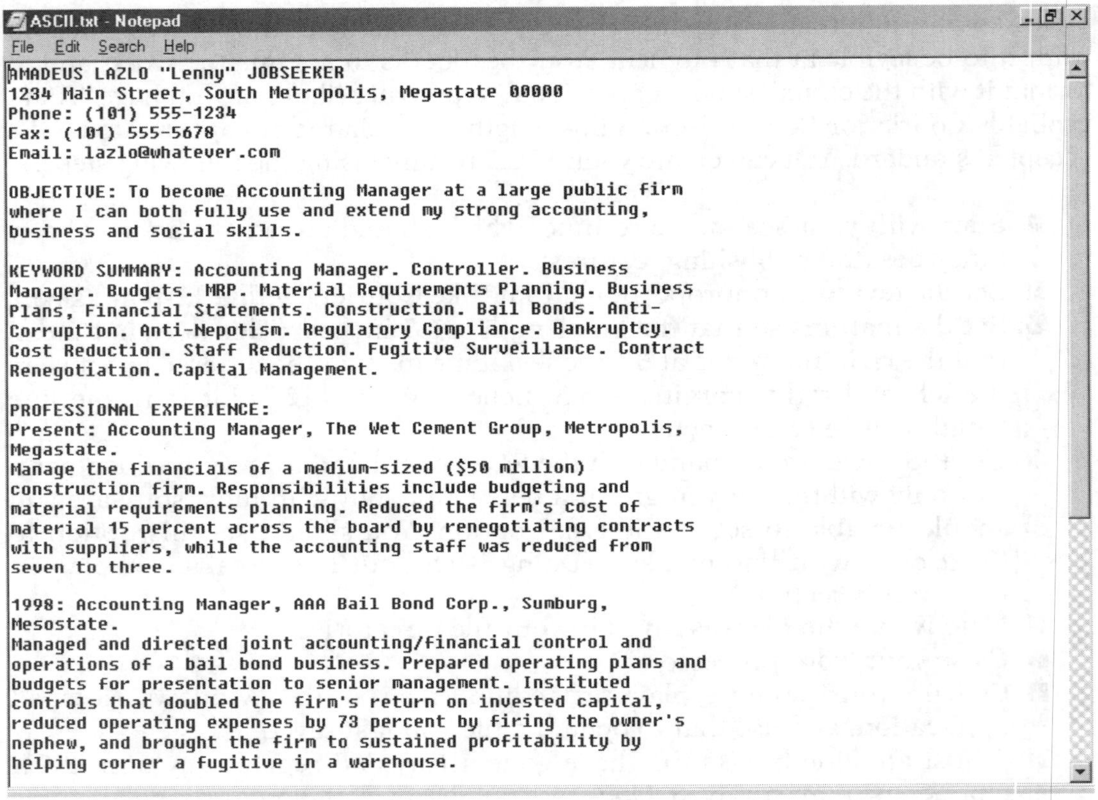

ASCII.txt - Notepad

File Edit Search Help

AMADEUS LAZLO "Lenny" JOBSEEKER
1234 Main Street, South Metropolis, Megastate 00000
Phone: (101) 555-1234
Fax: (101) 555-5678
Email: lazlo@whatever.com

OBJECTIVE: To become Accounting Manager at a large public firm
where I can both fully use and extend my strong accounting,
business and social skills.

KEYWORD SUMMARY: Accounting Manager. Controller. Business
Manager. Budgets. MRP. Material Requirements Planning. Business
Plans, Financial Statements. Construction. Bail Bonds. Anti-
Corruption. Anti-Nepotism. Regulatory Compliance. Bankruptcy.
Cost Reduction. Staff Reduction. Fugitive Surveillance. Contract
Renegotiation. Capital Management.

PROFESSIONAL EXPERIENCE:
Present: Accounting Manager, The Wet Cement Group, Metropolis,
Megastate.
Manage the financials of a medium-sized ($50 million)
construction firm. Responsibilities include budgeting and
material requirements planning. Reduced the firm's cost of
material 15 percent across the board by renegotiating contracts
with suppliers, while the accounting staff was reduced from
seven to three.

1998: Accounting Manager, AAA Bail Bond Corp., Sumburg,
Mesostate.
Managed and directed joint accounting/financial control and
operations of a bail bond business. Prepared operating plans and
budgets for presentation to senior management. Instituted
controls that doubled the firm's return on invested capital,
reduced operating expenses by 73 percent by firing the owner's
nephew, and brought the firm to sustained profitability by
helping corner a fugitive in a warehouse.

Figure 5.6 *ASCII resume displayed by Windows Notepad. The lines have been set to a length of 65 characters.*

To get around this problem, you can save your text file using the "text only" option, rather than "text only, with line breaks." That will turn each paragraph into one long line of text that will extend out beyond the right border of the screen as shown in Figure 5.8. You can still read all the text by following it with the horizontal scroll bar. Alternately, the software probably has a "word wrap" function that puts in a "soft" line break at the edge of the window. It's called "soft" because its position in the line will change as you resize the window and will not be preserved when you save the file.

Saving a file as plain text without line breaks is advantageous because you can copy and paste the text into another word processor. The original paragraphs will then re-create themselves because each line is a paragraph. But if

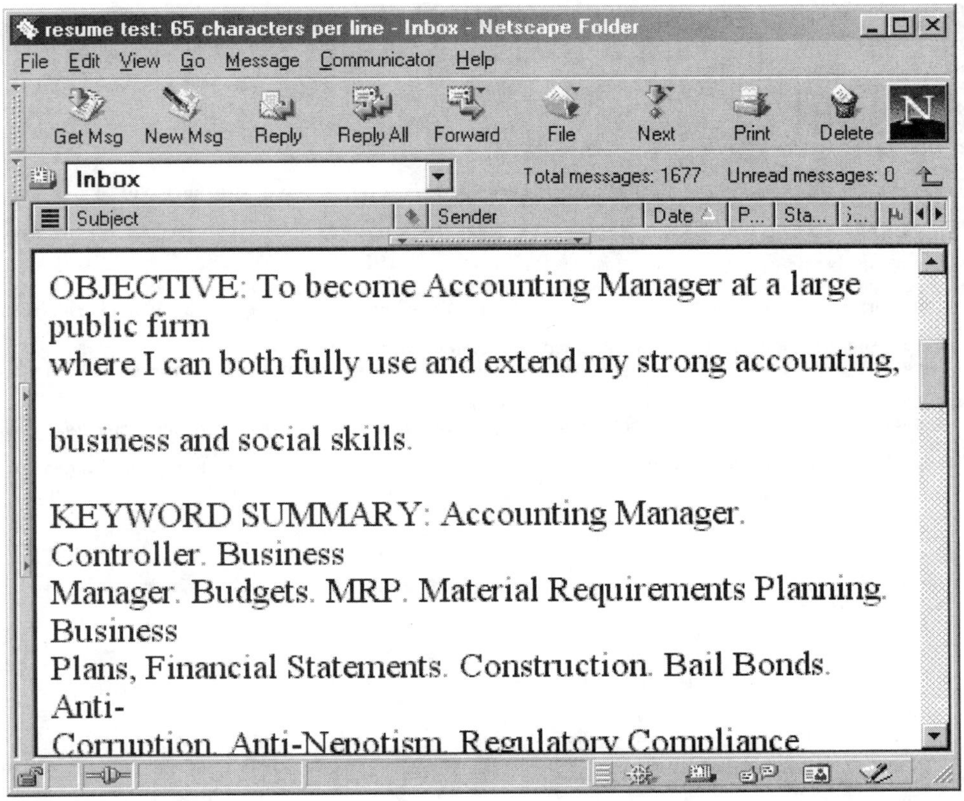

Figure 5.7 *This example shows what happens when text has been saved using the "with line breaks" option but then displayed in a window that is too narrow for the line length. The lines overflow, ruining the neat format achieved in Figure 5.6.*

you saved the file as "plain text, with line breaks," the file will be made up of short one-line paragraphs, and you will have to guess which lines constitute a paragraph. Then you will have to remove the end-of-paragraph character at the end of each line until you have re-created the original paragraph. (One reason you should put blank lines between paragraphs when sending text electronically is to make the paragraphs obvious.)

There may be times when people specifically ask that the resume or other material be sent without line breaks because they are going to reformat it. (If people ask you to use "hard carriage returns," they likewise mean that they want you to save the text without line breaks.) In that case, you need to save it as plain text, skipping the "with line breaks" option. You can compose the message as

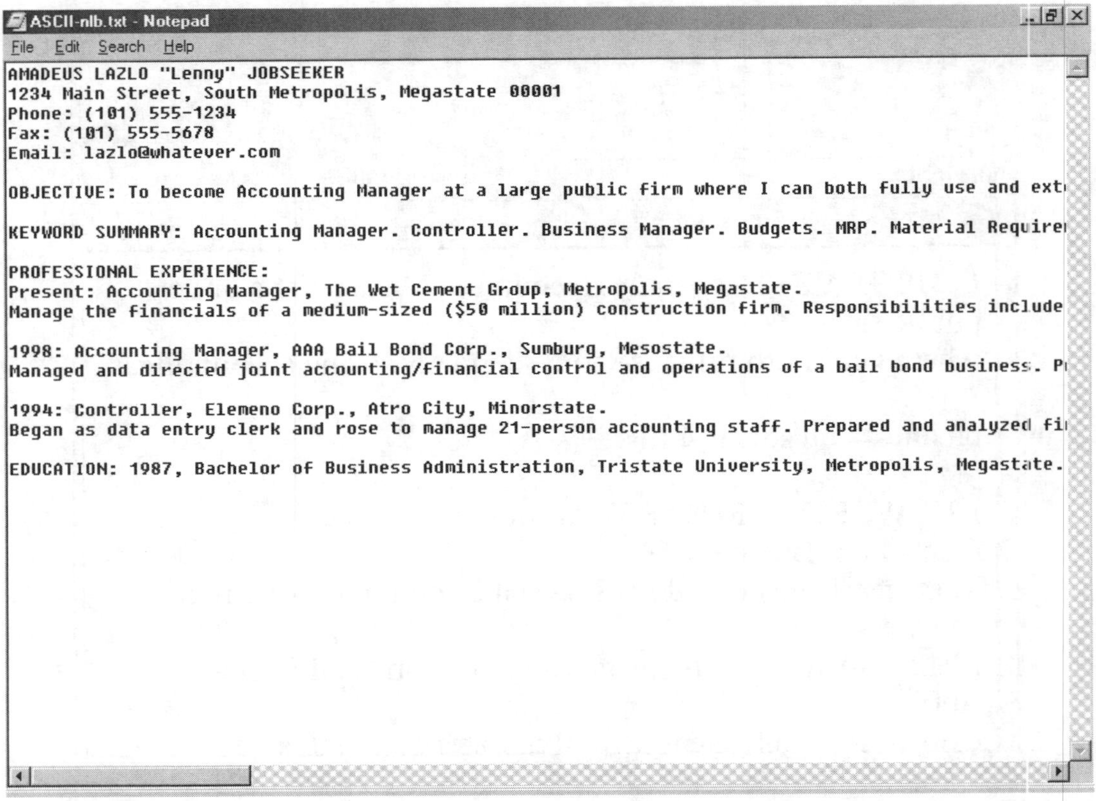
ASCII-nlb.txt - Notepad

File Edit Search Help

AMADEUS LAZLO "Lenny" JOBSEEKER
1234 Main Street, South Metropolis, Megastate 00001
Phone: (101) 555-1234
Fax: (101) 555-5678
Email: lazlo@whatever.com

OBJECTIVE: To become Accounting Manager at a large public firm where I can both fully use and ext

KEYWORD SUMMARY: Accounting Manager. Controller. Business Manager. Budgets. MRP. Material Require

PROFESSIONAL EXPERIENCE:
Present: Accounting Manager, The Wet Cement Group, Metropolis, Megastate.
Manage the financials of a medium-sized ($50 million) construction firm. Responsibilities include

1998: Accounting Manager, AAA Bail Bond Corp., Sumburg, Mesostate.
Managed and directed joint accounting/financial control and operations of a bail bond business. P

1994: Controller, Elemeno Corp., Atro City, Minorstate.
Began as data entry clerk and rose to manage 21-person accounting staff. Prepared and analyzed fi

EDUCATION: 1987, Bachelor of Business Administration, Tristate University, Metropolis, Megastate.

Figure 5.8 *Text save without line breaks and displayed in Windows Notepad. Each paragraph is now one line, and some of those lines run far beyond the right edge of the screen. You could still read the text by using the horizontal scroll bar at the bottom of the screen.*

described previously, copying and pasting the text of the resume into your e-mail message. But you should test the procedure by sending an e-mail to yourself to make sure that the software is not inserting line breaks.

In these cases, however, the recipient may actually want the resume e-mailed as an attached text file (using the .txt file extension.) See Chapter 9 for an explanation of e-mail file attachments.

Web Forms

Job-finding sites, such as detailed in Chapters 6, 7, and 8, often let you submit your resume so it can be referenced by potential employers—but they do it in a way that forces all the resumes on file at the Web site to conform to a set format. (This makes them much easier to search.) To do so, they don't let you input your resume as is. Instead, you fill out a series of screen forms.

The advantage is that you don't need to lose any sleep over how your resume is to be organized; that's been decided. You only need to call up your plain-text resume and flip back and forth between it and the browser screen containing the Web forms, copying and pasting information from your plain-text resume.

Most of the input forms do their own word wrapping, so you can use the default plain-text format, where each paragraph is one long line.

Web Page Resumes

Having your resume parked at a Web site for the world to read seems like a great idea, demonstrating that you are card-carrying member of the Internet revolution. Surely, you muse, having a Web site will put you on the same footing as the *Fortune* 1000, each of which also has a Web site. Anybody around the globe who knows how to use a search-engine can find you. And so on.

Actually, it's probably not worth the effort. The people who do the hiring are not going to sit at their computers painstakingly refining search-engine searches on the off chance they might find a needle in the haystack. Job prospects are supposed to come to them, not the other way around. Headhunters typically look for people who have jobs, not people who are looking for jobs.

On the other hand, you may be in a field for which a Web site could serve as your portfolio, to show off your skills—presumably, your skills as a Web site designer. In that case, you don't need directions for how to create and publish a Web site. However, the following pointers may prove valuable:

- The Web site should augment your resume, not replace it.
- Submit resumes as already described, but include the URL for your Web site.
- Compose the site with short, linked pages.
- Include links to off-site work examples, if possible.
- Use "meta tags" for your keywords.
- Keep in mind that organization outweighs technical achievement.

The Cover Letter

What you do not want to do is just cram your resume into an envelope (or e-mail screen) and send it off. You have to include a cover letter that explains why the recipient is getting this thing. The cover letter should include several elements:

- Refer to the job being applied for.
- Tell where you saw the job posting.
- Note that your resume is included, appended, or attached, as the case may be. If you included both a visual and scannable version in the envelope, mention that.
- Briefly summarize why you are the person for the job, referring the reader to your resume for further details.
- Give your contact information.
- When sending an e-mail cover letter, do not forget to include your name at the end. (Not that you shouldn't sign a paper cover letter, but people tend not to forget that.)

When summarizing your background in the cover letter, do not use the same level of details that the resume uses. (The reader will assume that you're putting these details into the cover letter because they are not in the resume, which means you have not taken the time to revise your resume.)

And of course, make sure that your cover letter is as polished as your resume. You have a spell checker, so use it.

Now that you have your resume ready, you can start using the many job sites on the Web, as detailed in the next three chapters.

CHAPTER 6

Leading Job Sites

Services Included in Job Sites

Your online job search is likely to revolve around a job site on the Web. These sites come in many flavors, but any one can be expected to have at least three elements:

- Lists of job openings that can be searched or browsed by a job seeker.
- A database into which a job seeker can post a resume, so that an employer can search for and find it. (Keep in mind that a user can copy the information to an off-line system, at which point the site has no control over its subsequent circulation.)
- Ancillary services of interest to job hunters, such as salary calculators, career guides, links to relocation services and resume writing services, and so on.

Job sites should also be open to the public, although some niche sites are only open to members of a professional organization and would be of interest only to them. Use should be free to job hunters. Basic revenue should come from employers, who pay to advertise job openings and to search the site's resume database, although sometimes even that is free. Some sites may charge job seekers fees for ancillary services. (The sites of some recruitment firms resemble job sites, but the posting of jobs is not open to the public. In addition, some job sites allow recruiting firms and headhunters to advertise their jobs on the site but not use the resume database.)

Other services that you may see (or may want to look for) include the following:

- Privacy features that prevent your resume from being seen by your current employer or anyone else you specify. (Lacking that, there should be a warning that such a feature is not available, and you should not post your resume there if you're concerned.)
- E-mail notification of new job postings that meet your criteria. (People who are not actually looking for a job often use such features to monitor the level of demand in their field.)
- Facilities to manage your job search effort, such as storage for your job search criteria and facilities for tracking your applications. (This would require user registration, which most sites offer as a free option.)

The 10 Leading Sites

There are hundreds of job sites out there—one source counted 8,000, but was evidently counting corporate sites with help-wanted sections. This chapter takes a look at the 10 leading examples, derived from the list published in February 2001 by Alexa Internet, an Internet audience-measurement service in San Francisco. At that time, it established the 10 largest job-related Web sites, as shown in Table 6.1. (Incidentally, page views are not the same as the number of people who visit a site, which would be far fewer because each person usually views many pages during a particular visit.)

Notice that Monster.com got almost as much traffic as the next six sites combined. Note also that a plateau occurred at the second and third positions and again at the fourth through seventh positions. This indicates that the field had achieved some measure of maturity, displaying a dominant player followed by other, smaller players who clustered together in tiers.

Also note that during the previous 13 months, each of the 10 sites had experienced a healthy increase in traffic; none had seen their page views increase by less than 29 percent. The average for the 10 was just under 50 percent. Keep in mind that these increases occurred during the same period that the dot-com gold rush was rapidly going bust, making job sites a bright spot in an industry that had proven wildly overhyped.

On the other hand, we're not talking about the insurance industry here—the rate of change is still quite rapid, as befits both a new industry and an Internet

Table 6.1 *The 10 Largest Job-Related Web Sites, February 2001*

Ranking	*Web Site*	*Estimated Page Views in January 2001*	*Traffic Increase over December 2000 (%)*	*Ranking among All Web Sites in February 2001*
1	Monster.com	614.9 million	41.5	13
2	HotJobs.com	178.3 million	51.4	57
3	Headhunter.com	157.3 million	62.5	68
4	Craigslist.org	98.9 million	41.7	117
5	Dice.com	71.5 million	48	159
6	JobsOnline.com	56.6 million	29	210
7	FlipDog.com	55.6 million	49.1	217
8	CareerBuilder.com	26.6 million	49.1	510
9	Vault.com	19.9 million	58.2	699
10	Net-Temps.com	18.9 million	56	773

Source: Alexa Internet, The Web Information Company, San Francisco, CA, www.alexa.com.

Table 6.2 *The 10 Largest Job-Related Web Sites, May 2001*

Ranking	*Web Site*	*Estimated Page Views in May 2001*	*Ranking among All Web Sites in May 2001*
1	Monster.com	561.1 million	39
2	HotJobs.com	231.6 million	128
3	Craigslist.org	134.4 million	234
4	Headhunter.com	122.7 million	267
5	Dice.com	75.4 million	448
6	FlipDog.com	59.2 million	566
7	JobsOnline.com	25.6 million	1,364
8	Vault.com	24.6 million	1,414
9	CareerBuilder.com	21.7 million	1,623
10	Net-Temps.com	21.6 million	1,628

Source: Alexa Internet, The Web Information Company, San Francisco, CA, www.alexa.com.

industry. At the author's request, Alexa Internet did a second survey of traffic at job sites, this time for May 2001. The results show that four months can make a big difference (see Table 6.2). (Again, page views are not the same as visitors. Monster.com itself claimed it had 7 million unique viewers during May 2001, who together made a total of almost 27 million separate visits to the site.)

Generally, the sites' ranking within the Web as a whole fell. Meanwhile, traffic on Monster.com slipped noticeably. (Possibly, the high-tech job market had stabilized after the dot-com bust, while the rest of the Web usage continued growing as usual.) But the total page views for all 10, taken together, fell less than 2 percent. Several sites experienced substantial gains (and moved up in the rankings relative to each other). The tier clusters appeared even more evident. Meanwhile, Monster.com still dominated the landscape.

The upshot is that the landscape may have changed even further by the time you read this. But there will still be something there. Job sites have proven themselves to be a genuine industry, not a dot-com fad, offering services of undeniable value to their users.

As for which site is best, the answer is simple: none. All have their wrinkles. But there is no rule against using more than one, and doing so will help your cause.

Please note that although the following sites can be considered the leading sites, they are also only the tip of the iceberg. Also, their inclusion should not be considered an endorsement. They are listed according to their Alexa Internet ranking for May 2001. More sites are listed in Chapter 8.

http://www.monster.com

Monster.com listed nearly four hundred thousand jobs in June 2001, with 11 million resumes and 16 million members. You can search for a job by location, job category, or company. The site also boasts that it offers more than two thousand pages of career, resume, and salary advice, as shown in Figure 6.1.

With a free "My Monster" account, you can compose five versions of your resume (and five cover letters) and "activate" them so they can be viewed by employers. Activated or not, a resume can also be declared "confidential" so that it hides your name and contact information, as well as the name of your current employer. The contact information will be replaced by a generic e-mail address at Monster.com. Responses sent to it will be forwarded to your regular e-mail address.

You can also create a "job search agent" that will e-mail you when a new job posting matches your criteria. The site also includes capsule descriptions of selected companies, with links to their job openings.

Monster.com also contains special sections for senior executives, college graduates, and those interested in working abroad. There is a section for freelancers, called Monster Talent Market, where employers post their available projects and where freelancers (called "free agents") bid on them. Free career-advice newsletters are offered in various fields.

Figure 6.1 *Monster.com's site, featuring its signature monster. (Reprinted from www.monster.com, by permission of Monster.com.)*

It also has an extensive relocation section, called monstermoving.com, with real estate and apartment search links, mortgage links, links to movers and truck rental services, city comparison charts, and plenty of advice.

Monster.com also offers a list of discussion forums moderated by experts in their fields (such as resume writing, interviewing, compensation, equal opportunity issues, military transition, and working overseas).

In addition, Monster.com has branch sites for specific countries, including Canada, the United Kingdom, Netherlands, Belgium, France, Germany, Italy, Luxembourg, Ireland, Spain, Australia, Singapore, New Zealand, Hong Kong, and India.

Chapter 7 provides a detailed description of how to use the basic features of Monster.com: Compose a resume and a cover letter, look for a job, apply for a job, and create a job search agent.

http://www.hotjobs.com

HotJobs.com boasts of being the number-two job site on the Web, a boast upheld by Alexa Internet. You can browse jobs directly from the opening page through its list of career categories, as shown in Figure 6.2. You can post a resume and limit access to it to specified employers to whom you are interested in applying. Alternatively, you can open it to all employers or even cut off all access and use the resume only for responding to job postings.

HotJobs did not offer any ancillary services to speak of, but does sponsor an ongoing series of job fairs in various cities where prospects and employers can meet face to face. There are also branch sites for Canada and Australia.

Figure 6.2 *The HotJobs site, which lets you browse jobs directly from the opening screen. (Reprinted from www.hotjobs.com, by permission of HotJobs.com.)*

(At the end of June 2001, HotJobs agreed to be acquired by TMP Worldwide, the parent company of Monster.com. TMP announced a policy of dual positioning for the sites, and HotJobs continued to maintain a separate operation.)

http://www.craigslist.org

Craigslist.org is basically a bulletin board system harking back to the days before the Internet took over, but translated to the Internet. (About time someone figured out how to do that.) As seen on its opening page (see Figure 6.3), the site provides links to a wide range of topics, each of which is a list of bulletin-board postings. These lists are for postings only; to cut down on flaming, discussion is segregated to another area. Job postings cost $75. Resume postings are free. Both resumes and jobs stay online for 30 days.

When creating a posting, you can specify whether it is a resume or a job (or an event announcement, item for sale, personal ad with gender preference, etc.). After you finish the posting, you receive an e-mail with a URL that contains a form that lets you edit the material before it appears, as well as perform later revisions. There is no mention of confidentiality, only a warning against including your phone number. (As ever, you could use a throwaway e-mail address, as explained in Chapter 9.)

You can search for jobs by clicking a selection in the category list on the opening screen. You will then get a list of postings, by date. You can also do a keyword search from the opening screen.

Craigslist does not have national coverage—the one that is shown in Figure 6.3 covers the San Francisco area. However, it has expanded to the other major cities on the West Coast and is spreading to other regions as well, such as Chicago, Boston, New York, Atlanta, Austin, and points in Australia. The opening page at www.craigslist.org contains the list.

http://www.headhunter.net

HeadHunter has not only claimed to be the fastest-growing job site but to have written the book on job searching. You can search by job type, company, industry, and field of interest (such as sales, nonprofit, or freelance)—in fact, by a total of 13 different criteria. From the opening page, you can launch a basic search using three criteria or browse by field of interest, as shown in Figure 6.4.

You can post your resume and decide if your name, phone number, and e-mail address will be shown—each can be set individually. If none of the three are displayed, an employer can still get back to you through an anonymous

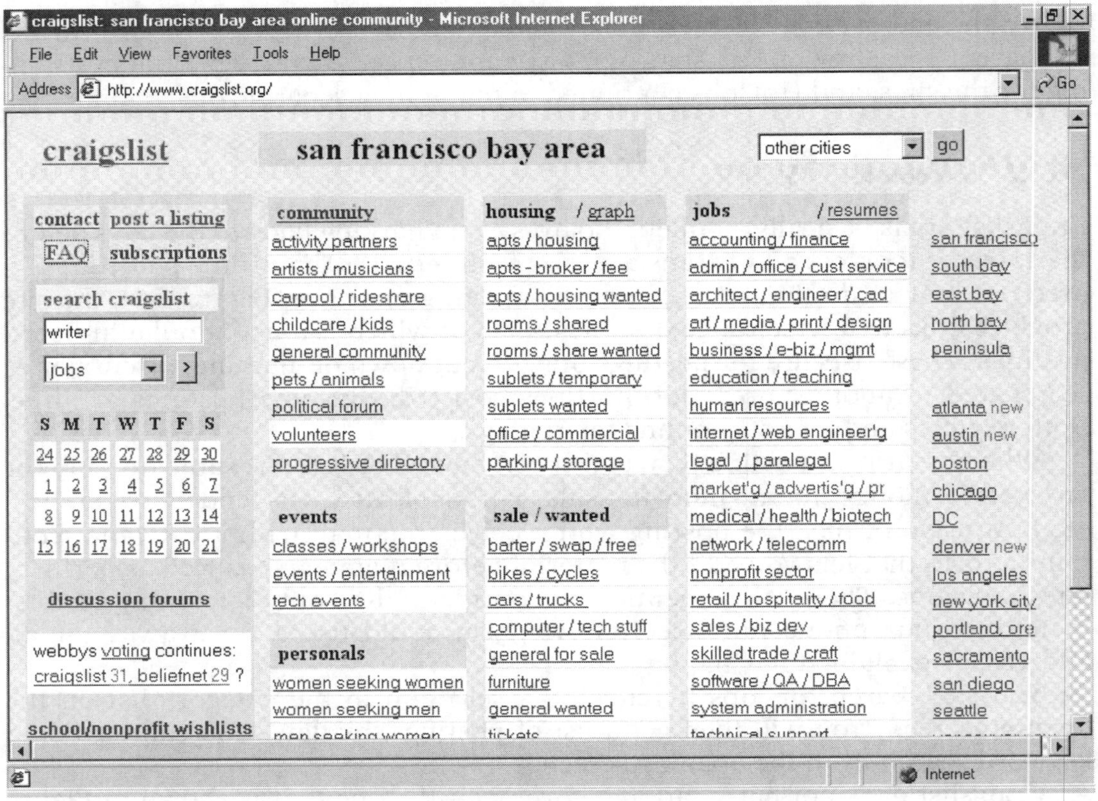

Figure 6.3 *The opening screen at Craigslist.org, which includes jobs as well as other attractions, such as personal ads. The default page serves the San Francisco area, but other cities can be selected from the list on the right. (Reprinted from www.craigslist.org, by permission of Craiglist.)*

e-mail feature. You can also keep employers from seeing your resume at all, using it only for applications.

If you do list your resume, the site sells a service called "resume upgrade," which ensures that you will appear at or near the top of any search results. This service starts at $10 per month. There was also a resume distribution service that would, for about $50, distribute your resume to about nine thousand recruiting firms. There's also e-mail notification of jobs that match your search criteria.

The site offers employers services similar to the "resume upgrade" to control where their postings appear when search results are listed.

The site's pages also include a "boss button." When you click it, up pops an innocuous screen with plain text. (Some computer games include a similar function, usually featuring a spreadsheet page.)

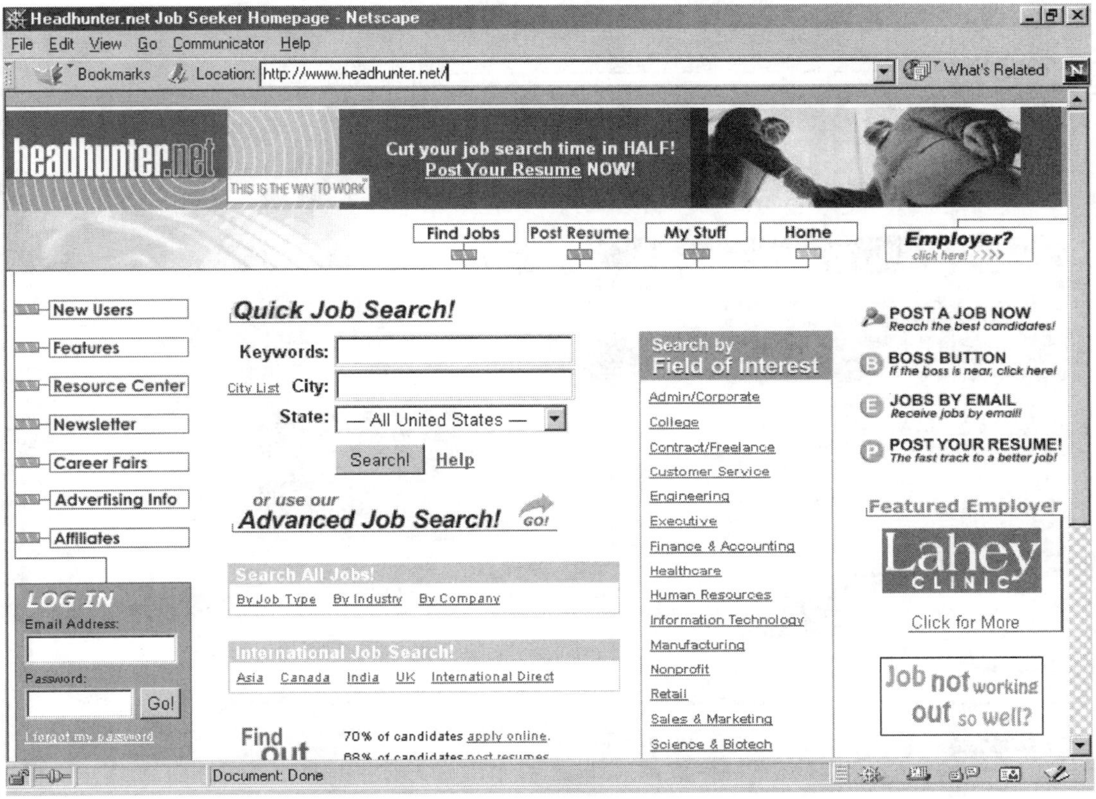

Figure 6.4 *The opening page at HeadHunter.net, showing its search facility and field of interest browser list. (Reprinted from www.headhunter.net, by permission of HeadHunter.net.)*

http://www.dice.com

Although connecting a gambling motif with job searching may be a little disheartening, it doesn't seem to bother people in the information technology field, which Dice.com serves. See Figure 6.5 for its opening screen, complete with lucky dice.

You can run a job search by keyword, metropolitan area, state, area code, and employment type (i.e., full-time, contract, contract to hire, etc.).

Rather than simply posting a resume, dice.com's "announce availability" feature lets you profile yourself by skills and years of experience. You're also asked your desired position, desired salary, and desired location, as well as citizenship status. You can input a plain-text resume if desired. However, the profile asks for complete contact information, and there appears to be no way to keep your boss from seeing your "announcement."

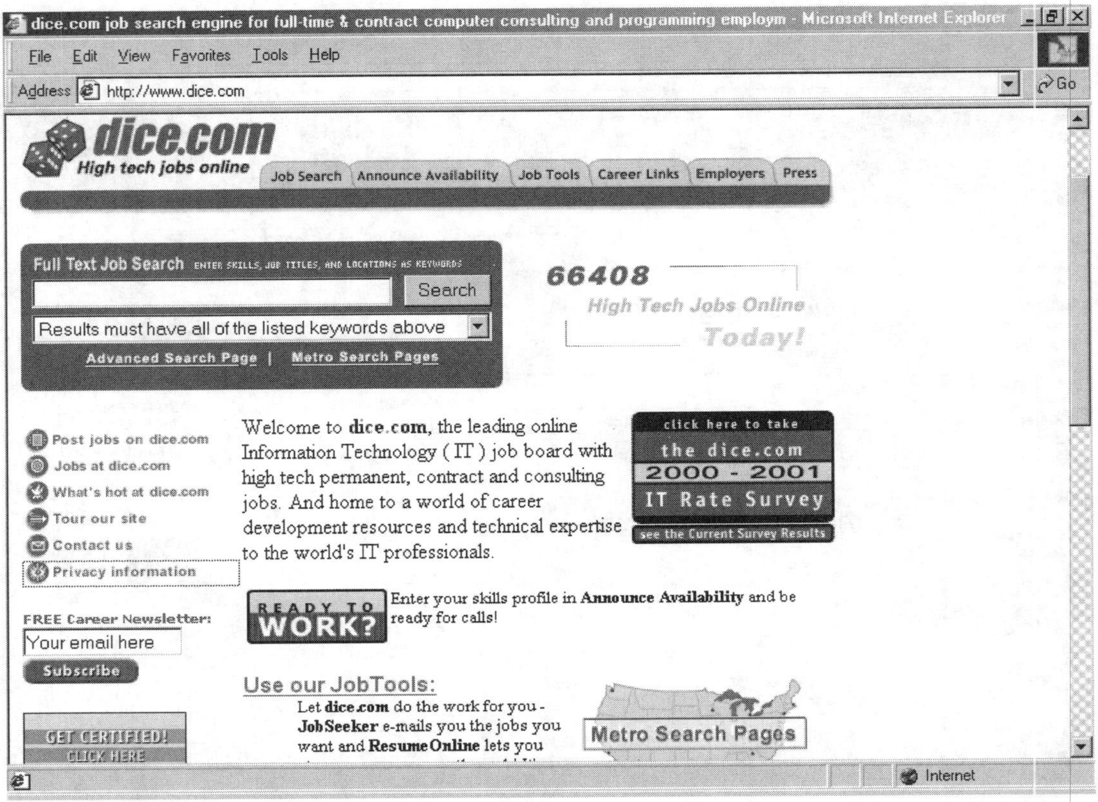

Figure 6.5 *Dice.com's opening screen—its high-tech users evidently hope to roll seven. (Reprinted from www.dice.com. © Dice.com, used by permission.)*

A "JobSeeker" function notifies you by e-mail of jobs that match your criteria. Ancillary services include preparation for certification exams and links to career-guidance sites.

http://www.flipdog.com

FlipDog claims to have the most jobs of any job site on the Web—they were listing more than six hundred thousand at this writing. (About a fifth were outside the United States.) It gets that number by using a search engine that harvests job postings from corporate Web sites, although employers also advertise directly at the site. The site's "job hunter" facility notifies you by e-mail when a job is posted that meets your criteria. (The name derives from the concept of a dog fetching a job, as shown on their opening page in Figure 6.6.) FlipDog allows recruiting agencies to list jobs, but you can exclude them when searching for a job.

You can post your resume, but the resume is used to generate a profile, which is what employers see. A profile can be active, passive, or private. An active profile includes contact information, allowing an employer to contact you directly. A passive profile contains no contact information; the user must contact the employer in response to a query. A private profile cannot be read by an employer unless you apply for a job.

The site also includes links for ancillary services and various resources for career guidance.

(In May 2001, FlipDog was acquired by Monster.com's parent company, TMP Worldwide. Terms and conditions of the acquisition were not disclosed, and operations at FlipDog continued at this writing.)

Figure 6.6 *The FlipDog site, with its canine job retriever. The numbers in the "Top Jobs Category" list refer to internal reference numbers rather than the total number of openings. (Used by permission.)*

http://www.jobsonline.com

JobsOnline is free to both job seekers and employers and is supported by advertising, as hinted by the opening screen, shown in Figure 6.7. This business model means that you are barraged with ads, often in the form of pop-up windows. Ad links on the resume-creation page invite you to leave the site and go subscribe to business magazines. Amazingly, registration includes having to opt out of receiving work-at-home network marketing promotions, plus lotto promotions. Subsequently, users have to opt out of another blizzard of offers during every log-in.

The job search facility (once reached through the ads) allows you to search only by metropolitan area and job category, plus the age range of the job listing. (Listings go back 60 days.) You can choose up to five items from the location and

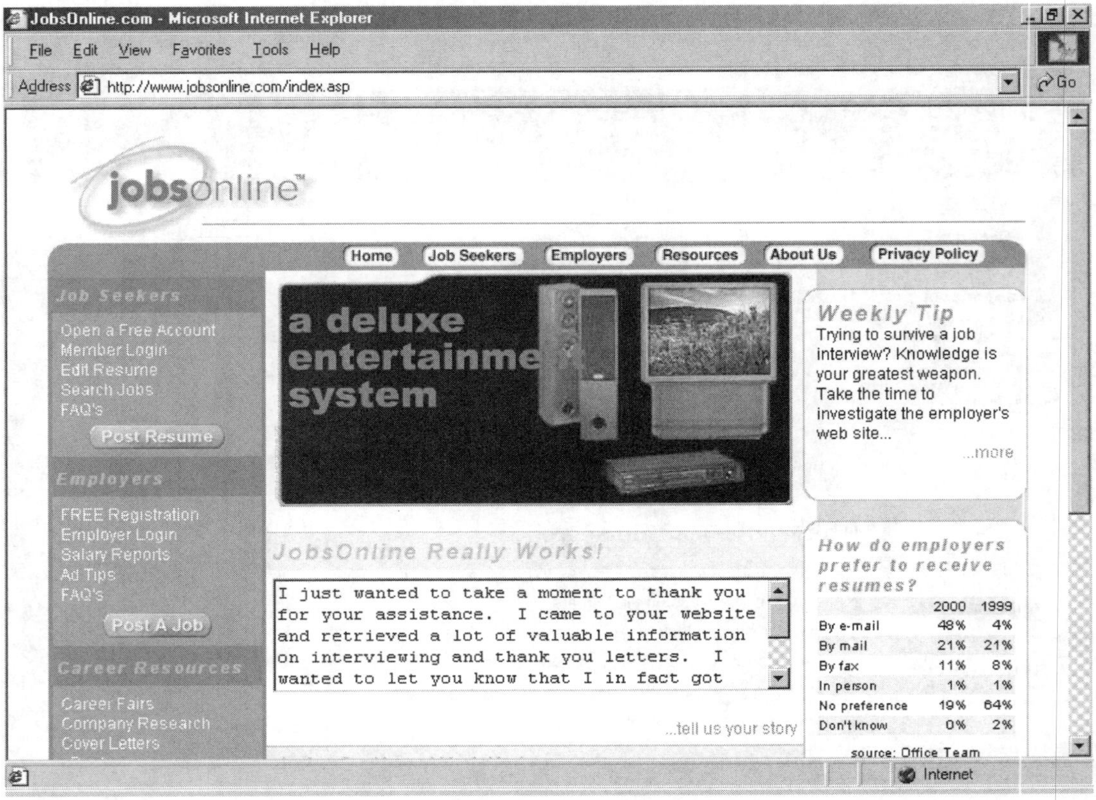

Figure 6.7 *The JobsOnline opening screen, complete with top-of-page advertisement. (Reprinted from www.jobsonline.com. © 2001 JobsOnline.)*

job category lists by using the standard control-click procedure, but that appears to be the extent of its sophistication—it provides no keyword search facility, for instance. Some of the items in the job category list, such as "homemaker" and "self-employed," would make more sense in a resume profile because no employer is likely to advertise for such jobs.

You can paste a plain-text resume and also compose a profile of your skills and experience. But the site makes no mention of confidentiality—there appears to be no way to keep your boss from seeing your resume. (Presumably, you could use a throwaway e-mail address—covered in Chapter 9—and leave out other contact information.)

There is the usual career advice material, such as resume-writing tips, and some of it looked good. Some ancillary services, such as relocation, are offered through partnered links.

http://www.vault.com

Vault.com—which serves the high-tech field—touts itself as the premier place to look for a job on the basis of its reams of career-related articles and columns, plus a series of company-specific "water-cooler" discussion forums. Its opening screen, shown in Figure 6.8, will give you a feel for what's there. It offers snapshot descriptions and background information (including links to financial data) of selected high-tech firms to aid those wanting to research a potential employer.

You can also look for a job and post a resume. For resume confidentiality, you can elect to use Vault's "single blind e-mail" arrangement, in which the employer does not see your e-mail address, but when Vault forwards the employer's e-mail to you (the candidate), you can see the employer's e-mail address. If you then respond to that e-mail, the employer will be able to see your address.

Job searching can be done via keyword, location of job, industry, job function, desired experience level, and job type (i.e., full-time, temporary, contract, etc.)

http://www.careerbuilder.com

Although CareerBuilder has the standard features of a job site, you may find the career-guidance material so fascinating and extensive that you forget to look for a job—at least for a while. Life at work, cover letters, interviewing, salary negotiations, and industry issues are all covered. See Figure 6.9 for the opening screen.

Some jobs are posted directly with CareerBuilder, but most of its listings appear to be generated by its ability to search other sites. It lists about seventy-five sites that its search engine links to, many of which appear to be the online versions of regional newspapers. Others are sites that serve a particular field. You can post a

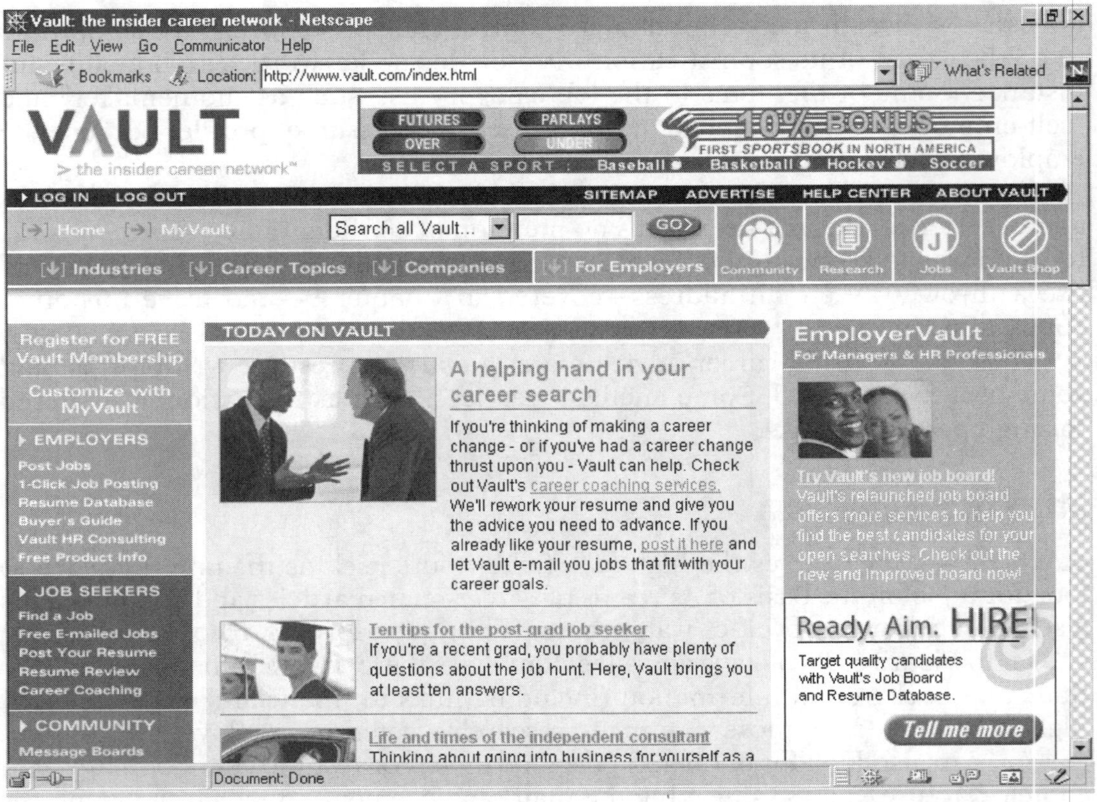

Figure 6.8 *The opening screen at Vault.com, which manages to promote its many services while not clubbing you with ads. (Reprinted from www.vault.com, by permission of Vault.com.)*

resume and restrict specified companies from reading it. You can also set up a personal "search agent" to notify you of suitable jobs by e-mail. The site also provides a folder for storing job leads, as well as a facility for writing customized cover letters.

http://www.net-temps.com

Net-Temps calls itself the "conduit between the online job market and the staffing industry," although it also lists full-time jobs, as indicated by its opening screen (see Figure 6.10.)

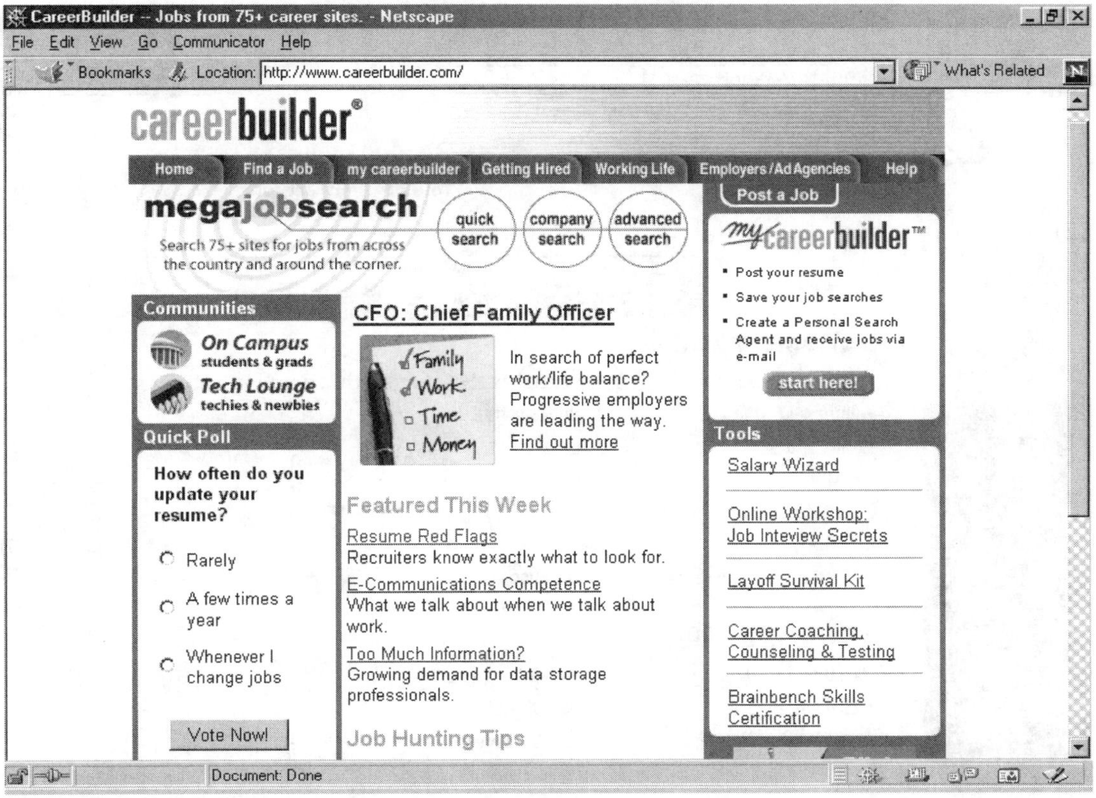

Figure 6.9 *CareerBuilder's opening screen. The job search facilities take a back seat to career tips—but you can still search for a job. (Reprinted from www.careerbuilder.com, by permission of CareerBuilder.com.)*

You can search for jobs by keyword, metropolitan area, and job type (i.e., contract, direct, or both). There is also a "job search agent" to notify you of jobs that meet your criteria.

You can post your plain-text resume, create a profile about yourself, and suppress contact information. The site also includes a salary research facility, career advice including resume writing, a weekly newsletter of career advice, discussion forums, and classified ads.

The next chapter looks at the mechanics of using a job site—in this case, Monster.com. Chapter 8 lists additional job sites.

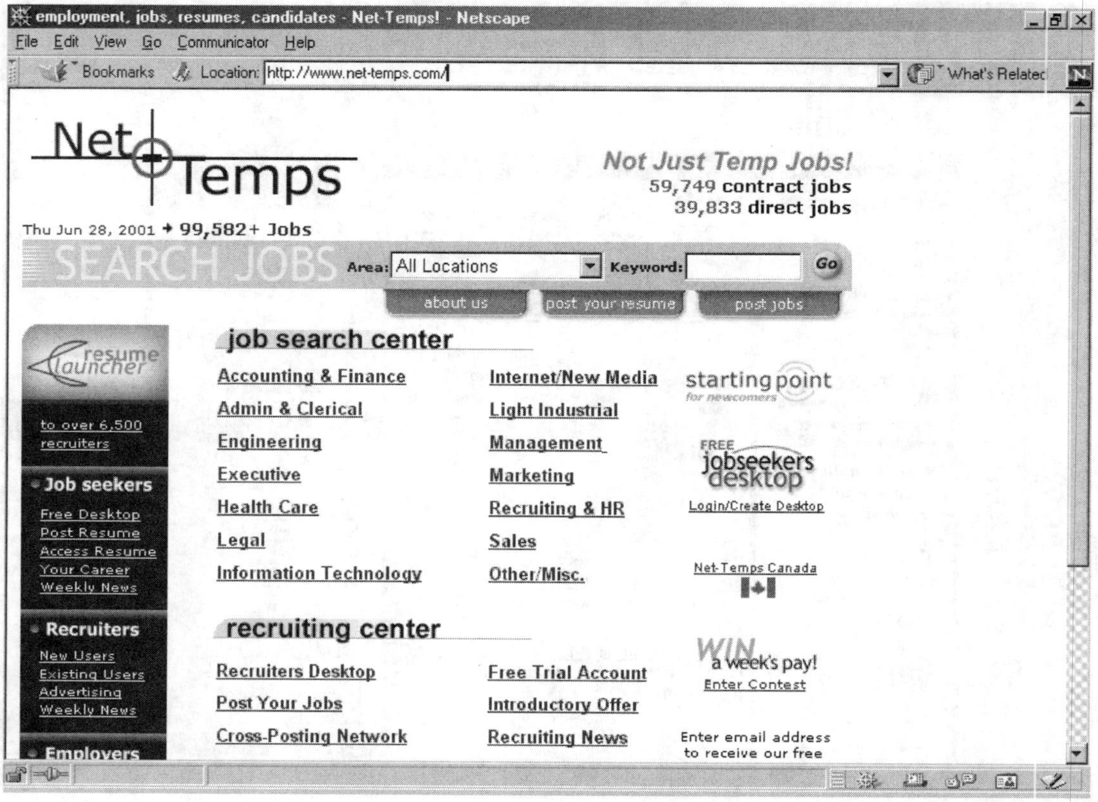

Figure 6.10 *The opening screen at Net-Temps, with a real-time total of the jobs it lists. (Reprinted from www.net-temps.com, by permission of Net-Temps.com.)*

CHAPTER 7

Sample Site

As the previous chapter makes clear, the Web has plenty of sites that cater to job hunters, offering searchable job postings and a place to post your resume so prospective employers can see it. This chapter examines the mechanics of actually using such a site, in this case, Monster.com, which is, at the moment, the largest job site on the Web.

Monster.com

Owned by a publicly traded firm called TMP Worldwide headquartered in New York City, Monster.com offers all the basic services discussed in the previous chapter—plus two others. The basic services are as follows:

- *Resume composition and posting.* You create your resume using Monster.com's format. However, you can base it on your plain-text resume, such as was discussed in Chapter 5. Your resume can be confidential, so your boss won't have a clue.
- *Job searching.* You can search help-wanted notices that employers have posted at the site, each with a job description and contact information. A posting stays active for 60 days or until removed by the employer who posted it.

- *Job search agents.* Notice of new job postings that meet your criteria will be e-mailed to you, so you won't need to run a new search every day.
- *Ancillary services.* It includes a large volume of background information of interest to job seekers, plus links to related services, such as apartment locators and movers.

Here are the two other services:

- *On-line applications.* Once you find a job you like, Monster.com will send your resume (via e-mail) directly to the employer.
- *Cover letters.* You can compose online cover letters that will accompany the resume sent to an employer when you make an online application.

As with most job sites, the service is free to job seekers. (At this writing the single-unit charge to employers for a job posting was $295.)

Here is the sequence of actions that a job seeker at Monster.com would probably take:

- Registration.
- Resume composition.
- Cover-letter composition.
- Looking and applying for a job.
- Other services.

Registration

If you register with Monster.com, you receive a personal folder in a branch site called My Monster, at my.monster.com, which will store your resumes, track your applications, and so on. Thereafter, you can simply return to my.monster.com, log in, and pursue your job search, at any time, day or night, seven days a week.

The Monster.com opening screen, reproduced in Figure 7.1, contains a toolbar below the top-of-screen advertisement and above the monster logo. It contains the entries "Search Jobs," "My Monster," Career Center," and "For Employers." Click on the "My Monster" entry. (Alternately, you can go directly to my.monster.com.) You should then get the My Monster opening screen (see Figure 7.2). From here you can log in if you are already registered or register yourself for the first time. To register, click the "Create your new My Monster account" link.

Clicking on this link should bring up the new account setup screen, as shown in Figure 7.3. The personal information it requests is pretty skeletal and self-

Figure 7.1 *The Monster.com opening screen. While you can search for a job from this screen, the serious job hunter should go to my.monster.com by clicking the "My Monster" entry in the black toolbar near the top of the screen. (Reprinted from www.monster.com, by permission of Monster.com.)*

explanatory, requiring only a name, country, e-mail address, user name, and password. However, the page requires that you state your "career level." The choices are student, entry level (less than two years experience), mid-career (more than two years experience—they must assume short careers), management, executive, and senior executive.

After making your choices, click "Submit" at the bottom of the page. (Monster.com accepts you without questioning the veracity of any of your information. It only asks that all the required fields be filled in.) You then should get your own My Monster folder screen (see Figure 7.4). The screen will list your resumes and search agents (you can compose five of each). For the resumes, it will also indicate how many employers have viewed it.

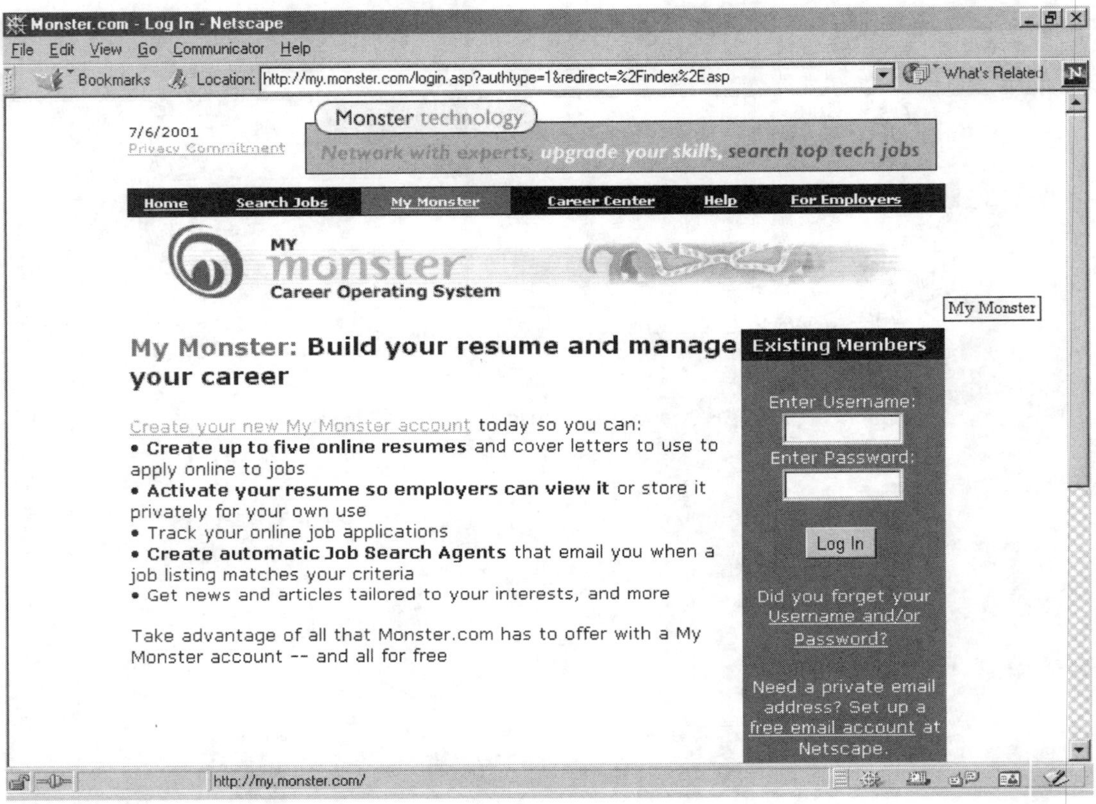

Figure 7.2 *The My Monster opening screen, where you can either register or log in if you are already registered. (Reprinted from my.monster.com, by permission of Monster.com.)*

At this point, the most important part of the page is probably the My Monster toolbar, located separately from the Monster.com toolbar (below the logo). Its entries include the following, some of which will be explained in more detail later in the chapter:

- *Account profile.* This link lets you change your account information. You may, for instance, want to change the e-mail address that responses will be sent to.
- *Agents.* From here, you can create a job search agent or edit an existing one. (Agents can also be created during the job search process.)
- *Applications.* You can apply directly for a job through Monster.com. The site records the applications you have made. (Applications are not made through this link but are made as part of the job search process.)

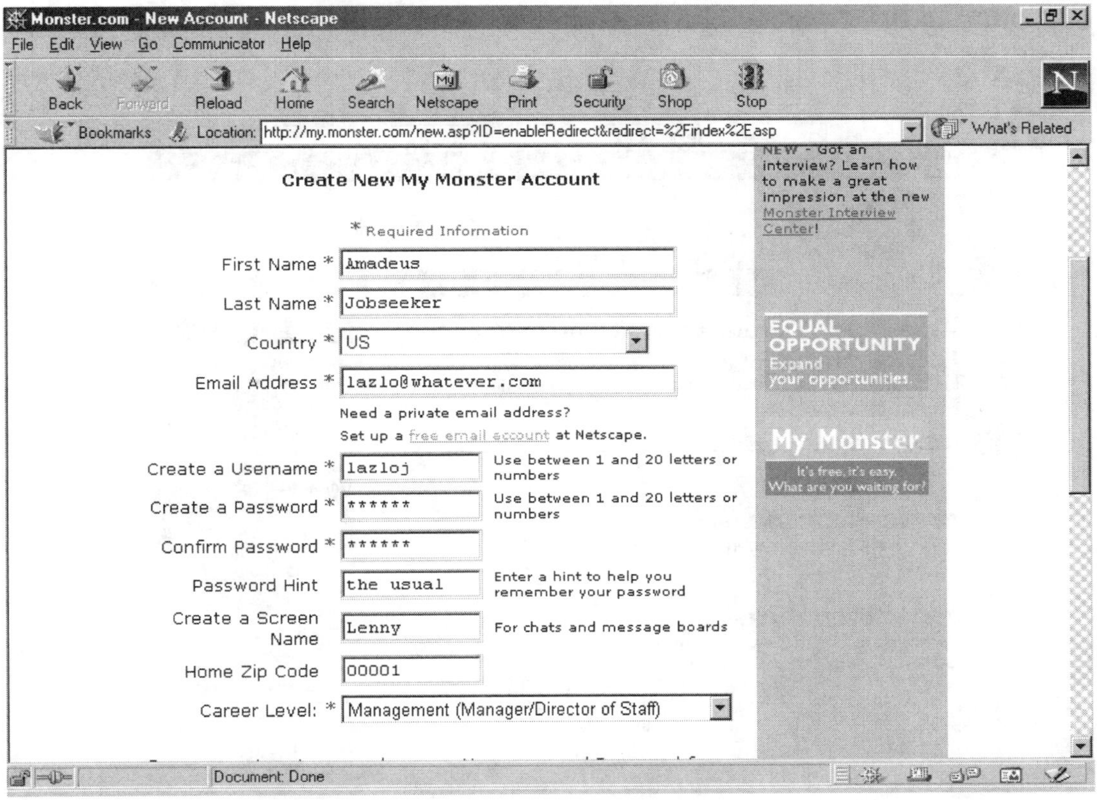

Figure 7.3 *New account setup screen. Your "career level" is chosen from a list rather than typed in. (Reprinted from my.monster.com, by permission of Monster.com.)*

- *Resumes.* From this link, you can compose, view, edit, activate, deactivate, duplicate, send, or delete your online resumes.
- *Letters.* Through this link, you can compose and edit cover letters to accompany your resume when it comes time to apply for a job through Monster.com.
- *Career talk.* This links takes you to chat rooms, discussion forums, and so on.

Composing Your Resume

Being visible to employers and applying for a job through Monster.com requires that you have a Monster.com resume. You begin the process by clicking the "Cre-

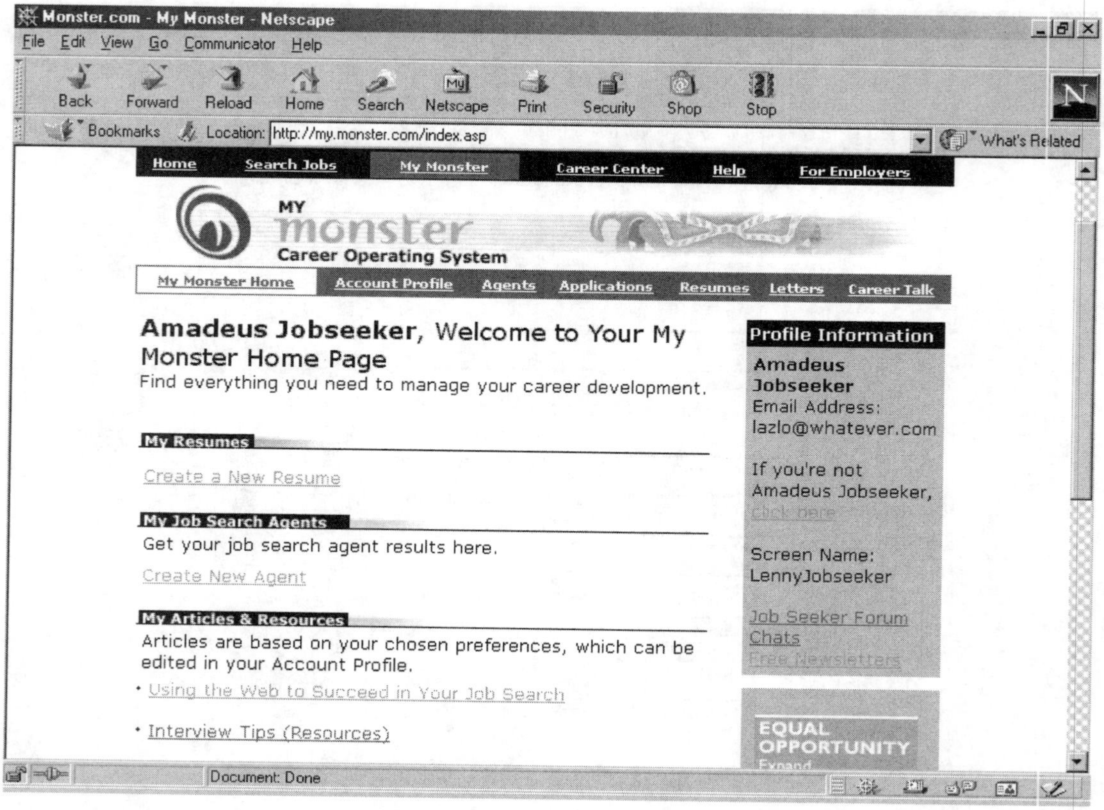

Figure 7.4 *The My Monster opening page, which you reach after creating a free account. From here, you can compose a resume and use other Monster.com services. (Reprinted from my.monster.com, by permission of Monster.com.)*

ate a New Resume" selection on the My Monster opening screen (see Figure 7.4). This brings up the instruction page, the top of which is shown in Figure 7.5.

Monster.com breaks the resume into a number of sections, each of which is the subject of a step in the resume-composition process. The steps are listed on the left side of the instruction page. (The steps will be listed on the left side of every screen in the resume-composition process, with highlighting to indicate which section you are currently in. You can also skip to a particular step by clicking it on the list.) There are 13 steps:

- Resume title (required) and objective.
- Candidate info (required).
- Target job.

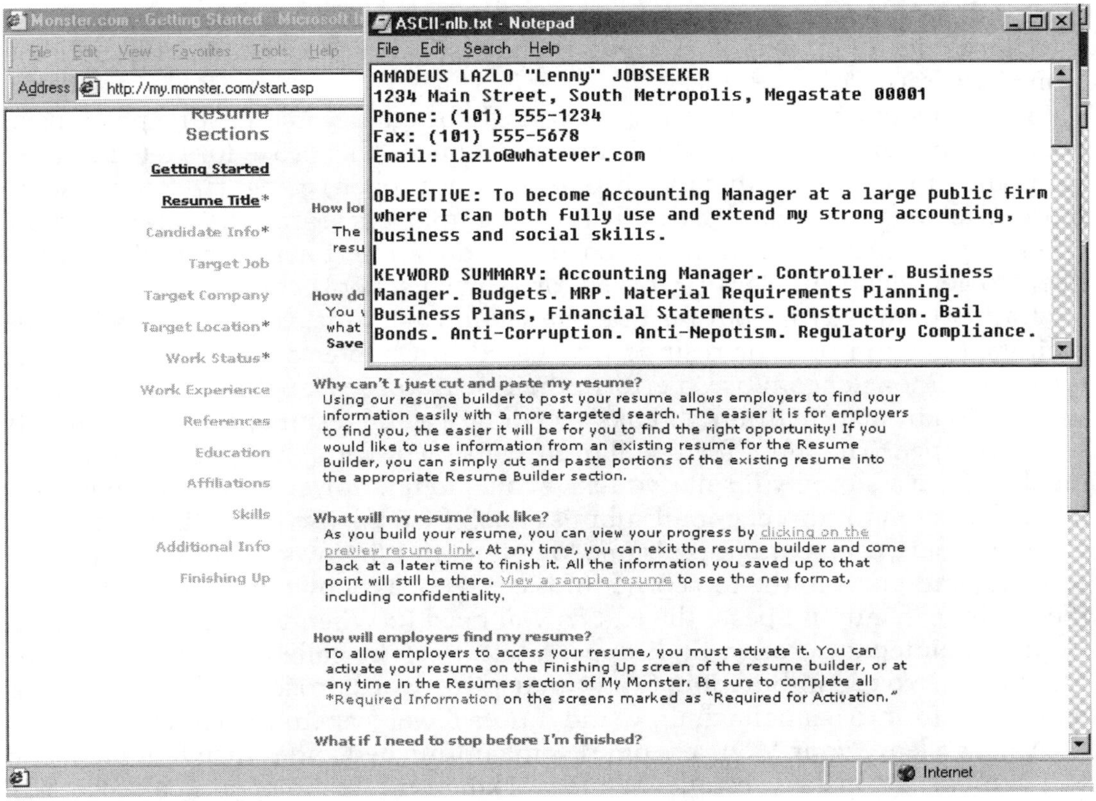

Figure 7.5 *The Monster.com resume-composition instruction screen with the example resume in Notepad, in a plain-text file without line breaks. You can use the Notepad word-wrap feature for better legibility, as shown, because it will not add line breaks. Otherwise, each paragraph is one long line extending off the right edge of the screen. (Reprinted from my.monster.com, by permission of Monster.com.)*

- Target company.
- Target location (required).
- Work status (required).
- Work experience.
- References.
- Education.
- Affiliations.
- Skills.
- Additional info.
- Finishing up.

Notice that only four of the steps are actually required (resume title, candidate info, target location, and work status). The rest can be left blank, although you won't have much of a resume.

The instruction page explains that you will be cutting and pasting portions of your resume rather than the whole resume at once. This procedure lets Monster.com (and other job sites that use this profiling approach) categorize your resume more efficiently in its database and also lets employers search the database more efficiently. (Otherwise, if they searched for education, for instance, they are as likely to get what schools you worked for as what schools you attended.)

Rather than rewrite your resume one section at a time, you should call up the plain-text version of your resume (discussed in Chapter 5). Because the input forms that Monster.com uses perform their own word wrapping, you should not use the "plain text, with line breaks" version of your resume; its text is already word wrapped. The input form will overlay its own word wrapping, and the end result will be a sloppily formatted text. (You should, however, use the "with line breaks" version for direct e-mail submissions.) Instead, use the default plain-text version, where each paragraph is one long line. In Windows, you can load it into Notepad and put it in the top corner of the screen, as shown in Figure 7.5. From there, you can cut and paste the text as you need it. When working on the input form, the Notepad screen will disappear, but it can be called up again using the Alt-Esc keystroke combination. (You can use any word processor, but Notepad is handier to fit into a small window, and it uses fewer system resources.)

You can leave your Monster.com resume unfinished and return to it later, and you can edit a finished resume. While working on a resume, you can also skip around within the steps.

Clicking the "Start" button at the bottom of the instruction page brings you to the first step.

Resume Title and Objective

The title is the first thing employers will see when they scan a list of resumes, so you want yours to be something that will stand out, but also give an accurate reflection of the contents—and of you, for that matter. In addition, you want to appeal to the target audience. Monster.com suggests things like "Senior Corporate Tax Accountant" or "The Cobol Man." Regardless, some kind of title is required; Monster.com won't permit a blank title line.

The title of most resumes is, of course, "Resume" or the name of the candidate. But now you have to come up with something different. When in doubt, it's probably best to fall back on a simple job description. If, for example, you are selling yourself as an accounting manager and you are confident that an "accounting manager" is what the employers will be looking for, then just title yourself "Accounting Manager." That's what was done in the screen shown in Figure 7.6.

The same page also asks for your objective. If your resume already happens to include one, you could just copy and paste it from the Notepad window, as was done in Figure 7.6. Objective statements are not used in professions where your objective would be self-evident. (If you find yourself pushing Monster.com's 2,000-character limit for your objective, sit down and rethink it. A single sentence should suffice.) To go to the next step, click the "Save" button at the bottom of the screen.

Note that the bottom of the screen shows a box by the statement, "Show My Resume in Another Window as I Create It." If you check that box before clicking

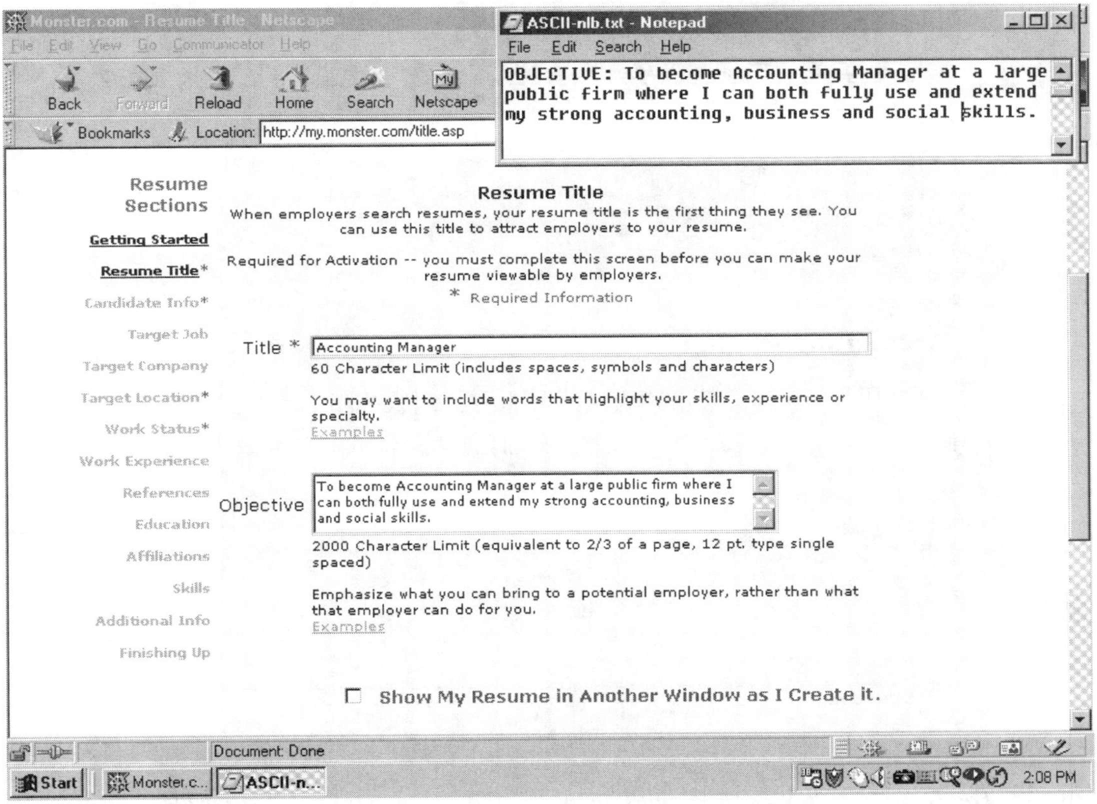

Figure 7.6 *The Resume Title and Objective screen of the resume-writing process. Text was copied from the Notepad window but just about any word processor would do. (Reprinted from my.monster.com, by permission of Monster.com.)*

the "Save" button, Monster.com will give you a pop-up window such as the one shown in Figure 7.7 to show you how the resume looks so far. You can minimize this screen and return to it as you get deeper into the composition process. Get an updated view of how the resume looks so far by clicking the "Click here to show an updated version of your resume" entry.

Candidate Information

Having saved the previous screen, you are now in the Candidate Information screen (see Figure 7.8). Together with the standard contact information, the form asks when you can start a new job. You can set a specific date or choose

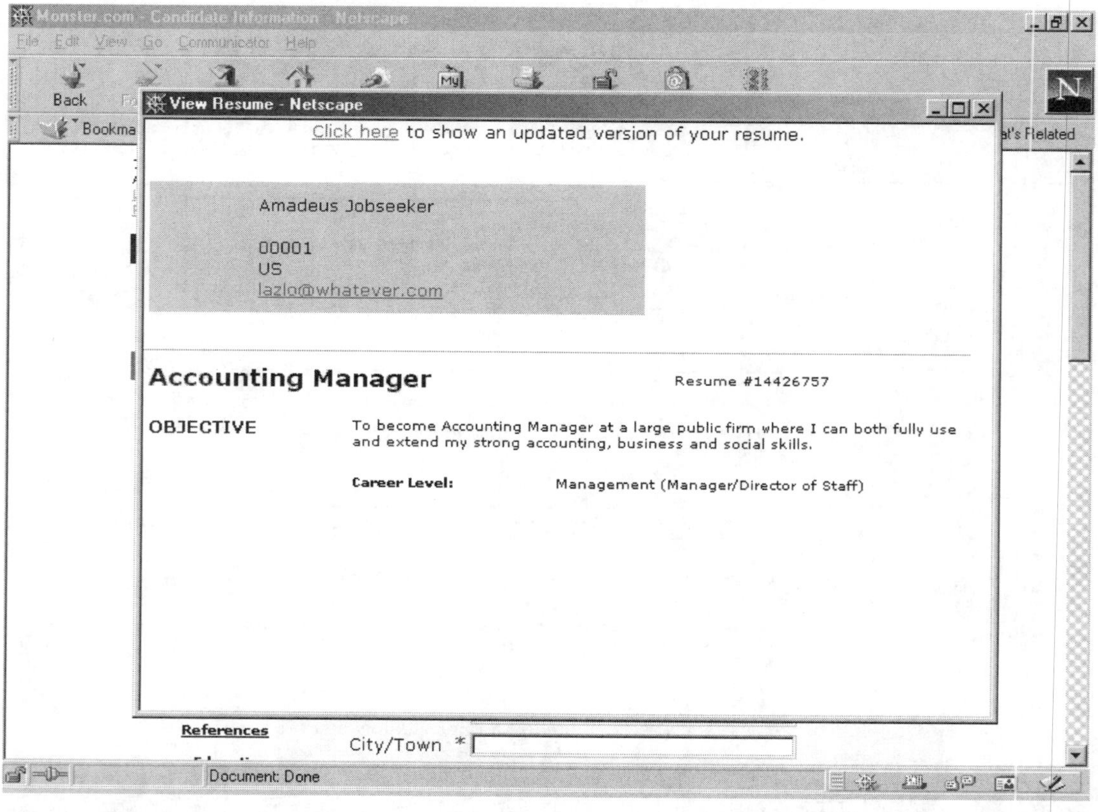

Figure 7.7 *The resume review screen, which can be updated as you get further along with your resume and have more to show. The material in the shaded block at the top is the identifying information that will be hidden from employers if you opt to make your resume "confidential." (Reprinted from my.monster.com, by permission of Monster.com.)*

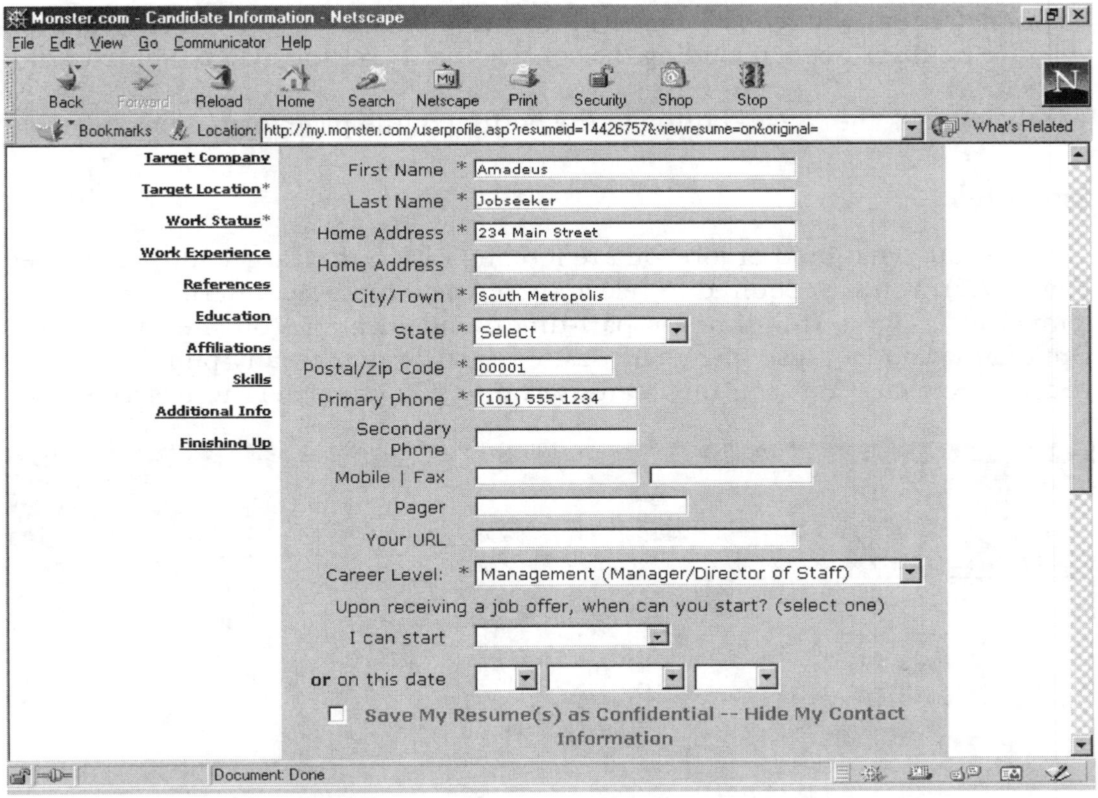

Figure 7.8 *The Candidate Information screen, where Monster.com asks for your contact information and where you decide if your resume should be confidential. (Reprinted from my.monster.com, by permission of Monster.com.)*

descriptors from a list: start immediately, in less than one month, in one to three months, in more than three months, or negotiable.

This screen is also where you decide if your resume is going to be confidential. If you check the box at the bottom of the screen, the contact information will not be shown when employers pull up your resume. Instead, they will see a Monster.com e-mail address. E-mail to that address will be directed to your regular e-mail address (i.e., the one you gave when you set up your account). Also, when you give your job history (a few steps from now), the name of your current employer will be hidden if you give "Present" as the end date of your last job. In addition, the names and numbers of any references you list will be hidden.

You can change the confidentiality setting later if desired.

Monster.com will let you create up to five online resumes. The information you give on this screen, including the confidentiality setting, will be shared by all of them.

Again, click the "Save" button at the bottom of the page to go on.

Target Job

You indicate what kind of job you are looking for on the Target Job screen (see Figure 7.9). You are required to select a job type (employee, intern, contract, or temporary), status (full-time or part-time), and location (on-site or off-site). Optionally, you can also give your desired salary range (many pundits suggest you not do that). You can then can use up to 500 characters to describe your

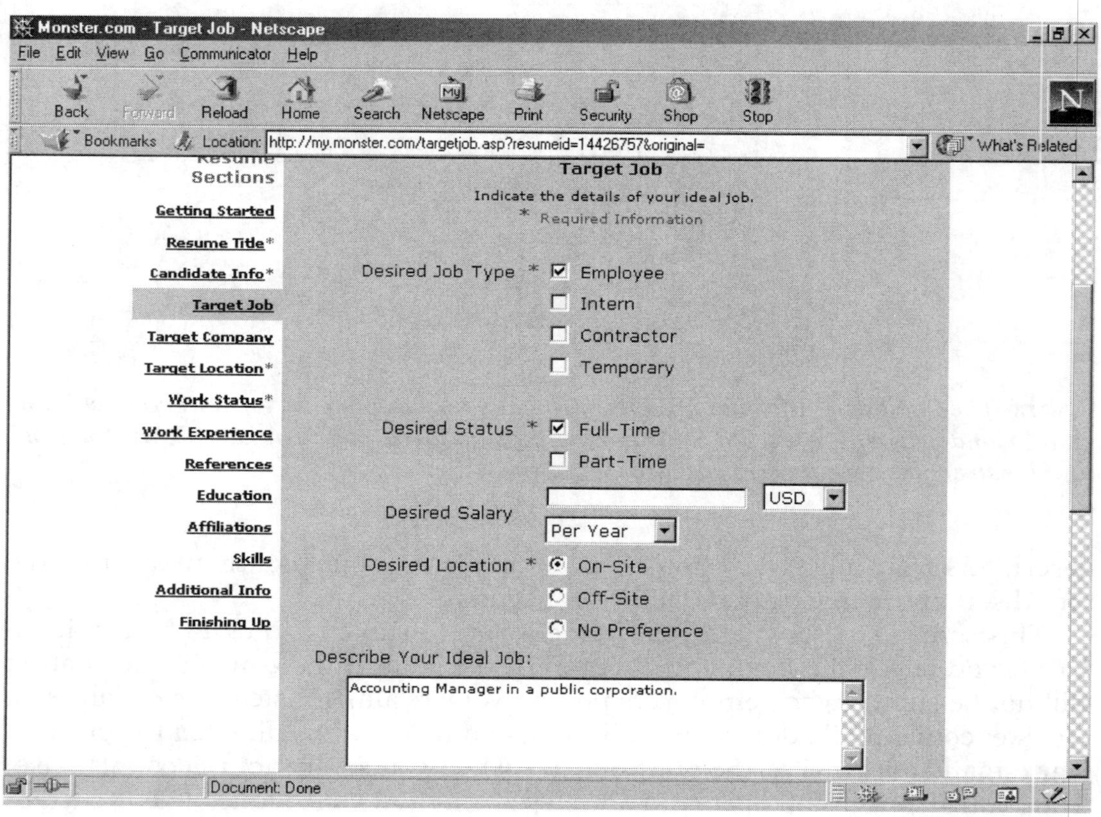

Figure 7.9 *The Target Job screen, where you indicate what kind of job you are looking for. The salary range and ideal job are optional. (Reprinted from my.monster.com, by permission of Monster.com.)*

ideal job. If "long lunch breaks" are the only thing that comes to mind, you should skip this section.

Having made your choice, click the "Save" button at the bottom of the screen to go on.

Target Company

The next step lets you indicate what kind of company you hope to work for. The Target Company screen (shown in Figure 7.10) is optional, and a lot of resumes include no such section because it might exclude you from consideration by an employer that you may otherwise be interested in. But if you do want to use this screen, you are required to choose from a long list what kind of company you want to work for, running from accounting to manufacturing to transportation.

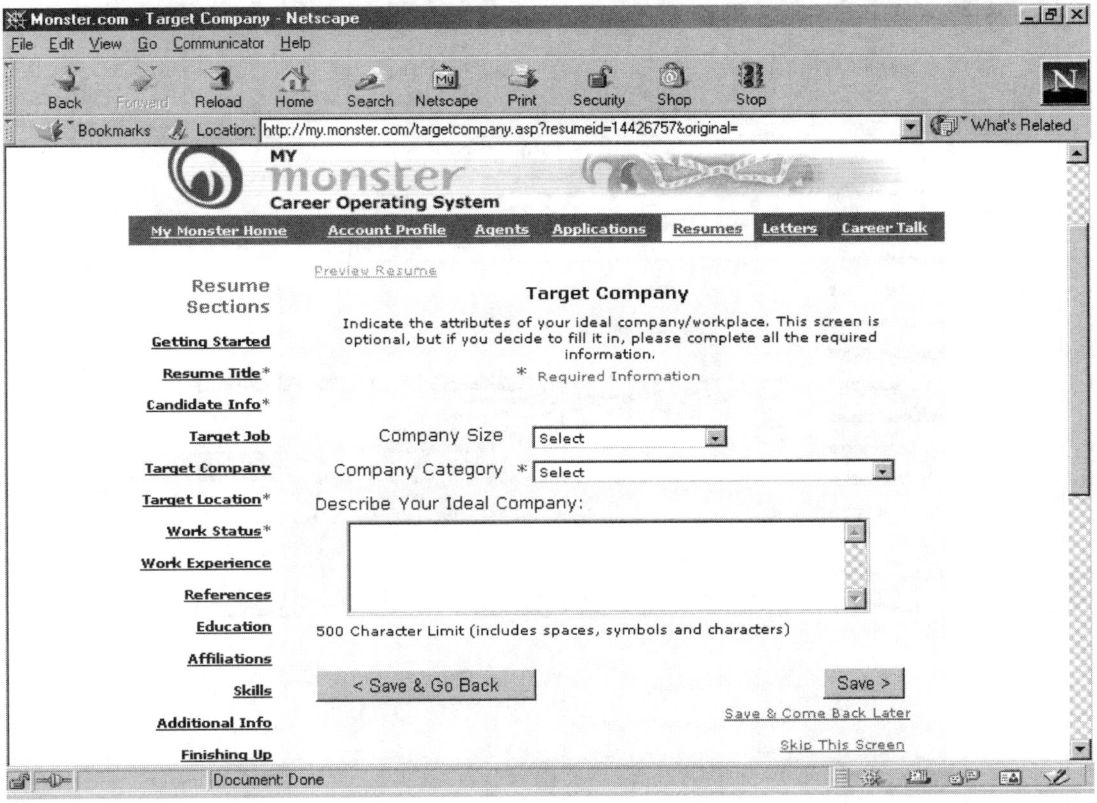

Figure 7.10 *The Target Company screen, where you state your ideal company. You can skip this screen entirely. (Reprinted from my.monster.com, by permission of Monster.com.)*

Optionally, you can select a company size: small (1–99 employees), medium (100–999), or large (1,000 or more). You also have the option of describing your "ideal company."

Target Location

At this step, you must state whether you are willing to relocate. Monster.com will not display your resume to employers unless you answer this question, so the time for a decision is at hand.

If you don't want to relocate, it's easy—just click the "No" button (see Figure 7.11) and go on. If you click the "Yes" button, then you can go on to select up to 20 places where you would be willing to work. You just highlight them on the list

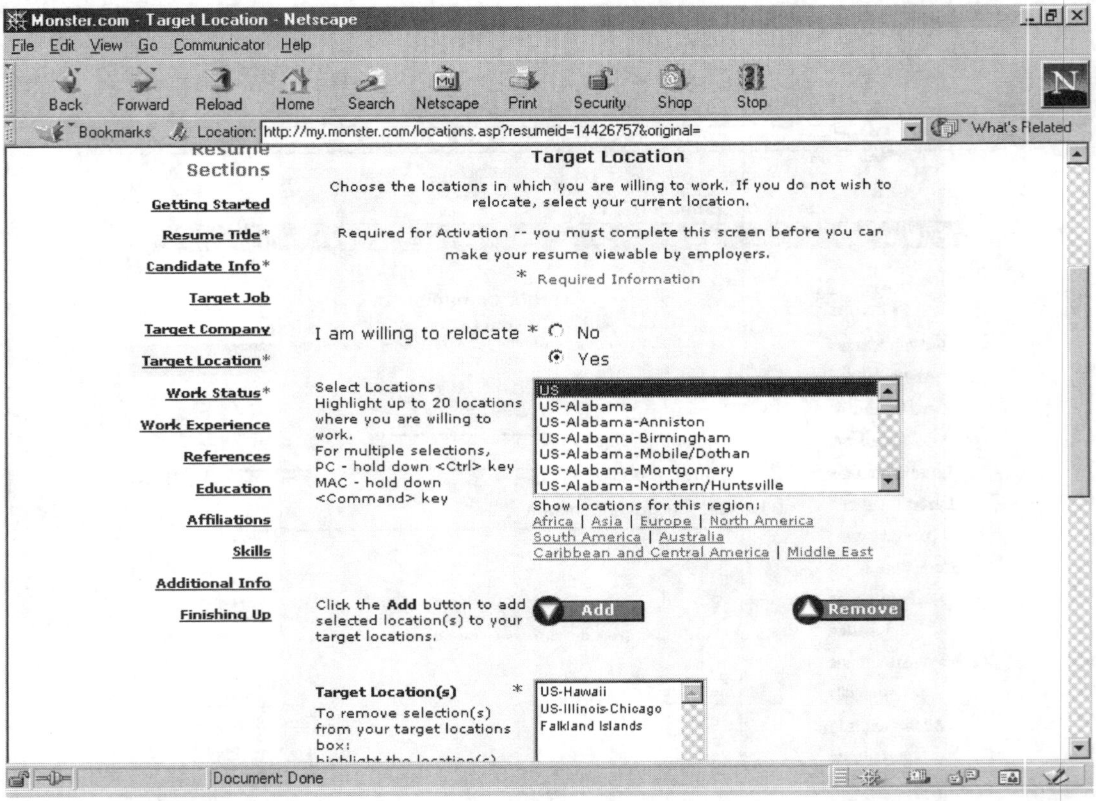

Figure 7.11 *Target Location screen, where you indicate whether you are willing to move and to where. You must give an answer before Monster.com will display your resume. (Reprinted from my.monster.com, by permission of Monster.com.)*

and click the "Add" button. The form gives you the whole world to choose from, with the possible exception of Antarctica.

Work Status

The Work Status screen (not shown) simply asks for your residency status. You state whether you are authorized to work in the United States for any employer, that you are authorized to work only for your current employer, or that you will need sponsorship to work in the United States.

Work status is another piece of information that is absolutely required—Monster.com will not display your resume without an answer.

Work Experience

Now you've reached the meat of the resume, the Work Experience section. Using this screen (shown in Figure 7.12), you can input your job history, one job at a time. Again, you can put your plain-text resume in a Notepad screen and copy and paste the material.

As mentioned already, if you use "Present" as the end date of your most recent job and opted for confidentiality, the company name will be hidden from employers who are shown your resume, making it less likely that news of your job search will get back to your current boss.

You have to fill in all the data fields—job description, title, and so on.

When you are finished with one job, you can go onto the next one by clicking the "Save and Add Experience" button. As you add each job, the header information of previously added jobs will be listed at the bottom of the page, below the input form. The jobs are automatically listed in reverse chronological order, even if you entered them in some other order.

At this point, if you bring up the View Resume window and click the "Click here to show an updated version of your resume" entry, you should see something like that shown in Figure 7.13. Because confidentiality has been chosen here, the contact information in the shaded block at the top of the screen consists only of a Monster.com e-mail address. The target location selection and work status information is shown, but in the Work Experience section, the most recent job shows "CONFIDENTIAL" as the employer.

After repeating the "Save and Add Experience" procedure for each of your past jobs, click the "Save" button at the button of the page to go on to the next step.

References

The next step asks you to list your references. Similar to the procedure in the Work Experience section, you reuse the same input form (not shown) for each

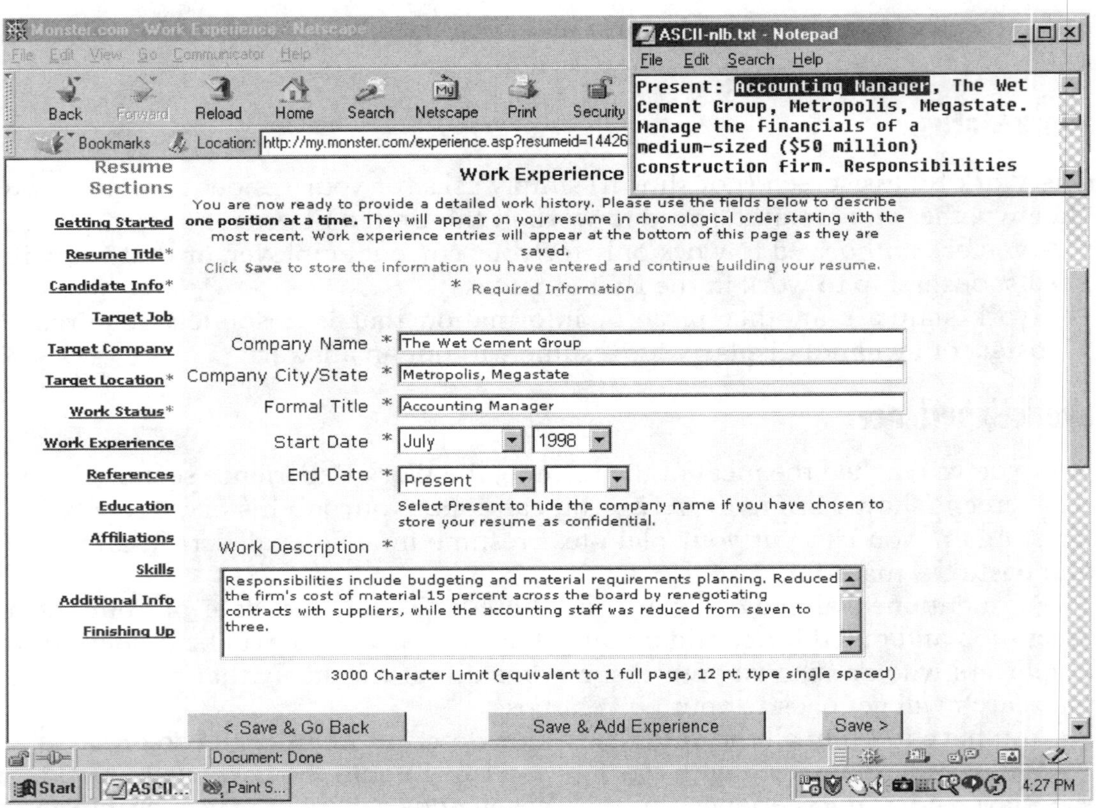

Figure 7.12 *Work Experience screen with one job filled in. The job description and other text were copied from the plain-text resume in the overlaid Notepad screen. (Reprinted from my.monster.com, by permission of Monster.com.)*

reference, much as you reused the Work Experience form for each job, clicking "Save and Add Reference" button after each reference and the "Save" button when you are through.

For each reference, you are asked to supply the name, title, phone number, company, and e-mail address, plus the reference type (i.e., whether it is a personal or professional reference). You must give the name, phone number, and type—the other items are optional.

Actually, the entire reference step is optional—you do not have to list your references with your resume. And you may not want to give out references until you know who is asking for them. That way, you can give out references selectively and warn the references that they will be called. But remember, you do have to have references lined up.

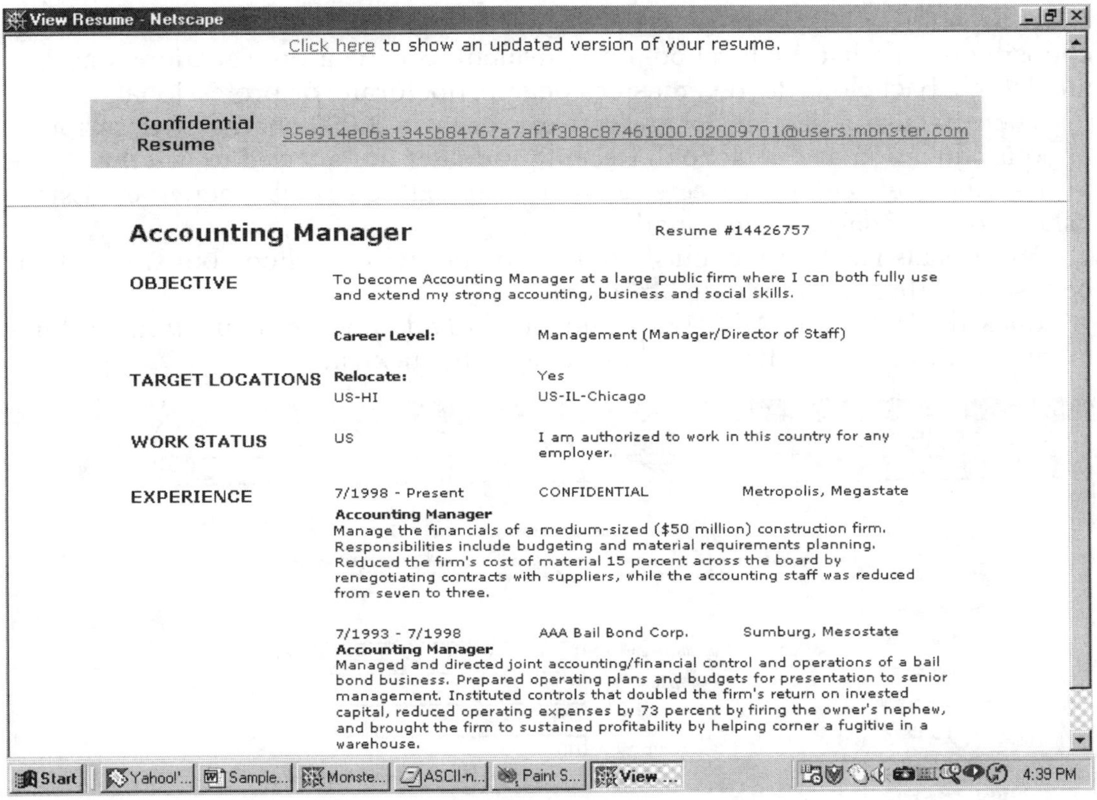

Figure 7.13 *The View Resume window after inputting the job history information, demonstrating some of Monster.com's resume-confidentiality features. (Reprinted from my.monster.com, by permission of Monster.com.)*

If you have opted for confidentiality, the reference section will not be displayed to an employer who is surfing the database. But it will be displayed if you send the resume directly to an employer.

Click "Save" when you are through or "Skip This Screen" if you don't want to list references.

Education

With the education step, you again reuse the same screen (shown in Figure 7.14) to describe each level of education that you want to list. You don't have to list your education, but if you do, the system requires that you input the school or program name, its location, and the degree or level attained. The latter involves choosing from a list: high school or equivalent, certification, vocational, associate degree, bachelor's degree, master's degree, doctorate, or professional.

There is also a section where you can input a 2,000-character description of your education at that school. Recent graduates are advised to use this space to describe their college careers, emphasizing extracurricular activities. Established professionals should usually skip it.

Sources also agree that you should not mention high school, but simply let it be assumed that you graduated from one.

Click the "Save and Add New Education" to add another educational attainment, or click "Add" to finish and move on to the next step.

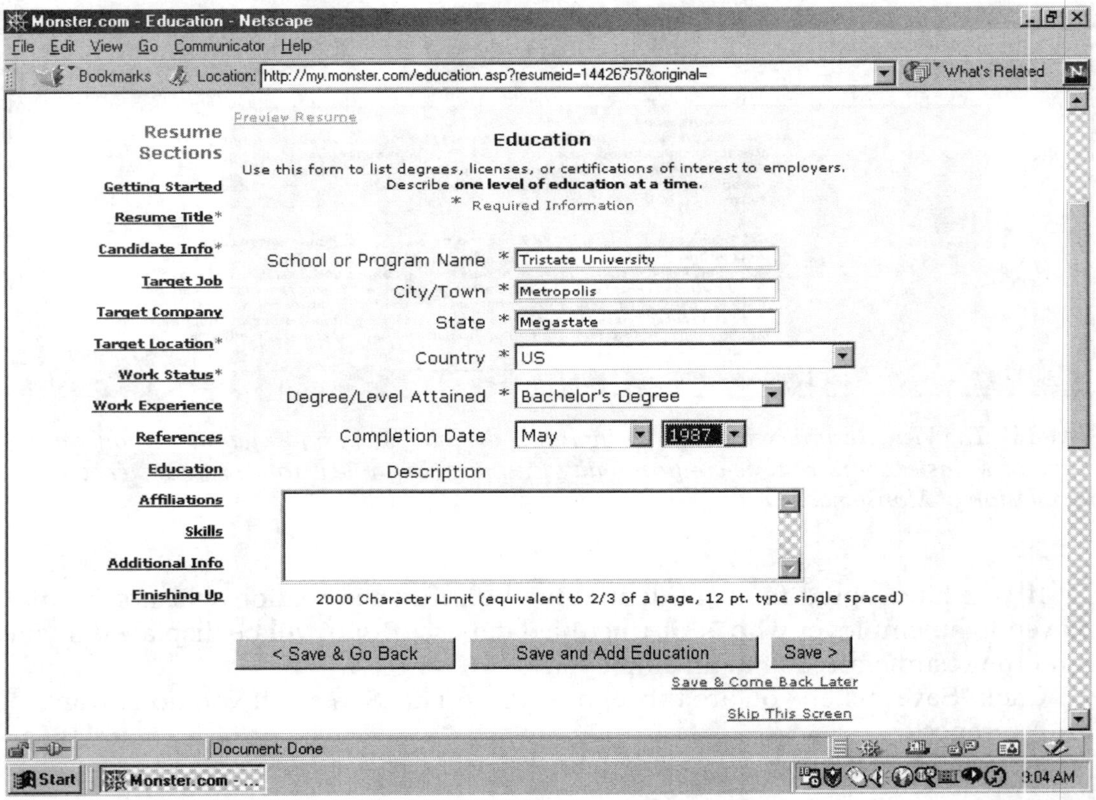

Figure 7.14 *The Education screen, used to list your college degrees and other educational levels, such as technical certifications. (Reprinted from my.monster.com, by permission of Monster.com.)*

Affiliations

Employers are often interested in what professional organizations you belong to. The Affiliations screen (not shown) lets you list each organization you want to mention. For each one, you must give the organization's name, your title in it, and the dates you belonged. ("Present" can be used as the end date.)

Alternatively, you can skip the whole screen and go on. If the only thing you can think of to list is your paid listing in a vanity who's-who book, you should skip this screen.

Again, you reuse the form for each affiliation, clicking the "Save and Add Affiliation" button to add a further organization or the "Save" button to finish and move on to the next step.

Skills

Especially in information technology fields, job applicants will want to list the job-related skills that they have acquired, especially knowledge of specific computer languages. This can be done using the Skills screen, shown in Figure 7.15.

If you list a skill, you must fill in all the data items: the name of the skill, how long ago you last used it (the options on the list are never, currently used, one year ago, two years ago, three years ago, or four-plus years ago), your skills level (beginner, intermediate, or expert), and the number of years of experience you have with that skill. ("Never" is an option in the "last used" field because you can have received training for something and not used it professionally.)

As with previous steps, you reuse the form for each skill, clicking the "Save and Add Skill" button to add another skill or the "Save" button to finish.

If you have done a keyword version of your resume, as described in Chapter 5, it may be useful to review it and see if any of the keywords should be reflected in a skills listing.

If you don't have any skills you want to list, you can simply skip this screen and go to the next section.

Additional Information

Everyone has additional information—the hobbies and awards and achievements that don't fit anyplace else. You can put them in the Additional Information section (see Figure 7.16). Notice that you have space for 3,000 characters, which is about two double-spaced typewritten pages—far more than you should expect anyone to read.

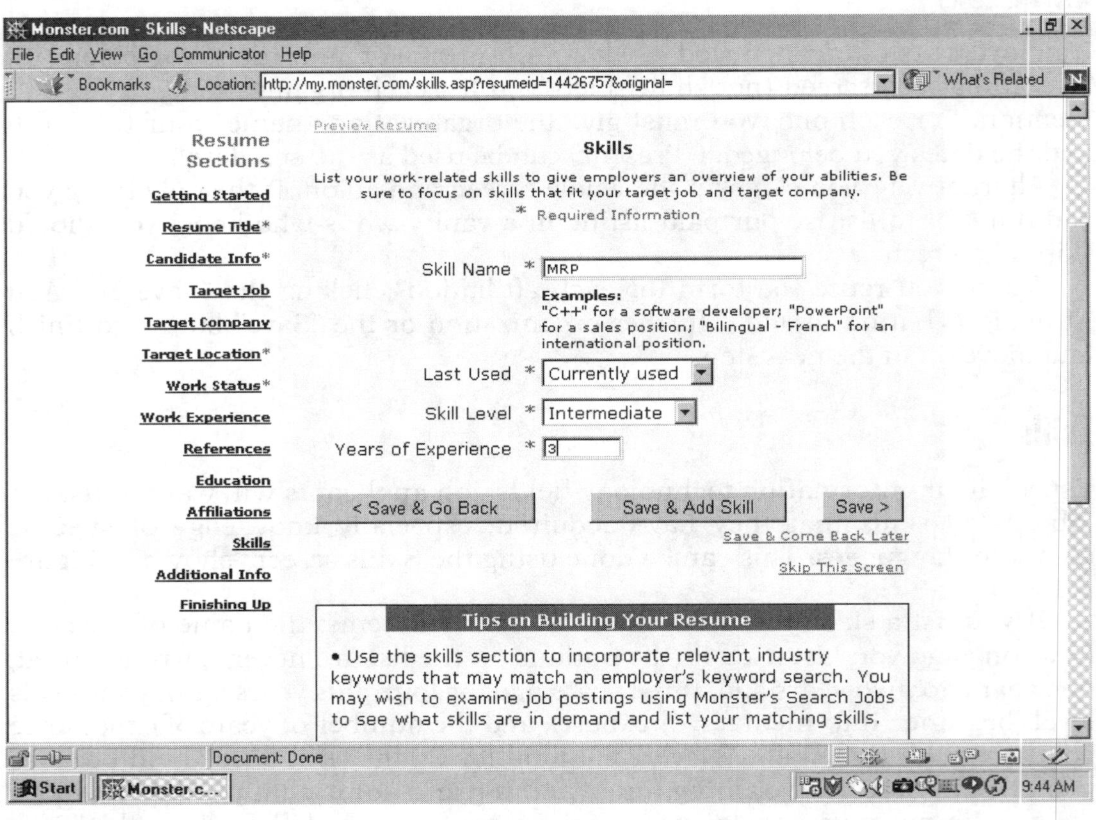

Figure 7.15 *The Skills screen, where you can list the job-related skills you have acquired. (Reprinted from my.monster.com, by permission of Monster.com.)*

If you have nothing additional to say, you can just click the "Skip This Screen" entry and go on. To add information to your resume after entering it on this screen, click the "Save" button.

Finishing Up

The last step lets you do just that—finish up. This screen (not shown) includes buttons that let you activate the resume so that employers surfing the resume database can see it. Or you can save it for further editing in "inactive status," where only you can see it.

This step also includes a "Preview Resume" option. For the sample resume, clicking the preview option generated the resume shown in Figure 7.17.

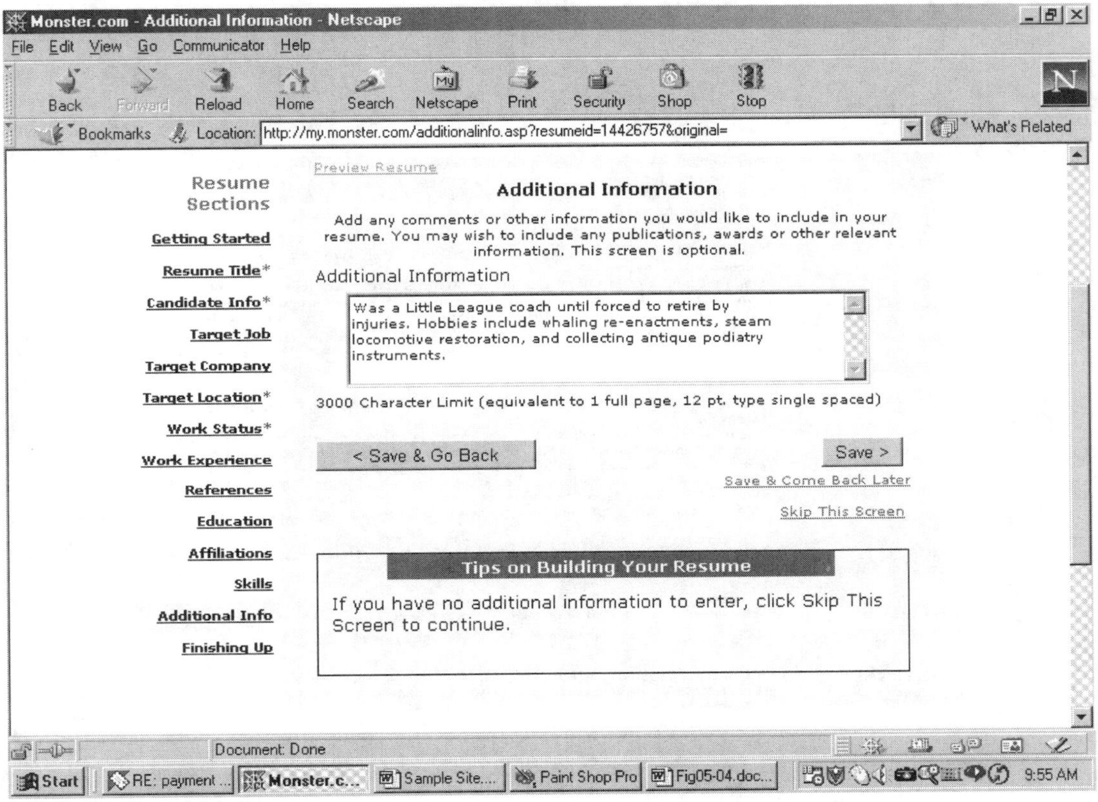

Figure 7.16 *The Additional Information screen, where you can mention things that don't fit anywhere else in your resume. (Reprinted from my.monster.com, by permission of Monster.com.)*

Results

If you return to your My Monster folder screen, clicking on the "Resumes" entry in the My Monster toolbar will bring up a screen like that shown in Figure 7.18. It will list the resumes you have stored so far, together with their status and the number of times each has been viewed by an employer. The system will not supply the name of the employers who did the looking, because confidentiality is a two-way street.

You can compose and store five resumes on the system, but only one at a time can be active in the database.

From this screen, you can view and edit a resume, duplicate it (to create a new version that you will edit), delete it, activate or deactivate it, or renew it (by

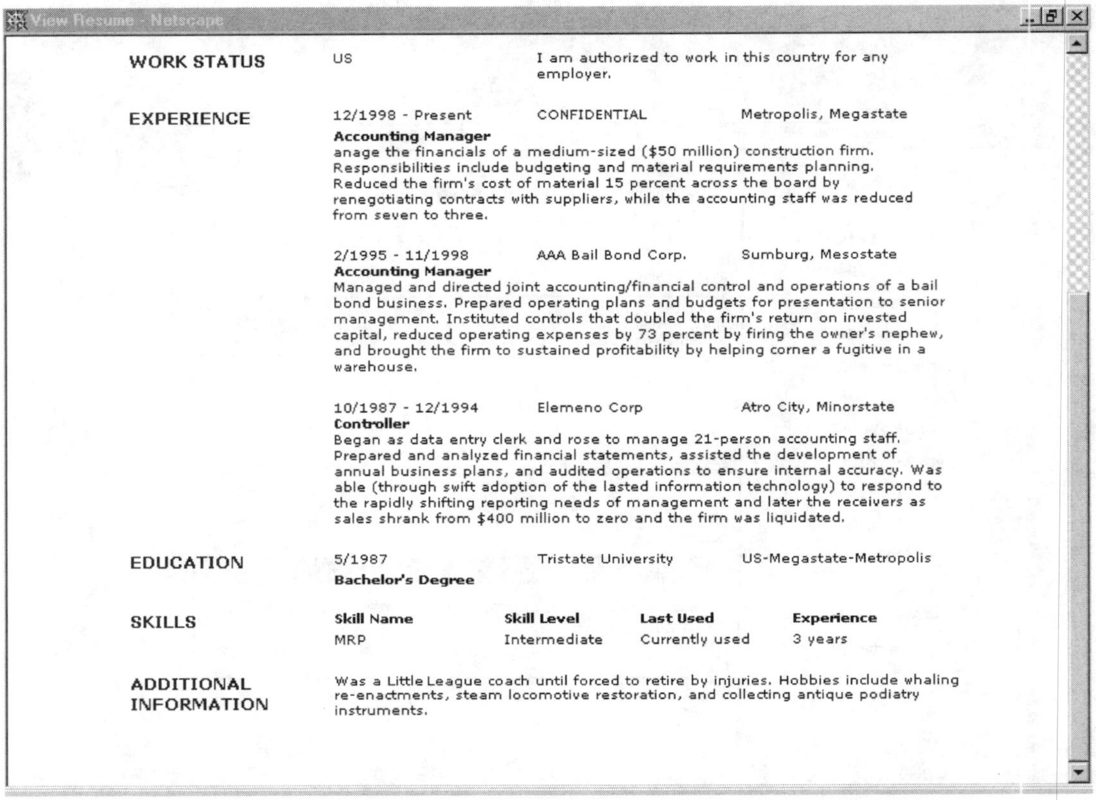
View Resume - Netscape

WORK STATUS
US — I am authorized to work in this country for any employer.

EXPERIENCE
12/1998 - Present — CONFIDENTIAL — Metropolis, Megastate
Accounting Manager
anage the financials of a medium-sized ($50 million) construction firm. Responsibilities include budgeting and material requirements planning. Reduced the firm's cost of material 15 percent across the board by renegotiating contracts with suppliers, while the accounting staff was reduced from seven to three.

2/1995 - 11/1998 — AAA Bail Bond Corp. — Sumburg, Mesostate
Accounting Manager
Managed and directed joint accounting/financial control and operations of a bail bond business. Prepared operating plans and budgets for presentation to senior management. Instituted controls that doubled the firm's return on invested capital, reduced operating expenses by 73 percent by firing the owner's nephew, and brought the firm to sustained profitability by helping corner a fugitive in a warehouse.

10/1987 - 12/1994 — Elemeno Corp — Atro City, Minorstate
Controller
Began as data entry clerk and rose to manage 21-person accounting staff. Prepared and analyzed financial statements, assisted the development of annual business plans, and audited operations to ensure internal accuracy. Was able (through swift adoption of the lasted information technology) to respond to the rapidly shifting reporting needs of management and later the receivers as sales shrank from $400 million to zero and the firm was liquidated.

EDUCATION
5/1987 — Tristate University — US-Megastate-Metropolis
Bachelor's Degree

SKILLS

Skill Name	Skill Level	Last Used	Experience
MRP	Intermediate	Currently used	3 years

ADDITIONAL INFORMATION
Was a Little League coach until forced to retire by injuries. Hobbies include whaling re-enactments, steam locomotive restoration, and collecting antique podiatry instruments.

Figure 7.17 *A preview of the example resume rendered by Monster.com. This screen shows the bottom half of the resume with material entered after the work experience step—education, skills, and additional information. (Reprinted from my.monster.com, by permission of Monster.com.)*

reseting its deactivation date to a year after yesterday; it otherwise automatically deactivates a year after it was created).

You can also send your resume to anyone, including a friend, an employer, or yourself. And you should do that to make sure it looks fine when rendered as e-mail. It will come as plain text, with the text indented from the headers as shown in Figure 7.17. The text will not have line breaks; that is, each paragraph is one long line, which the recipient's e-mail program can word wrap or not.

A confidential resume that you send will show the Monster.com e-mail address for your account, but it will also show your real return e-mail address. So, if you sent the resume to an employer, the employer could get back directly

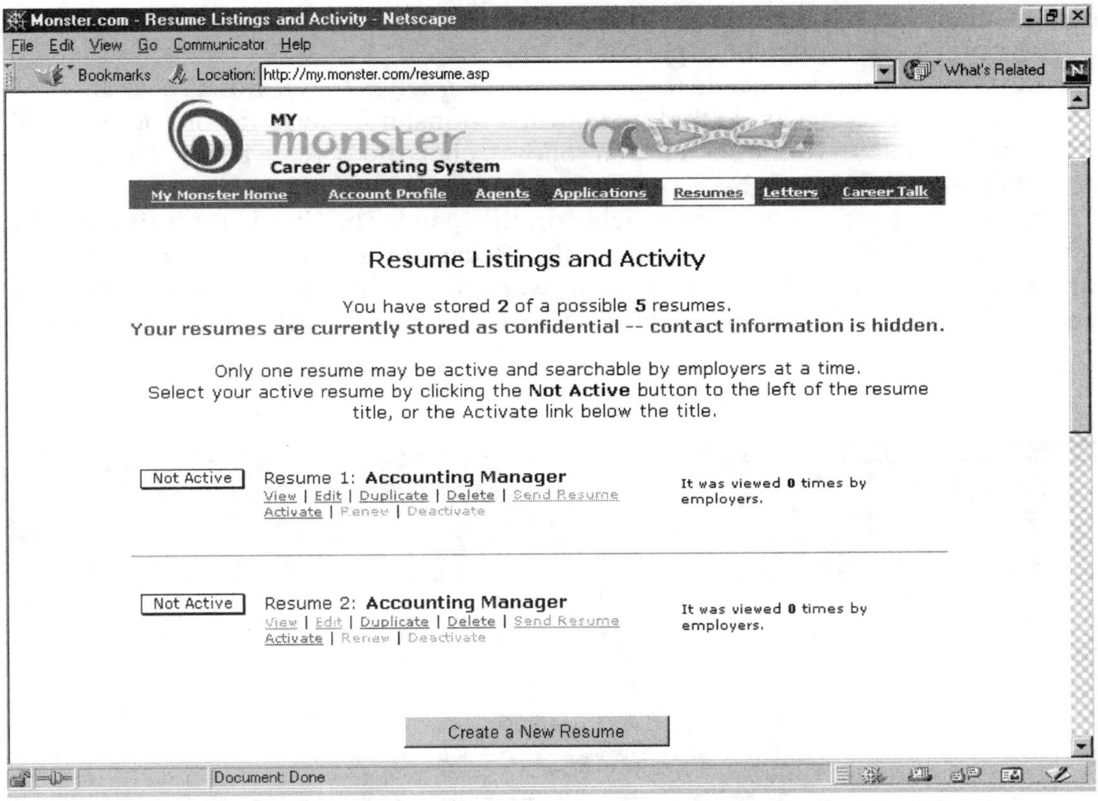

Figure 7.18 *Resume toolbar screen after creating resumes. In this case, two resumes have been created but both are currently inactive, meaning that no employers have viewed them yet. (Reprinted from my.monster.com, by permission of Monster.com.)*

to you—but also possibly figure out who you are. If that is a problem, you can use a throw-away e-mail address, as discussed in Chapter 9.

Cover Letters

You should always include a cover letter when you send a resume to someone, explaining why they are getting this resume and what job you are interested in. (It may be self-evident to you and may even be self-evident to the recipient, but it may not be to the person who actually opens and sorts the mail.) In the off-line world, you can generate the letter the same way you generate a copy of your resume. But in the online world, you need an online cover letter. Because Monster.com can send your resume to an employer as part of the application process (explained in the next section), you want it to be able to generate a cover letter that it can also send.

And Monster.com can do that. In your My Monster folder, click on the "Letters" entry in the toolbar. In the screen that follows, click the "Create a New Letter" button. You should then see the "Create a Letter" page, as shown in Figure 7.19.

Note that there are two entry fields on this page. The first is for a title for the letter that will be for your reference only. (Because the system lets you compose and store five different letters, you will want to be able to tell them apart.) The second field is for the text of the letter. You are limited to 4,000 characters, which

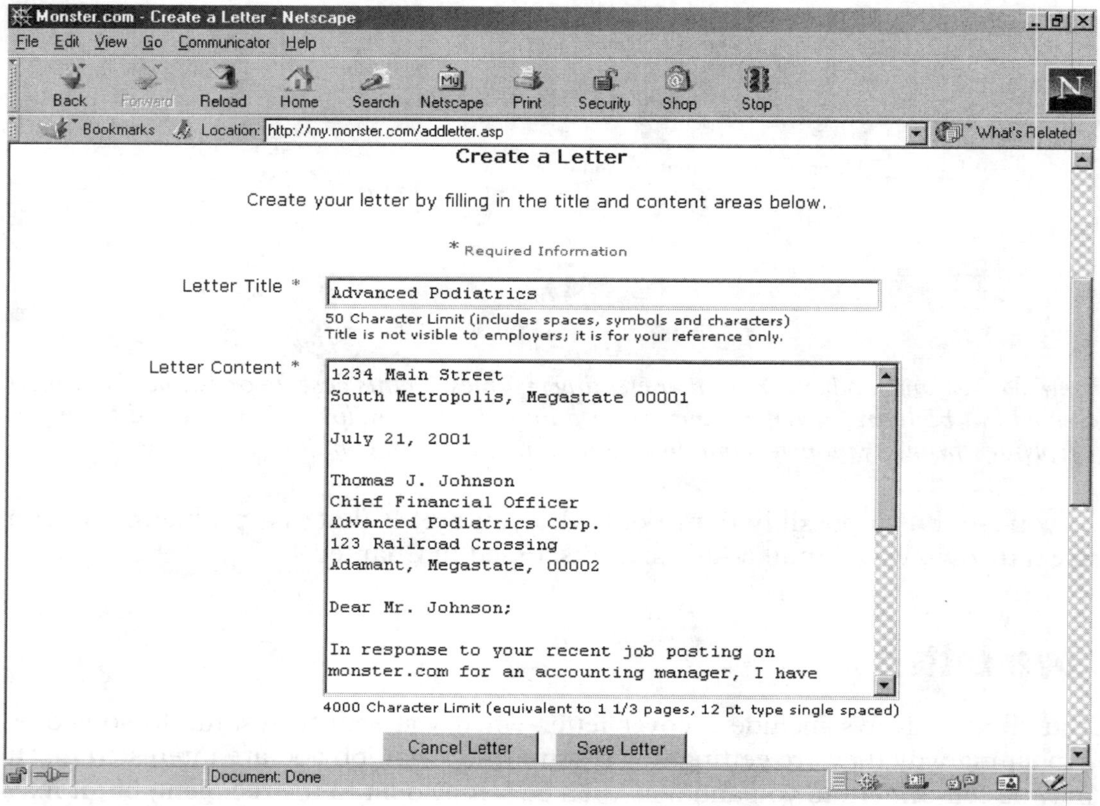

Figure 7.19 *Cover-letter composition screen at Monster.com. When applying for a job online, the cover letter can be sent with your application. The letter is plain text and can be composed in a word processor and then pasted into the text entry window. The title is for your personal reference only. (Reprinted from my.monster.com, by permission of Monster.com.)*

is far more than you need for a one-page letter (and a cover letter should be less than a page long if you expect the recipient to actually read it).

You should compose the text in a word processor and then copy and paste the text into the input field. Keep in mind that the end result will be a plain-text letter; don't rely on any of your word processor's desktop publishing features, such as boldfacing, underlining, and font changes.

You can then click the "Save Letter" button to save your composition. After that, the "Letters" section of the folder will list the new cover letter (and up to four others that you compose) by the title you gave it. You can look at a preview of a given letter, edit it, duplicate it, delete it, or send it.

If you send the letter, it is sent by itself to whatever e-mail address you supply. When you apply online, Monster.com will send a cover letter you select, with a resume you select, to the employer.

Looking and Applying for a Job

You can perform a job search by clicking the "Search Jobs" item in the Monster.com (not my.monster.com) toolbar. In other words, you don't have to be a registered user with a My Monster folder to perform a job search.

After clicking on "Search Jobs," you should get a screen like the one shown in Figure 7.20, which will allow you to browse or search. If you search, you can save the parameters as an "agent." If you find something suitable, you can apply.

Searching and Applying

The example screen (Figure 7.20) shows a search in progress. You can search by metropolitan area, job category, and keyword. You can also search via any combination of these. If you don't care about location or category, you can set either of these two to "select all."

The example search produced more than a thousand hits (of accountants or auditors in the Chicago area), as shown in Figure 7.21. This is too many to be practical, but Monster.com then lets you perform a subsearch, meaning that you can search the results of the first search with new parameters. Two parameters are allowed: age of the posting and keywords. Keywords, as is usual, can be preceded with "not" to exclude rather than include them.

Inputting MRP (material requirements planning, one of the sample applicant's skills) as the keyword for the subsearch results in exactly one result (not shown). Clicking on it will bring up an actual job posting, as seen in Figure 7.22. Notice that there is contact information, so that the applicant could approach the employer outside Monster.com. But there is also an "Apply Online" button.

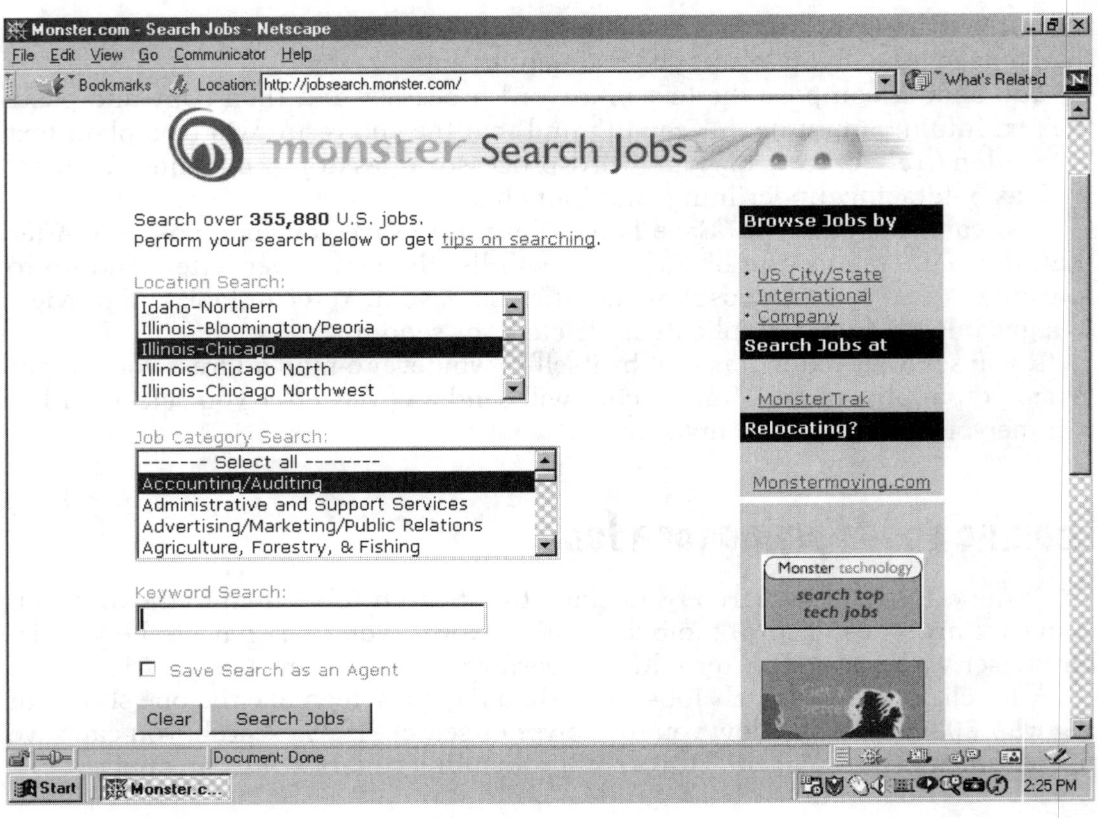

Figure 7.20 *The Monster.com job search screen. You can search the database via location, job category, or keyword parameters, or you can browse. (Reprinted from my.monster.com, by permission of Monster.com.)*

Clicking this button brings up the "Apply Online" screen, in your My Monster folder, as shown in Figure 7.23. (If you are not a registered user, you will have to register at this point.) From the "Apply Online" screen you can select which cover letter (if any) and which resume to send. (In the example, there is no appropriate cover letter, and the applicant would want to go back to the Letters section of the My Monster toolbar and write one, run the search again, and then do the application.)

Clicking the "Apply for this position now!" button will transmit your resume and cover letter to the e-mail address of the contact person selected by the employer when the job was posted.

In some cases, however, clicking the "Apply Online" button at the bottom of a job posting will link you to the employer's own Web site, where you can fill out an actual application. Often, you will be invited to paste your plain-text resume.

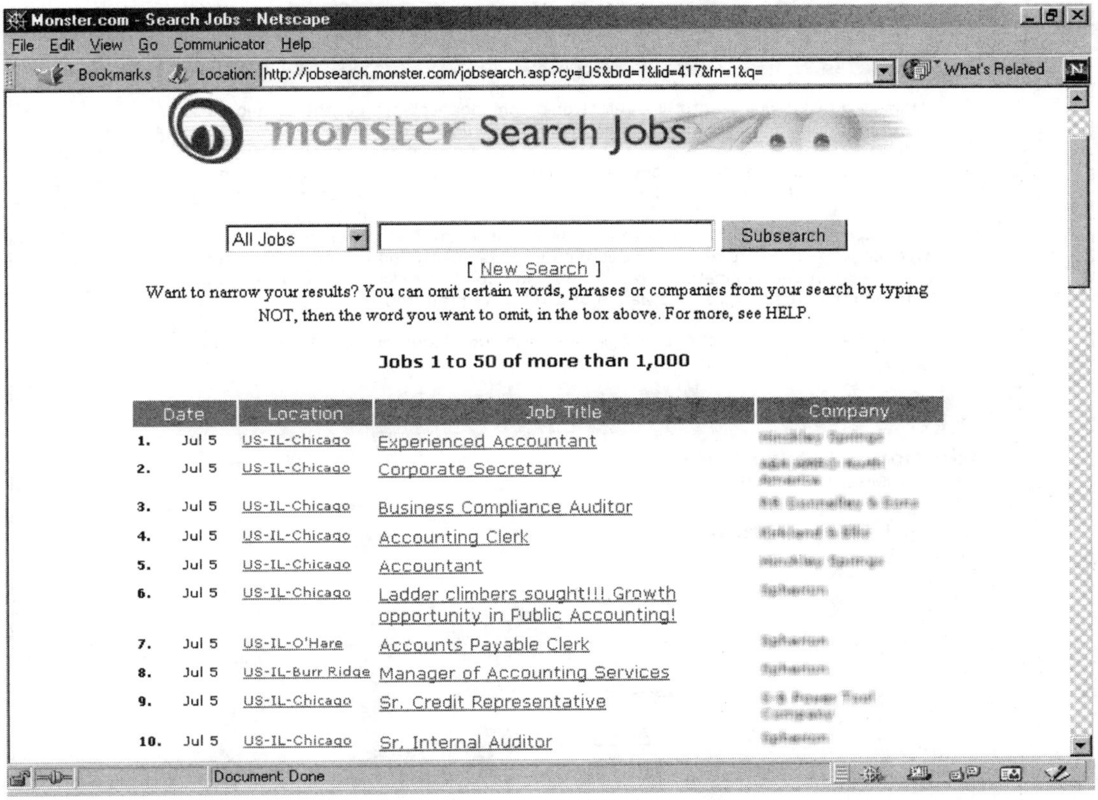

Figure 7.21 *The results of the search from Figure 7.20, with identifying information blurred out. The job seeker can then make a subsearch of the original results by limiting the age of the postings or by using keywords. (Reprinted from my.monster.com, by permission of Monster.com.)*

Browsing and Applying

Back at the opening "Search Jobs" screen, note that you can also browse for jobs by city or state, by country, or by company.

Clicking on the "US City/State" browsing option brings up a map of the United States. Clicking on the state you want will bring up a screen (such as shown in Figure 7.24) where you can do any of three things: pick from a list of metropolitan areas in that state, launch a keyword search against the job postings in that state, or pick from a list of companies that are advertising for jobs in that state. (The list of companies can be very long and may be broken down into alphabetical segments.)

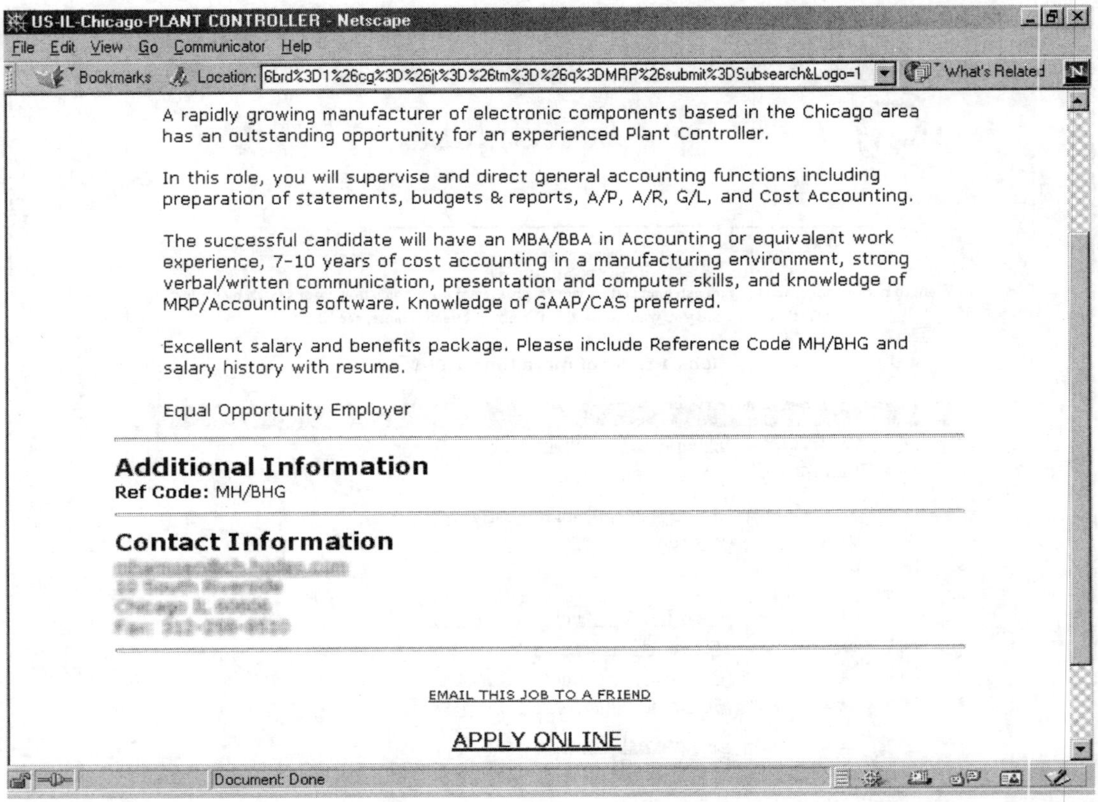

Figure 7.22 *Job posting reached as the result of a job search. (Reprinted from www.monster.com, by permission of Monster.com.)*

If you pick a metropolitan area, you can then run a keyword search against the job postings in that area or browse a list of companies that have job postings in that area.

At that point, you will get lists of jobs, as described in the previous section, and you can proceed to apply online.

If you browse by company, Monster.com currently gives you the same screens that you would get if you choose to browse by city/state because companies are listed on the same pages.

If you choose the "International" option in the browse commands, Monster.com will let you select what country or region in which you want to work (and what country or region you are moving from) and let you search for jobs there. You will also be offered links to tips on living, working, and moving there.

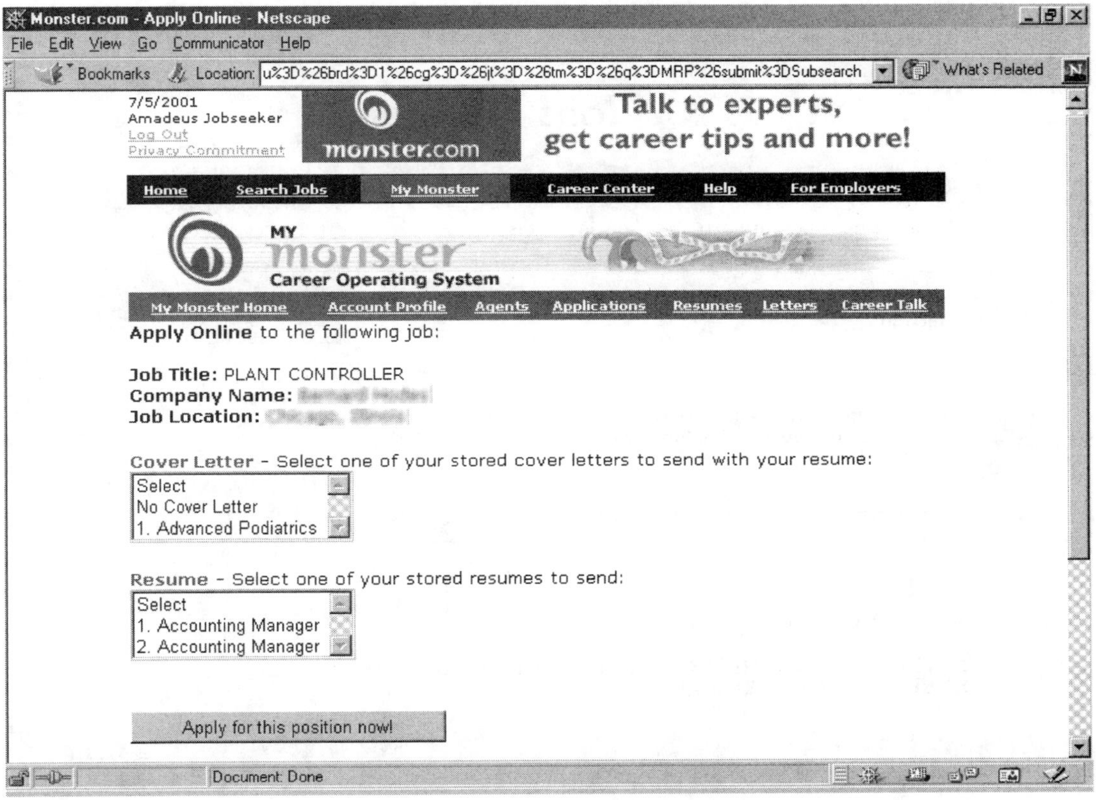

Figure 7.23 *The "Apply Online" screen, where you can respond to a specific job posting by sending your resume and optionally a cover letter directly to the employer who posted the job. (Reprinted from my.monster.com, by permission of Monster.com.)*

Checking on Applications

If you click on the "Applications" entry in the My Monster toolbar, you will get a page listing the applications you have made online through Monster.com, showing the date of each, the job title, and the company name. If you have a long list, you can sort it by either of the three data items by clicking its column header.

For each application, the job description will be linked to the job title. You can read the description by clicking on the job title—unless the employer has removed the posting, presumably because it has been filled. In that case, nothing will be linked to the job title.

Note that it is up to the employer to actually respond to your application—employers are urged to acknowledge applications, but there is no requirement

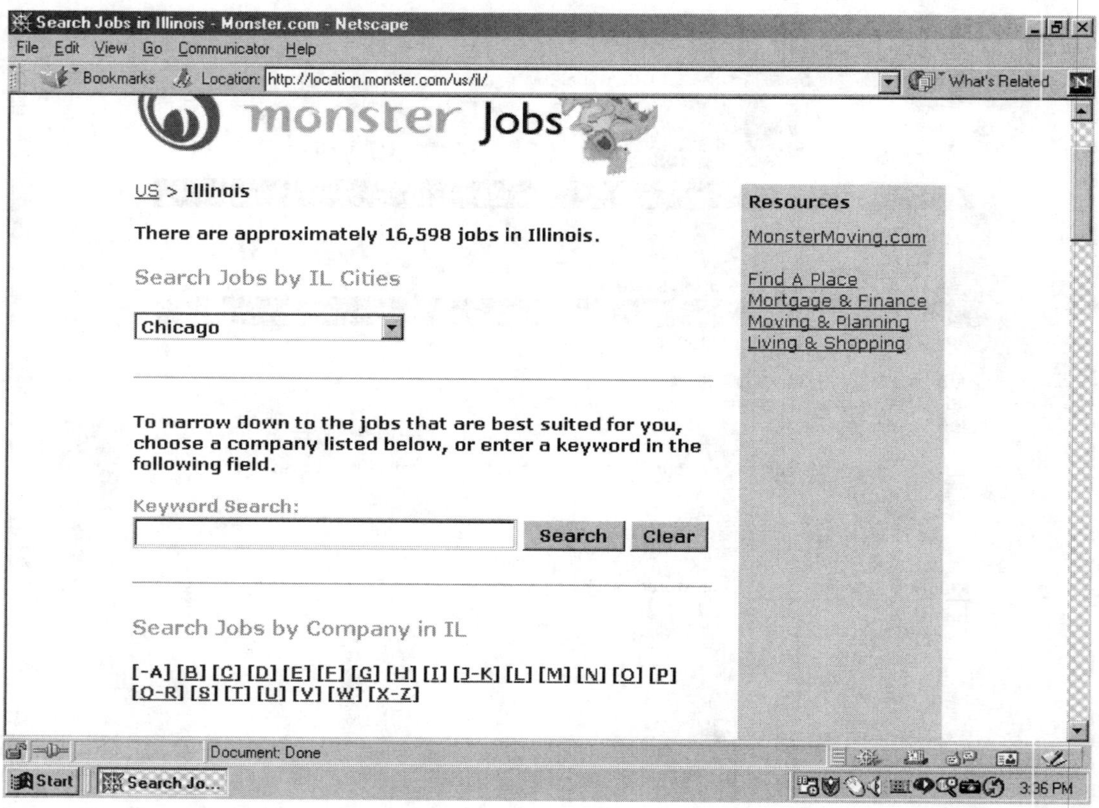

Figure 7.24 *The Search Jobs screen after electing to browse Illinois. You can select an Illinois city, input a keyword to search Illinois jobs, or browse an alphabetical list of companies with job openings in Illinois. (Reprinted from www.monster.com, by permission of Monster.com.)*

that they do so. In the absence of an acknowledgment, it is up to you to decide whether to follow through by some other media, such as a phone call.

Creating Search Agents

If you click the "Save Search as an Agent" box (shown in Figure 7.20) before running a search (as opposed to browsing), you will be switched over to the Create Job Search Agents screen, shown in Figure 7.25.

As well as providing the same search criteria you would use on the default search screen, the screen allows you to choose what kind of job you want your agent to look for (full-time or part-time, contract or employee) and how often e-mail notification should be sent—daily, weekly, biweekly, monthly, or none. (You should use "none" when you want to check the results in your My Monster folder rather than receive e-mail notification.) Your agent then looks for new postings that meet your search criteria and will send you e-mail notification. (After receiving notification, you go to your My Monster folder to see the job posting.)

If you did not already have a My Monster account, the system will move you to the My Monster registration screen to set one up before creating the agent.

You can also create agents by going to the "Agents" entry in the My Monster toolbar, as shown in Figure 7.26. There, you have three commands for each of the five agents you can create: view, edit, and delete. View lists the latest jobs that meet your search criteria, Edit lets you alter the agent's criteria, and Delete lets you delete the agent.

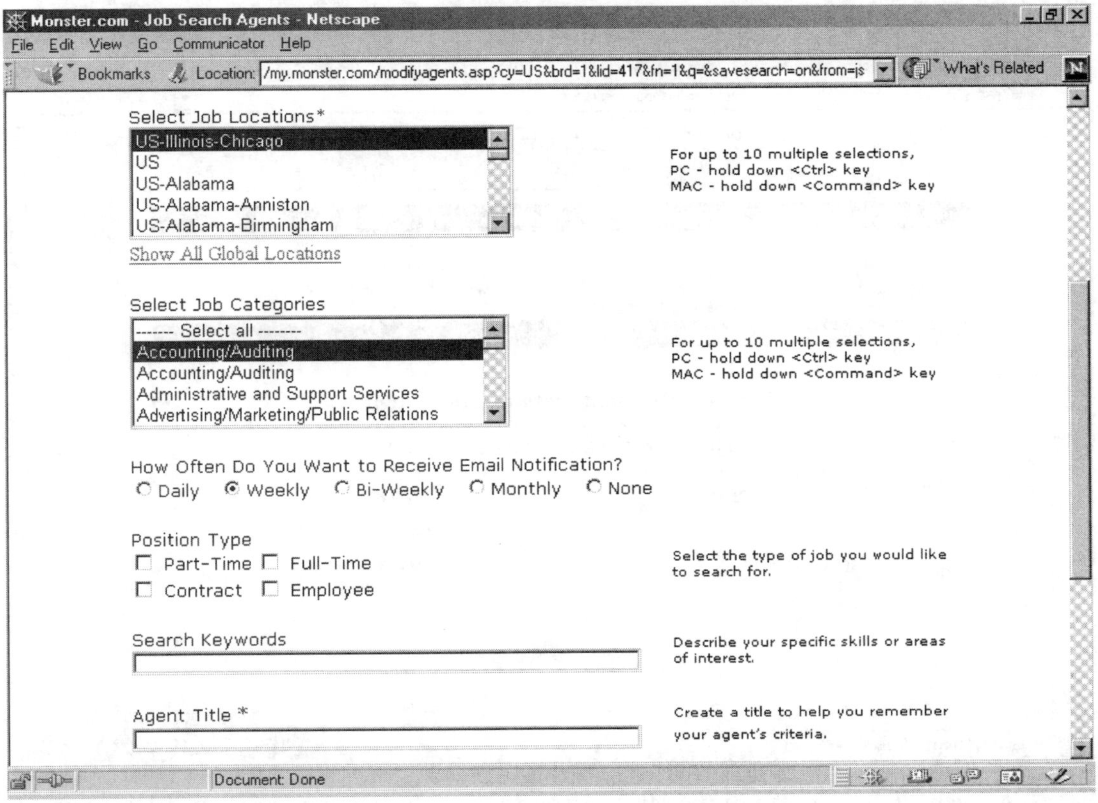

Figure 7.25 *The job search agent-creation screen, where you select from Monster.com's search parameters and state the type of position you're looking for and how often you want e-mail notification. (Reprinted from my.monster.com, by permission of Monster.com.)*

Other Services

Clicking the "Career Talk" entry in the My Monster toolbar brings up a list of chat rooms, discussion forms (some hosted by experts), and free newsletters of interested to job seekers.

Clicking the "Career Center" entry in the Monster.com toolbar puts you in touch with a wealth of material that may help you in your job hunt, including material on writing effective resumes and cover letters, researching salaries and companies, handling interviews, and so on. There's an entire branch site—

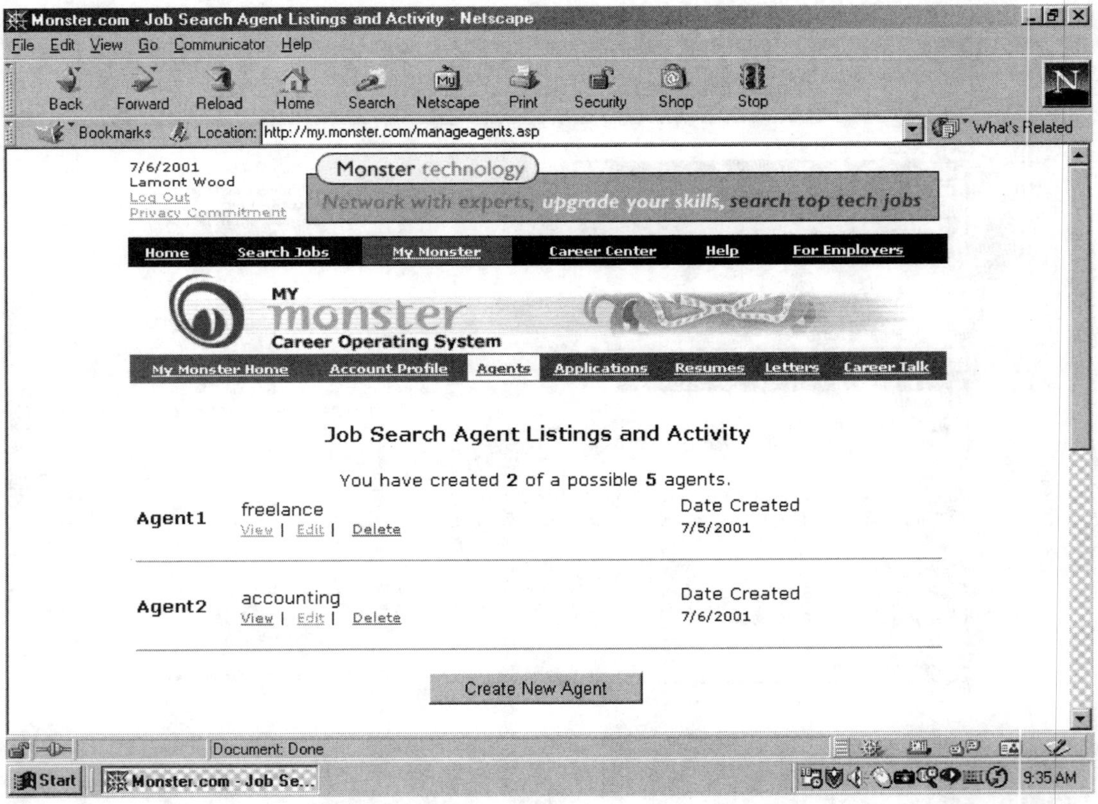

Figure 7.26 *Agent-listing screen in the My Monster folder, where you can edit or delete your job search agents or view what they've found. (Reprinted from my.monster.com, by permission of Monster.com.)*

MonsterMoving.com—devoted to relocation issues, such as finding a house or apartment, mortgage, and moving company, not to mention figuring out what city you really want to live in.

Yes, you could read all day—but remember, you're supposed to be looking for a job.

CHAPTER 8

Other Job Sites

Chapter 6 looked at the 10 largest job sites on the Web, as defined by Alexa Internet of San Francisco. This chapter examines more sites, broken down into various categories:

- The next 10 sites.
- Portals.
- Want ad sites.
- Sites that list corporate job sites.
- Selected niche sites.

These sites are just intended to serve as a sample of what's out there. And as always, inclusion does not constitute endorsement. To see more jobs sites, try Yahoo!'s "Business and Economy/Employment and Work/Jobs" section.

The Next 10 Sites

Alexa Internet actually lists 20 top job sites. The following sections discuss the ones that ranked 11 to 20 as of May 2001.

http://www.jobsinthemoney.com

Jobsinthemoney.com touts itself as the "market-maker in professional finance positions," meaning that it carries jobs in banking, accounting, and finance.

http://www.salary.com

Mentioned in Chapter 4, www.salary.com states that it offers "recruitment and employee valuation products for organizations with market-driven pay practices." It's a job site by virtue of its e-recruiting service, "an extension of the powerful Salary Wizard compensation data source that enables corporations to reach candidates who have self-selected into a specific industry and ZIP code."

http://www.aecjobbank.com

The initials AEC in www.aecjobbank.com stand for architecture, engineering, and construction, making this a "building industry employment" site.

http://www.computerjobs.com

The name, www.computerjobs.com, says it all. This site lists available jobs by region and skill—Texas and database systems were the leaders at this writing. In a reverse of the usual practice of e-mailing prospects about job openings, the site will e-mail promising new resumes to employers.

http://www.jobs.com

The job site www.jobs.com claims a regional focus, although the focus is on 25 different major cities and 100 metropolitan areas.

http://www.jobtrak.com

The job site www.jobtrak.com is actually a branch of Monster.com, specializing in the needs of college students and recent graduates.

http://www.6figurejobs.com

Looking for a job as a chief executive officer? Well, some companies are looking to hire, and if you have the right credentials, www.6figurejobs.com claims to be able to put you in touch with them, for free, with confidentiality assured for both parties.

http://inside.techies.com

"Technology professionals" is what inside.techies.com says it specializes in.

http://www.brassring.com

The Web site www.brassring.com specializes in career management tools (such as resume composition) for people in the information technology field. But it also has the usual job and resume databases.

http://www.wetfeet.com

Although www.wetfeet.com is also a general job site, its specialty appears to be internship programs, offered through a branch site called http://internships.wetfeet.com.

Portals

Portals are lists of Web sites that address a particular topic, with links to those sites. Portals are a good place to start in any field because a Web site is in the best position to keep up with the changing landscape of the Web. The following portals address career and job-hunting Web sites.

http://www.dbm.com

This general job portal, www.dbm.com, called the Riley Guide, lists career information and job sites by every category the organizers could think of, from aboriginal affinity groups (no kidding) to zookeepers.

http://www.job-hunt.org

This portal for job searchers, www.job-hunt.org, lists job sites by category, often with subjective reviews. (Sites with rigorous privacy policies get the best reviews.)

http://www.careers.org

The careers portal www.careers.org, is basically a list of job and career sites. But it's an exhaustive list, and branches into almost anything you'd need during an job search, including online dictionaries, plus online entertainment when you get tired of working.

http://www.jobhuntersbible.com

The portal www.jobhuntersbible.com is the online supplement to job-hunter book *What Color Is Your Parachute*. It includes ancillary material like self-assessment tests, resume writing tips, and corporate research.

http://www.ahandyguide.com/Directory/Business/Employment/

The portal at www.ahandyguide.com has a large collection of employment sites (among many other things).

Want Ad Sites

There are also Web sites that aggregate the want ads of various online newspapers. Because most newspapers worth mentioning have an online version these days, the results can be impressive. Again, this list should not be considered definitive.

http://www.jobbankusa.com

Job Bank USA is a general job site at www.jobbankusa.com that also includes a "meta search" facility to search the help-wanted ads of online newspapers, by state.

http://www.nationaladsearch.com

National Ad Search at www.nationaladsearch.com inputs Sunday help-wanted ads from the daily newspapers in the 65 largest cities in the United States, specializing in managerial, executive, professional, and technical positions. Ads stay online for three weeks. You can read 100 ads for $10.

http://www.jobfactory.com

The "JobSpider" at www.jobfactory.com searches online newspapers and everything else it can find (corporate sites, recruiter sites, newsgroups, etc.) for help-wanted notices. At this writing, it listed more than 3.1 million jobs, making it one of the largest job databases on the Web.

http://www.employmentwizard.com

Employment Wizard at www.employmentwizard.com reports that it gets it job listings from local newspapers, plus some directly from employers.

Listings of Corporate Job Sites

Perhaps you want to check the jobs available in a particular company, instead of just look for a job. You could go to its Web site and look for the "jobs" or "career opportunities" section, if there is one. (Chapter 12 will help you find corporations' Web sites.)

But if you want to browse corporate job sites, or the corporate job sites of particular industries, then the following sites are for you.

http://www.careerexposure.com

The site at www.careerexposure.com lists corporate Web sites with job listings under the main headings of financial services, manufacturing, high technology, services, retailing, transportation, energy, miscellaneous, and international. Each main heading includes a list of subheads, and each subhead has a list of corporate Web sites. You can also post your text-only resume.

http://www.yahoo.com

Yahoo! lists more than three hundred corporate job sites in its Business and Economy/Employment and Work/Jobs section.

http://www.jobsafari.com

JobsSafari.com claims to be the largest listing of corporate job sites. You can search by name or browse by location.

http://www.job-hunt.org/companies.shtml

Job-Hunt.org, mentioned earlier, has its own listing of corporate Web sites.

http://www.careerresource.net/employer

The list at www.careersource.net/employer represents a volunteer project by a doctoral student at Rensselaer Polytechnic Institute, but there is no assurance that it will continue to be maintained.

Selected Niche Sites

Job sites are especially common in the high-tech arena, where the participants make a point of doing everything by computer. But the trend has moved into other fields as well, as you can see by the following lists. Again, these sites should be taken as a sample of what's out there, rather than a definitive list. And with a trend toward consolidation appearing to emerge, the list will very likely have changed by the time you read this. (The sites are listed alphabetically by niche. Sites listed previously are also included.)

Academia

- http://www.academic360.com.
- http://www.academploy.com (Academic Employment Network).
- http://www.acphysci.com (Academic Physician and Scientist).
- http://www.aacc.nche.edu/career/careerline.asp (American Association of Community Colleges).
- http://chronicle.com/jobs (the *Chronicle of Higher Education*'s help-wanted section).
- http://www.higheredJobs.com.
- http://www.matrix.msu.edu/jobs (Job Guide for the Humanities and Social Sciences).
- http://www.recruitingteachers.org (National Teacher Recruitment Clearinghouse).

Banking, Accounting, Finance

- http://aba.careersite.com (American Bankers Association).
- http://www.accountemps.com.
- http://www.accounting.com.
- http://www.bankconnect.com.
- http://www.bankjobs.com.

http://www.bloomberg.com/careers.
http://www.careerbank.com.
http://www.fincareer.com.
http://www.investmentbankingjobs.com.
http://www.jobsinthemoney.com.
http://www.lifecareer.com.
http://www.loanprocessorjobs.com.
http://www.nbn-jobs.com (National Banking and Financial Services Network).

College Students and Recent Graduates

http://www.aftercollege.com.
http://www.black-collegian.com.
http://www.campchannel.com/jobboard (jobs at summer camps).
http://www.collegegrad.com.
http://www.collegepro.com (summer jobs as house painters).
http://www.collegerecruiter.com.
http://www.coolworks.com (seasonal jobs at resorts).
http://www.futurecollegegrads.com.
http://www.graduatingengineer.com.
http://www.jobtrak.com (part of Monster.com).
http://www.jobweb.com.
http://www.resortjobs.com.
http://www.summerjobs.com.

Consulting

http://www.ceweekly.com (*Contract Employment Weekly*).
http://www.consultlink.com.
http://www.cx.com (The Consulting Exchange).
http://www.guru.com.
http://www.imcusa.org (Institute of Management Consultants USA, Inc.).

Engineering

http://ci.mond.org/jobs.html (Society of Chemical Industry).
http://engineerjobs.com.
http://environmentalcareer.com.
http://jobs.ieeeusa.org/jobs (Institute of Electrical and Electronics Engineers, Inc.).

http://www.aecjobbank.com.
http://www.aiche.org/careerservices (American Institute of Chemical Engineers).
http://www.contractengineering.com.
http://www.eco.org (Environmental Careers Organization).
http://www.ejobs.org (environmental jobs).
http://www.engineeringjobs.com.

Factory Automation

http://www.automationtechies.com.

Freelancing

http://www.freelance.com.
http://www.freelanceonline.com.
http://www.freelancesearch.com.
http://www.sologig.com.

General

http://ww1.joboptions.com.
http://www.4work.com.
http://www.ajb.dni.us (America's Job Bank; an aggregate of state employment agency listings).
http://www.bestjobsusa.com.
http://www.brassring.com.
http://www.careerbuilder.com.
http://www.careercity.com.
http://www.careerjournal.com (*Wall Street Journal*).
http://www.careermag.com.
http://www.careermart.com.
http://www.craigslist.org.
http://www.cruelworld.com.
http://www.flipdog.com.
http://www.gotajob.com.
http://www.headhunter.net.
http://www.helpwanted.com.
http://www.hotjobs.com.
http://www.jobs.com.
http://www.jobsonline.com.

http://www.monster.com.
http://www.nationjob.com.
http://www.salary.com.
http://www.wetfeet.com.

Information Technology

http://inside.techies.com.
http://internetjobs.com.
http://itcareers.careercast.com (ITWorld.com).
http://jobs.brainbuzz.com.
http://jobs.cio.com (*CIO* magazine).
http://jobs.internet.com (Internet.com's job site).
http://softwaredeveloper.com.
http://www.careercity.com.
http://www.coboljobs.com.
http://www.computerjobs.com.
http://www.computerworld.com/cwi/careers (*ComputerWorld*).
http://www.cplusplusjobs.com.
http://www.databasejobs.com .
http://www.developers.net (software developers).
http://www.dice.com.
http://www.hireability.com.
http://www.prgjobs.com (jobs for programmers).
http://www.techjobbank.com (Tech Job Bank).
http://www.vault.com.
http://www.visualbasicjobs.com.

Internships

http://www.inroadsinc.org (internships for minorities).
http://www.internsnet.com.
http://www.internweb.com.
http://www.twc.edu (The Washington [D.C.] Center for Internships).

Law

http://www.acca.com/jobline/index.html (American Corporate Counsel Association).
http://www.attorneyjobsonline.com.

http://www.lawenforcementjob.com (law enforcement jobs portal).
http://www.lawjobs.com.

Management

http://www.6figurejobs.com.
http://www.brilliantpeople.com.

Medicine

http://medcareers.com.
http://www.4nursingjobs.com.
http://www.hospitaljobsonline.com.
http://www.pharmajobs.com (pharmaceutical jobs).
http://www.medhunters.com.
http://www.medzilla.com.

Other

http://lhkeeper.com (National Listing for Lighthouse Employment).
http://www.cincpac.com/afos/testpit.html (Archeological Fieldwork Opportunities).
http://www.diversitydirect.com (minority and disabled job seekers).

Sales and Marketing

http://jobs4sales.com.
http://marketingjobs.com.
http://salesclassifieds.com/.
http://www.ama.org (American Marketing Association).
http://www.retailjobnet.com.
http://www.salesjobs.com.
http://www.thejobboard.com.
http://www.topsalespositions.com.

Science

http://www.ams.org (American Mathematical Society).
http://www.sciencejobs.com.

http://www2.sciencecareers.org (American Association for the Advancement of Science).

Temping

http://www.appleone.com (light industrial).
http://www.kellyservices.com/kcn.
http://www.net-temps.com.
http://www.worknow.com (Olsten Staffing Services).

CHAPTER 9

Using E-Mail

You must have e-mail—don't think that you can do without it. There might be situations where you can pull off a job search without ever sending or receiving an e-mail message, but those are, increasingly, flukes. Having e-mail will make you as responsive and flexible as the other job seekers who have it. Not having it will make you stand out as that candidate who seemed sadly unprepared for twenty-first century office work.

This chapter looks at the following:

- The basics of e-mail.
- The mechanics of using e-mail.
- The all-important etiquette of e-mail.
- How to get free private e-mail.

E-mail Overview

E-mail (electronic mail) involves material sent from your computer to the computer of a recipient. There are many parallels with paper mail. The paper process would involve these steps:

- You prepare a letter on paper.
- You put it in a stamped, addressed envelope.
- You drop it in a mailbox, where a third party (the postal service) carries it to the mailbox of the recipient.
- The recipient opens it.

Here are the equivalent electronic steps for e-mail:

- You write a message using your e-mail software (or compose it in a word processor and then paste it into your e-mail software).
- You give the e-mail software the address of the recipient and click the "Send" button.
- Using your Internet connection, the software transmits it to a third party—typically, the e-mail server of the recipient's ISP (or corporate computer department).
- At some point, the recipient checks his or her e-mail, and the message is transmitted to the recipient's computer by the e-mail server where it has been waiting.

E-mail addresses take the form of the user name followed by an @ symbol (pronounced "at") and then the domain name. John Smith at domain.com might have the address johnsmith@domain.com or jsmith@domain.com—or for that matter, uncle.duddy@domain.com. Ultimately, the assignment of user names is, alas, completely idiosyncratic. Therefore, you cannot guess what a person's e-mail address is going to be.

Other important points:

- Transmission takes places over the Internet. The recipient may get the message through a corporate computer network, but that network has an e-mail "gateway" to the Internet.
- The recipient receives a copy of the original message, which stays on the sender's computer.
- While not necessarily instantaneous, transmission is very quick. However, the message does not arrive until the recipient checks for and receives incoming mail.
- The sender does not have to worry about routing. Simply knowing the e-mail address of the recipient is enough. The Internet itself will find a route or generate an error message to the sender saying that the message could not get through.
- As the message winds its way from sender to recipient, you have no control over what corners of the Internet it traverses. There can be no guarantee of privacy.

- You should not even have an expectation of privacy if you are using your employer's computer system. Your employer owns the computer and therefore its contents, which it can examine at will. If it is a government office, the e-mail is public record.
- Thanks to a feature called "file attachments," you can send any kind of computer material via e-mail—within limits. But as you will see, you must always be thinking about those limits.

The Big Upside

There is one little-known fact about Internet e-mail that can be extremely important to a job seeker: You should be able to get your e-mail from any point on the Internet, no matter where on the Internet your e-mail resides. As long as you have Web access, you should be able to tell your mail server to forward your mail to you. (You'll need to know the name of your mail server and be able to provide it with the password that protects your e-mail account.)

That means that if you are logged on to the Web through ISP number 1 but use ISP number 2 for your e-mail account, you can still receive your e-mail. The mail server on ISP number 2 will respond to queries from the user on ISP number 1 and forward any messages.

More specifically, if you use your office account to receive e-mail, you may (rightfully) feel hesitant to use your office e-mail address for job search purposes. After all, you're using company facilities for private purposes. Also, you're making it very easy for them to discover that you are looking for a job, and that is highly impolitic in some organizations. And, if you have a separate home e-mail address, you may also feel hesitant about using it, too, because it is easily traced back to you and will give you away.

But it is easy to get a temporary e-mail account to use for your job search. You can then check the messages in that account and download messages from it any time you are on the Web. It does not matter if you gained that access from the office, your home, or the public library.

How and where to get a temporary e-mail account is covered in the "Free E-Mail" section at the end of this chapter.

The Big Downside

The file attachment facility of Internet e-mail means that you can send anything at all along with your e-mail message, as long as it is a computer file. The attachment can be your beautifully formatted resume in its original word-processing format, a picture of you, a recording of your voice, or a digital video clip of you reporting the weather. Or it can be all these things, because you can attach multiple items. The next section looks at the mechanics of doing this.

You must, however, be very cautious about using this feature, and you may end up not using it at all in the course of your job search. There are two reasons for this:

- Files can be huge. And the Internet inflates their size even further by converting them from an eight-bit to a seven-bit format (for wider compatibility). But most e-mail systems limit the amount of file storage rationed to each e-mail user. If your message causes the mailbox to overflow, it will be refused. In addition, your own e-mail server may impose a limit on the size of the files it will send over the Internet.

- Attached files can contain viruses—programs written by vandals that can wreck a computer system. Therefore, a corporate e-mail system may refuse messages with attachments or strip off the attachments. But no way has been found to hide a virus in a plain-text message with no attachment.

Therefore, before sending a file attachment, you should check with the recipient. Just as you would not presume upon a mere acquaintance for an arduous favor, you should not presume to send a file attachment to someone known to you only as an e-mail address.

If this is the one point about e-mail etiquette that you pick up, it will suffice. Other points are made in the "E-Mail Etiquette" section. But first, take a look at the mechanics of e-mail.

The Mechanics of E-Mail

There are actually two kinds of e-mail applicable to an Internet-based job search:

- Standard e-mail using the POP (post office protocol) method that makes use of standard e-mail software. You can fetch your mail from any place on the Internet, and your files reside on your hard disk.
- Web-based e-mail, making use of your browser and the facilities on the Web site, of the e-mail service provider. Your files reside on the Web site, and you are limited to the facilities that it provides.

The free e-mail services listed later in this chapter are often Web-based. Setting up an account requires only that you have Internet access. Setting up an account and using it merely involves following the directions given at the site.

A POP services allows more options and is the kind you will be setting up if you get, for instance, a new home e-mail account through an ISP. The following sections look at the steps involved in setting up and using POP e-mail with the two most common PC e-mail software packages: Microsoft Outlook Express and Netscape Navigator.

Before you get started, you'll need the following:

- Access to the Internet for your computer, through a dial-up modem or broadband connection.
- E-mail software on your computer.
- An account with an ISP (or your employer, school, etc.) that includes an e-mail mailbox.
- The user name, password, and mailer server name that goes with that account.

If you have a Web access account, you probably already have everything on the list, including the e-mail account. But you may want to get a new one, for the reasons given previously. Then you may want to reconfigure your e-mail software to use the new e-mail account, such as the ones listed in the last section of this chapter.

Regardless of the reason you are getting an e-mail account, the next step is to configure and use your software.

Outlook Express

After you have your computer and its Internet connection set up so that you can get Web access, the next step is to configure your e-mail server.

In Outlook Express, click the "Tools" entry in the command menu near the top of the screen. In the pop-up menu that will appear, choose the "Accounts" option. You should get a screen labeled Internet Accounts. Click the "Mail" tab and then the "Add" button, choosing the "Mail" option, as shown in Figure 9.1. The software "wizard" will then walk you through the account setup procedure. Among the things you'll need are your e-mail address, mail server name, and password.

To compose a message, click the "Message" entry in the command menu near the top of the screen and select the "New Message" option. The composition window should then appear, as shown in Figure 9.2. You can type your message directly into the window or copy the text from a word processor and paste it into the Outlook Express composition window.

To attach a file to a message, click the "Attach" icon (with the paperclip image) in the tool bar near the top center of the window. You should then get the Insert Attachment screen, as shown in Figure 9.3. After locating and highlighting

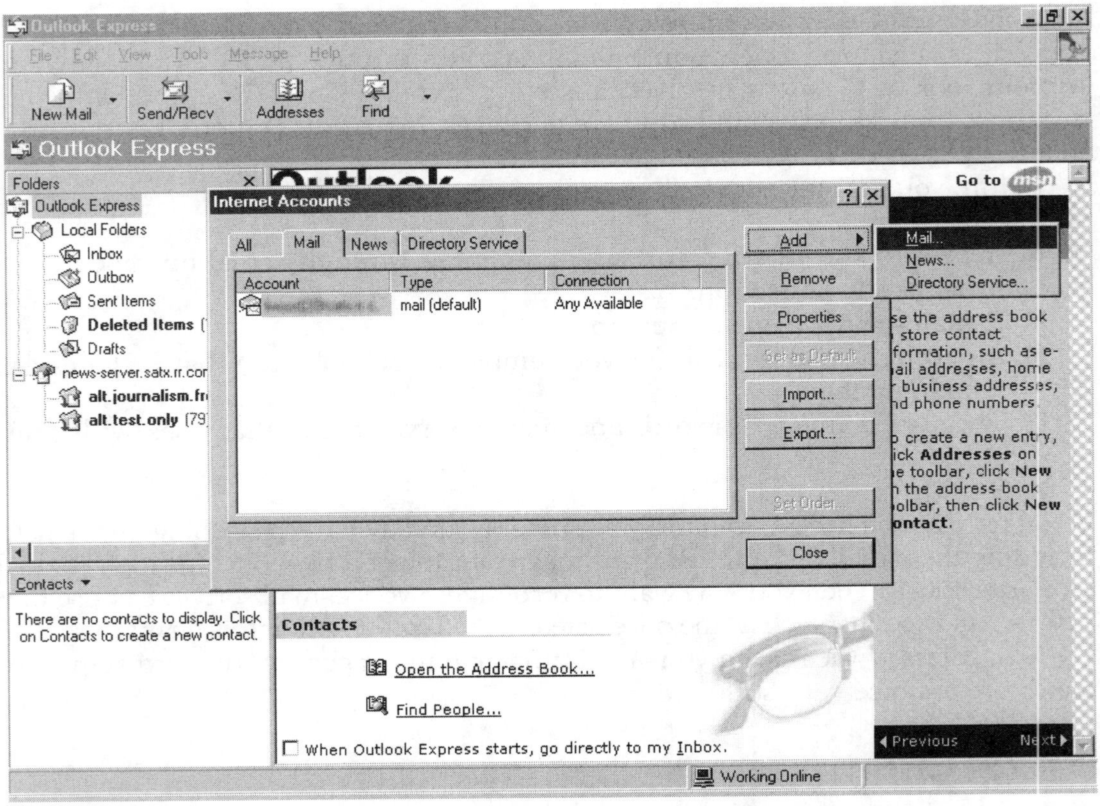

Figure 9.1 *The Internet Accounts windows in Outlook Express, where you set up your e-mail account information. The "Add" button invokes a "wizard" that walks you through the process. You reach this screen through the "Accounts" option of the "Tools" entry in the command menu. (Screen shot reprinted by permission from Microsoft Corporation.)*

the file you want to attach, click the "Attach" button. The Insert Attachment window will go away, and you'll be back in the composition window—but a new line has appeared before the Subject line, showing the attached files (complete with file-type icons) as shown in Figure 9.4.

You can select more than one file for attachment in the file selection window by using the standard Windows commands: control-click to select multiple noncontiguous files and Shift-click to select a block of files starting with the previously selected file.

You send the message by clicking the "Send" icon in the upper-left corner of the window. The message window will go away, leaving you in the main Outlook Express window.

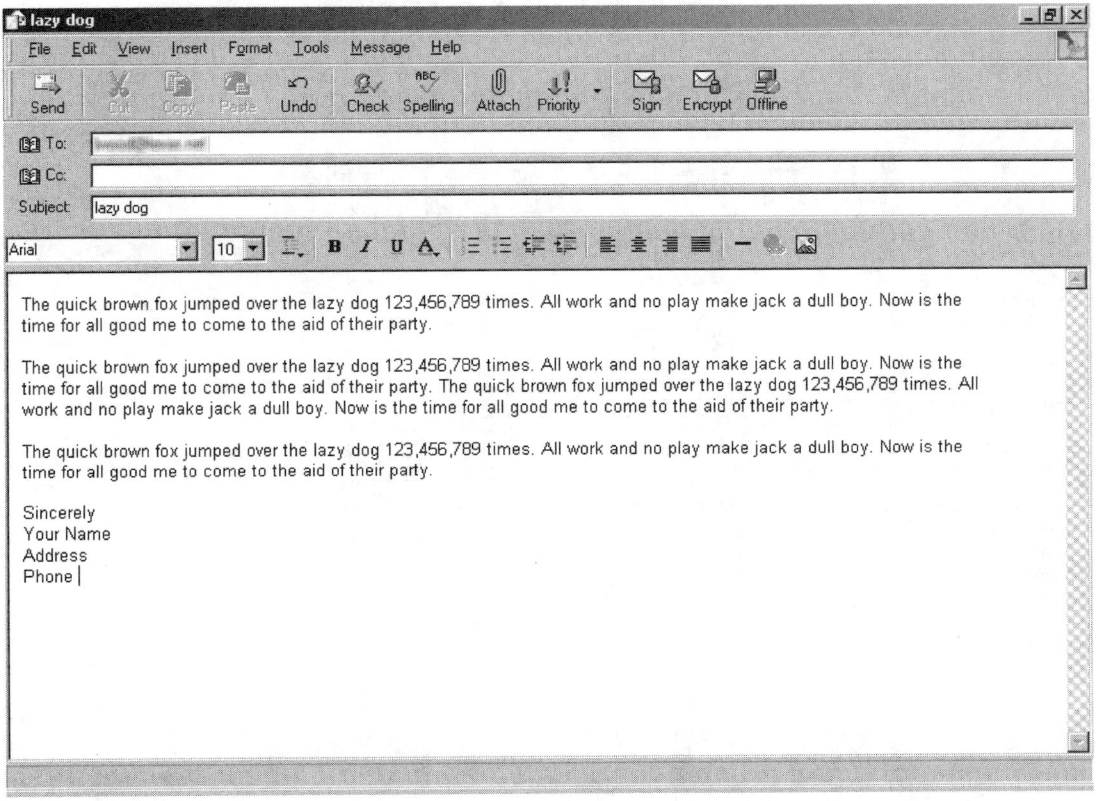

Figure 9.2 *The message window in Microsoft Outlook Express, which lets you compose an e-mail message. Alternately, you could copy the text on a word processor and paste it into this window. The text has been formatted according to the "Etiquette" section later in this chapter, with blank lines between paragraphs and an identifying signature line. (Screen shot reprinted by permission from Microsoft Corporation.)*

You can check your mail by clicking the "Send/Recv" icon in the toolbar near the top of the screen. Outlook Express will then give you a message stating how many unread messages are available, as shown in Figure 9.5. In addition, the folder window will show how many items are in the inbox; if any are unread, the inbox will be shown in boldface.

By clicking on the "Inbox" icon in the folders windows, you can bring up the Inbox screen, shown in Figure 9.6. The Subject line, the name of the sender, and the arrival time are shown for each message. When a message is selected, the contents appear in the lower window.

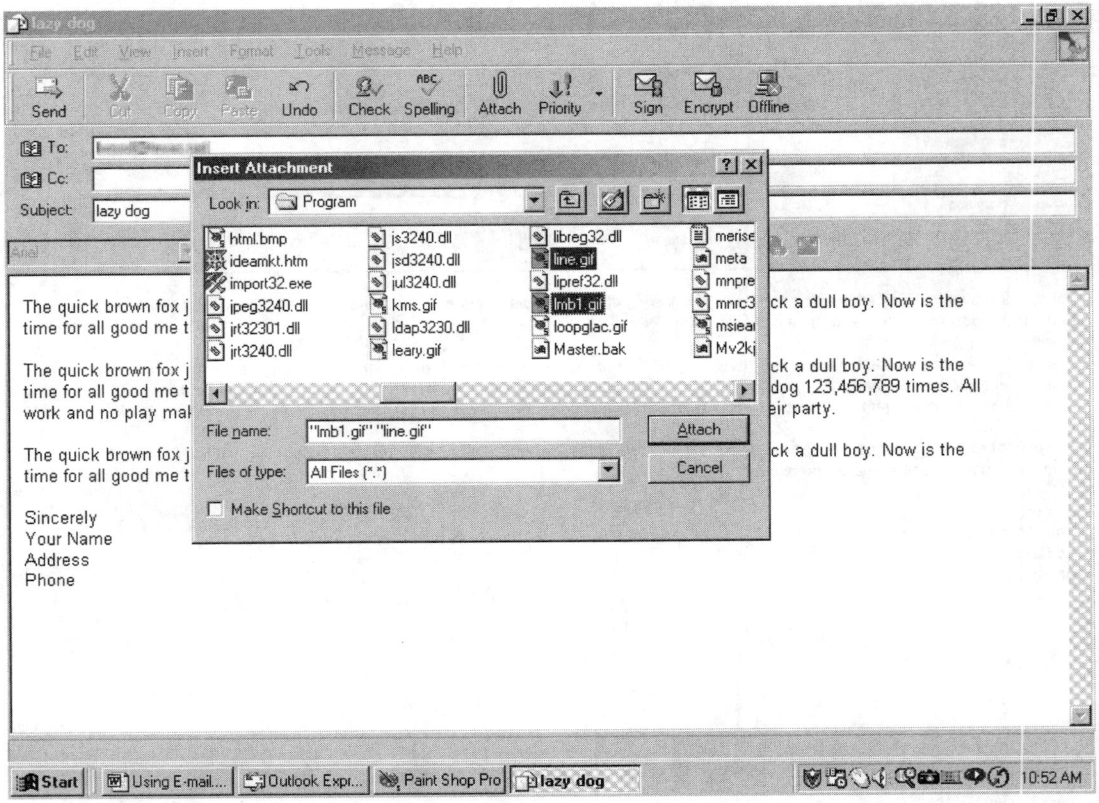

Figure 9.3 *The Outlook Express message window with the Insert Attachment window for designating which files are to be attached to the message. Two separate files have been attached using the control-click command. (Screen shot reprinted by permission from Microsoft Corporation.)*

The paperclip icon above and to the left of the message contents indicates the presence of file attachments. Outlook Express will attempt to display the contents of the attachments at the bottom of the message (not shown). Alternately, you can elect to save the attachments to disk (or open them if appropriate) by clicking the paperclip icon.

Netscape Communicator

As with Outlook Express, after your computer and its Internet connection are set up so that you can get Web access, the next step is to configure your e-mail server.

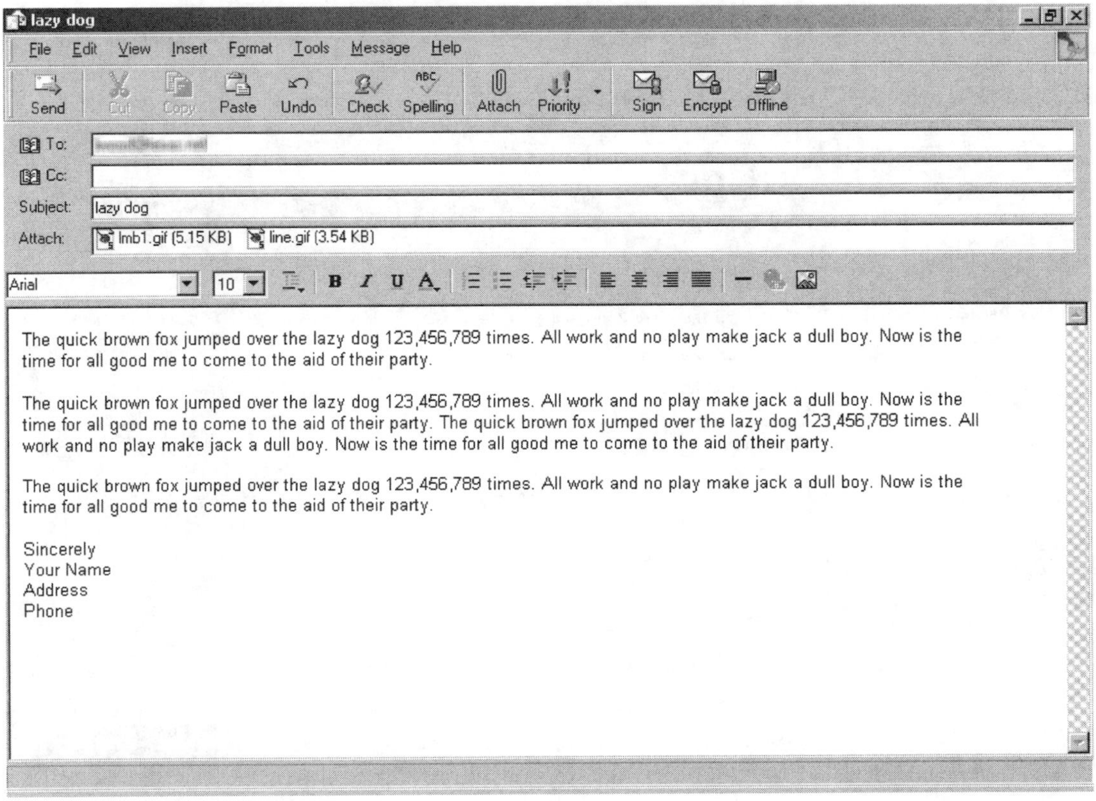

Figure 9.4 *The Outlook Express message window after attaching files to the message. A new display line has appeared below the Subject line to list the names of the attached files. (Screen shot reprinted by permission from Microsoft Corporation.)*

Go to Netscape Messenger (the e-mail part of Netscape Communicator) by clicking the "Address Book" icon on the bottom-right border of the screen or by clicking the "Communicator" entry in the command menu at the top of the screen and then selecting the "Messenger" option from the resulting pop-up menu.

Within Messenger, click the "Edit" entry in the command menu and select the "Preferences" option. A screen that includes a list of the various functions offered by the "Preferences" command should appear. If it is not already done, click the plus sign beside the "Mail & Newsgroups" item on the screen. Select the "Mail Server" item on the list. Your screen should look like the one shown in Figure 9.7. Input the name of your server and click "OK."

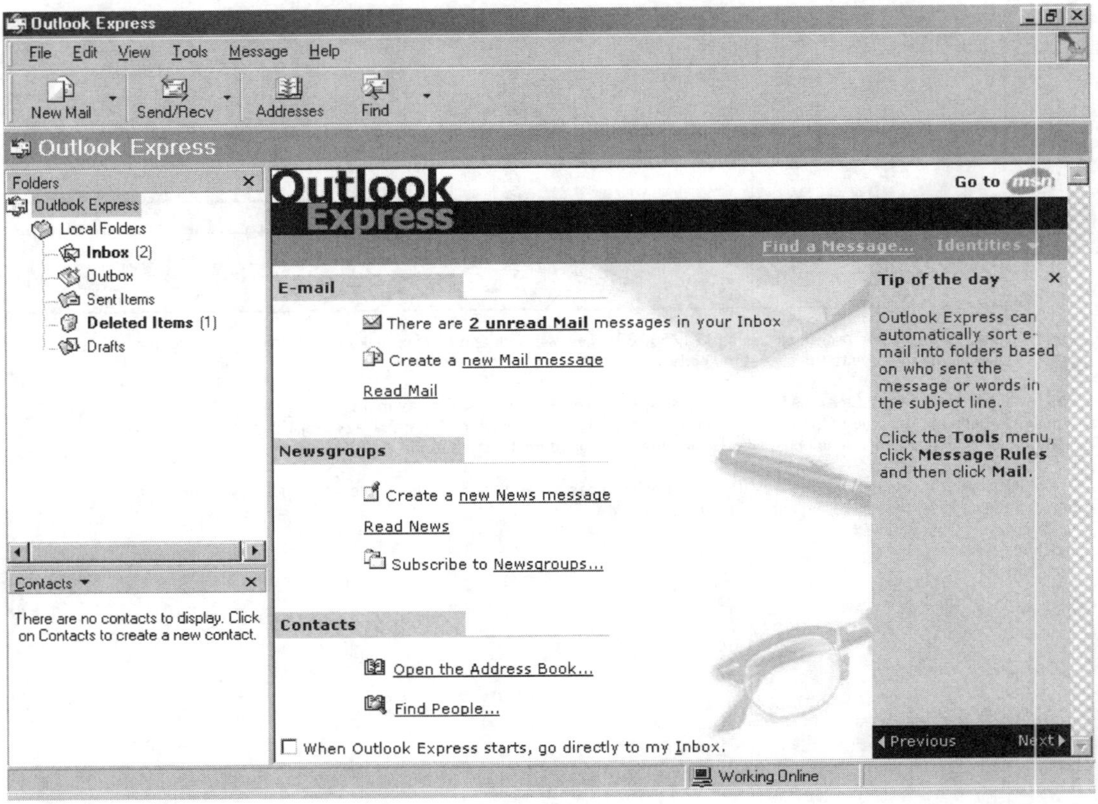

Figure 9.5 *Outlook Express indicating the arrival of unread messages, as indicated by both the message on the main screen, and by the boldface Inbox label. (Screen shot reprinted by permission from Microsoft Corporation.)*

Next you need to select the "Identity" item on the "Preferences" list. You will get a screen like Figure 9.8. Input your name and e-mail address as directed, and click "OK."

To compose a message, click the "New Msg" icon near the top left of the screen (clearly visible in Figure 9.12). The Composition window should then appear, as shown in Figure 9.9. You can type the message directly into the composition screen or cut and paste it from a word processor.

To attach a file to a message, click the "Attach" icon (with the paperclip image) near the top center of the window, and then select the "File" option in the pop-up windows that will appear. You will then get a standard Windows file selection screen, as shown in Figure 9.10. After locating and highlighting the file you want to attach, click the "Open" button. The file will not be opened (that's a

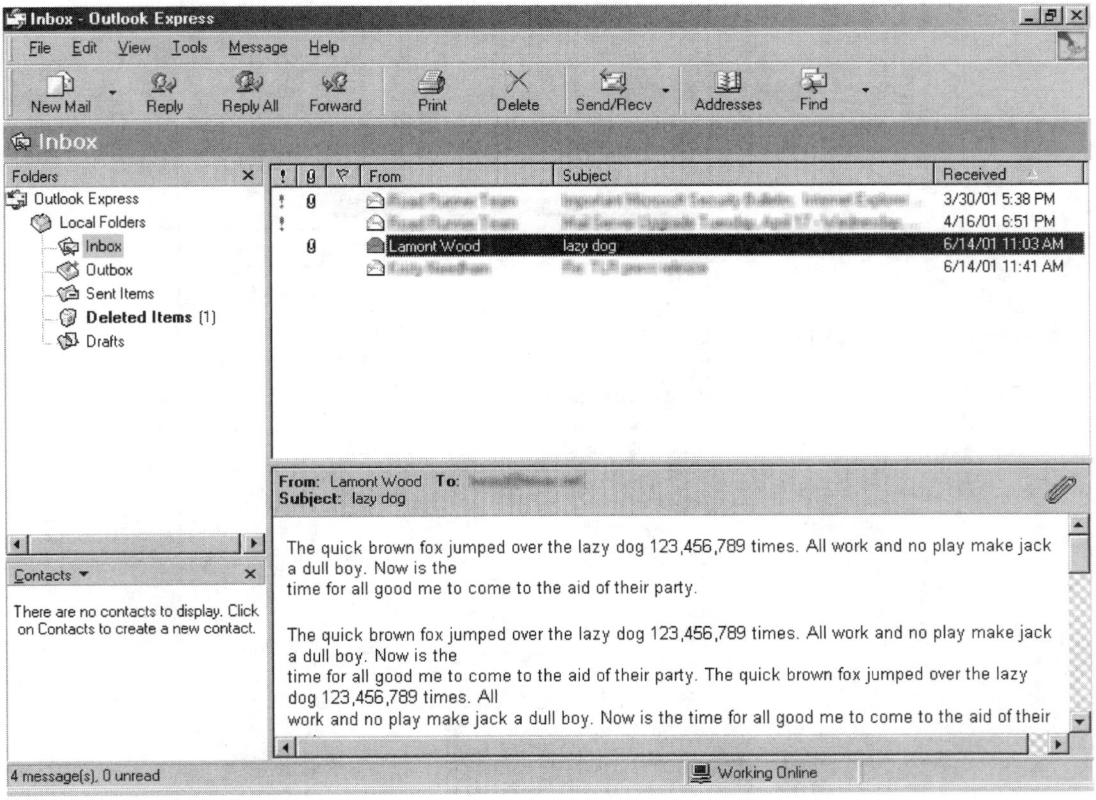

Figure 9.6 *The Inbox screen in Outlook Express, showing the arrival of the message shown in Figure 9.4. The paperclip icon indicates that the message has attachments. (Information about some of the messages has been blurred out.) Notice that the text's formatting differs from that of the outgoing message because the text is now in a smaller screen. (Screen shot reprinted by permission from Microsoft Corporation.)*

misnomer) but will instead appear on the line where the recipient's e-mail address formerly appeared the composition screen, as shown in Figure 9.11. (Clicking the "file card" logo to the left of that line will cause the e-mail address to be redisplayed.)

You can select more than one file for attachment in the file selection window by using the standard Windows commands: Control-click to select multiple non-contiguous files and Shift-click to select a block of files start with the previously selected file.

Once you are ready, you can send the message by clicking the "Send" button near the top left of the screen.

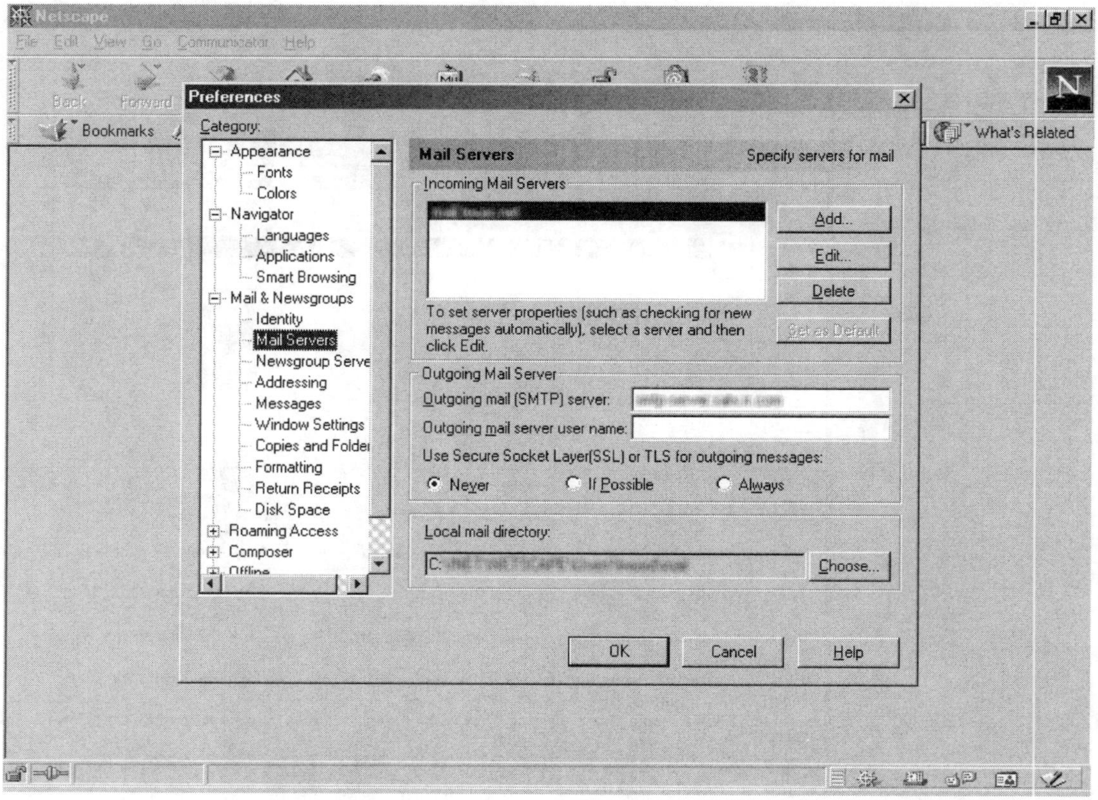

Figure 9.7 *Screen for setting the identification of your mail server in Netscape Communicator, reached through the "Preferences" option of the "Edit" command. Note that you can have a separate mail server for outgoing and incoming mail. You could, for instance, send from an office mail server that permits file attachments, while receiving through an anonymous third-party service that, however, will not let you send attachments. (The server names and file address have been blurred out in the screen shot.)*

Back at the main Netscape Messenger screen, you check your mail by clicking the "Get Msg" button near the top left corner of the window. As shown in Figure 9.12, new messages will appear as additional entries in the top screen. (Unread messages will be listed in boldface.) Notice that, in addition to the subject line, you can see the sender's name, the date and size of the message, and whether a reply to the message has been made.

When you select a message in the top screen, the body of the message will appear in the bottom screen. Attached files are listed below the body of the message (not seen); you can jump to that list by clicking the paperclip icon at the top

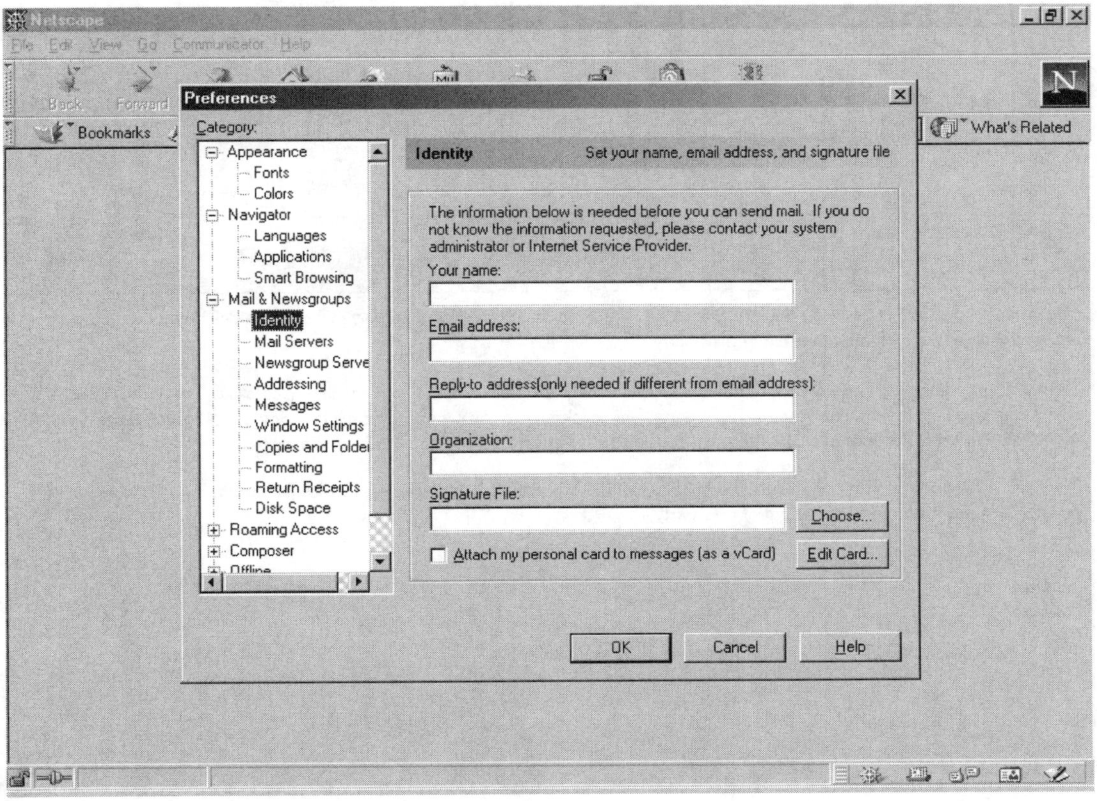

Figure 9.8 *Screen for establishing your own identity in Netscape (i.e., giving it your e-mail address). It too is reached through the "Preferences" option of the "Edit" command. You can also use it to automatically attach a signature file or vCard to your messages.*

of the message. When you click on the name of a file attachment, Netscape will try optionally try to run it (if that's possible) or just save it to disk. If you have it saved, make note of what subdirectory it is going to so you can examine it later. But if you forget, you can always use the Find command under the Windows Start button.

Being able to send e-mail leaves a bigger question—what to say, and especially, how to say it. The next section examines the etiquettte involved.

E-Mail Etiquette

Do you remember the caveat made earlier about using file attachments? Good. That will keep you out of trouble. But there is more to e-mail etiquette than real-

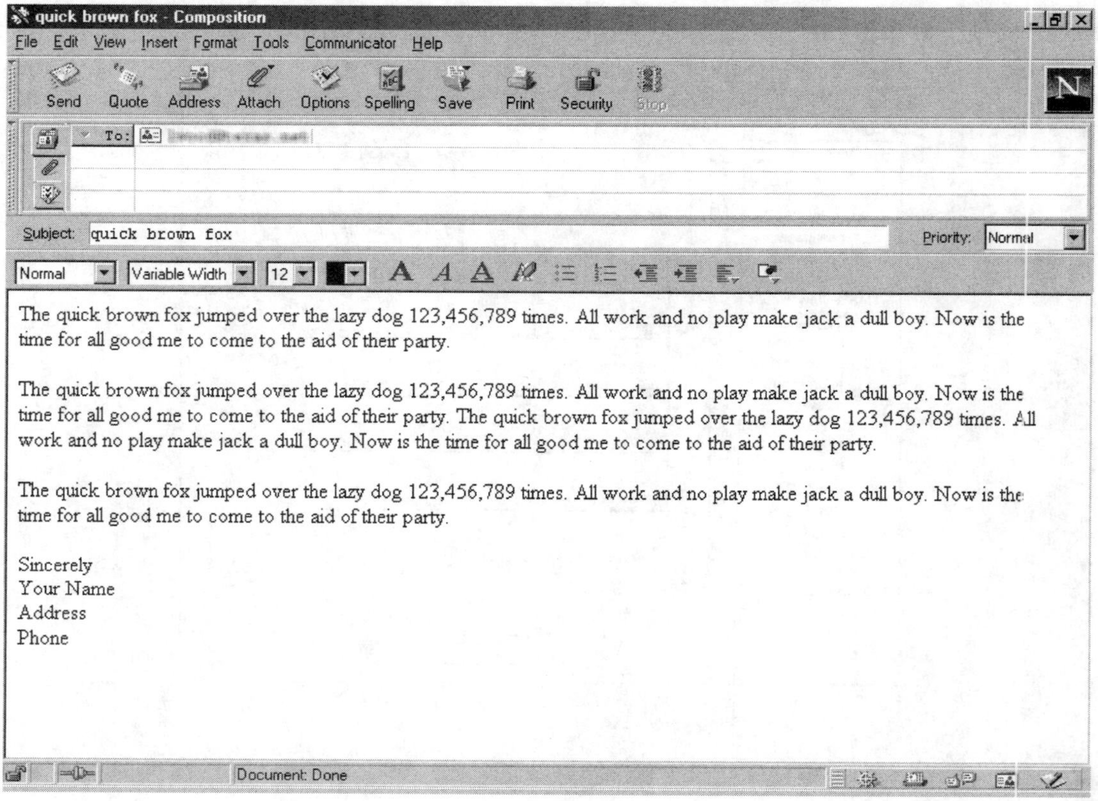

Figure 9.9 *The Composition window in Netscape Communicator, which lets you compose a message. Alternately, you could copy the text on a word processor and paste it into this window. The text has been formatted according to the "Etiquette" section later in this chapter, with blank lines between paragraphs and an identifying signature line.*

izing that file attachments must be used with care, just like there is more to phone etiquette than realizing that you should not dial random numbers for entertainment.

In fact, a comparison with phone etiquette is instructive. You probably received guidance concerning phone etiquette from the time you were old enough to respond to a ringing phone. Your parents knew that there was both great power and potential for abuse embodied in Alexander Graham Bell's invention, which lets you talk directly into the ear of a complete stranger. Personal e-mail was not an issue when you were that age, but if it had been your parents would have told you that, yes, it gives you the power to put a message onto the screen of a complete

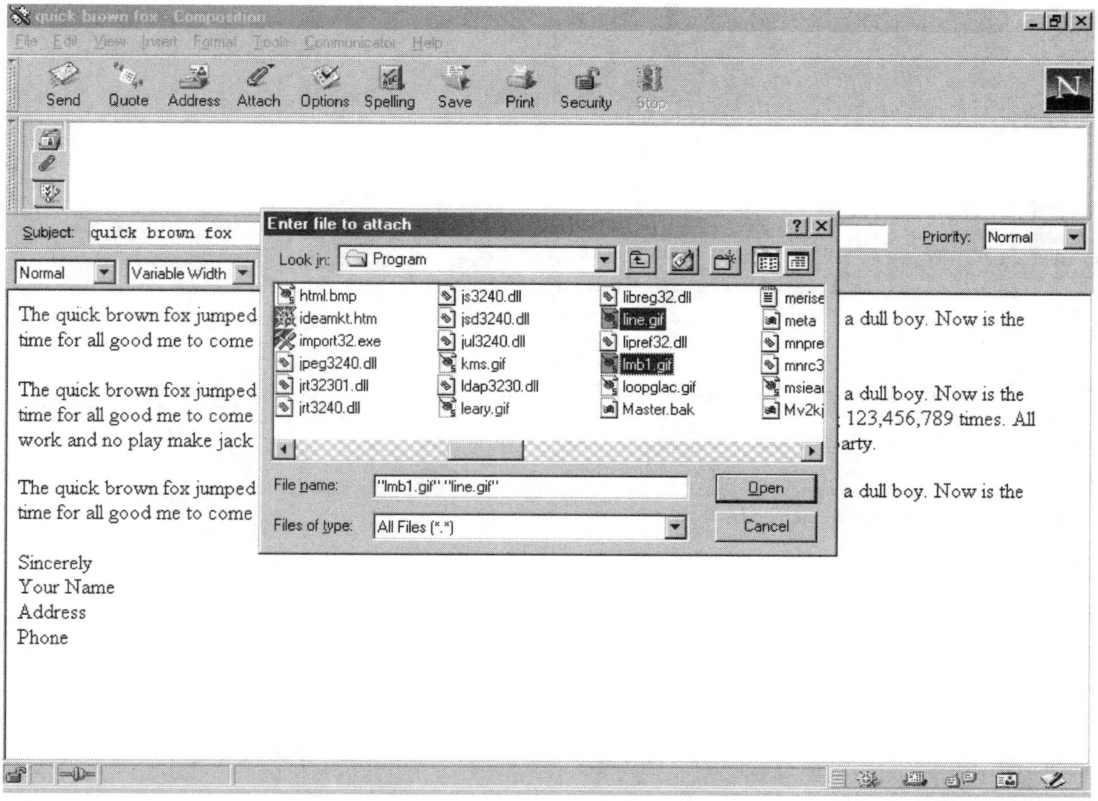

Figure 9.10 *The Netscape Composition window with a file selection window for designating which files are to be attached to the message. Two separate files have been attached using the control-click command.*

stranger's personal computer. And nonabusive use involves respect for that power, not to mention respect for the other person. Keep the following points in mind.

Don't Presume

Just because you have unearthed someone's e-mail address does not mean you should use it. You probably aren't thrilled to get unsolicited e-mail and phone calls and may write off the people behind them as nuisances. So don't risk branding yourself as a nuisance in the eyes of your recipient. Instead, use e-mail to contact someone when you see an implied invitation to do so. That can amount to the inclusion of the e-mail address in an ad or its presence on a business card that the person gave you.

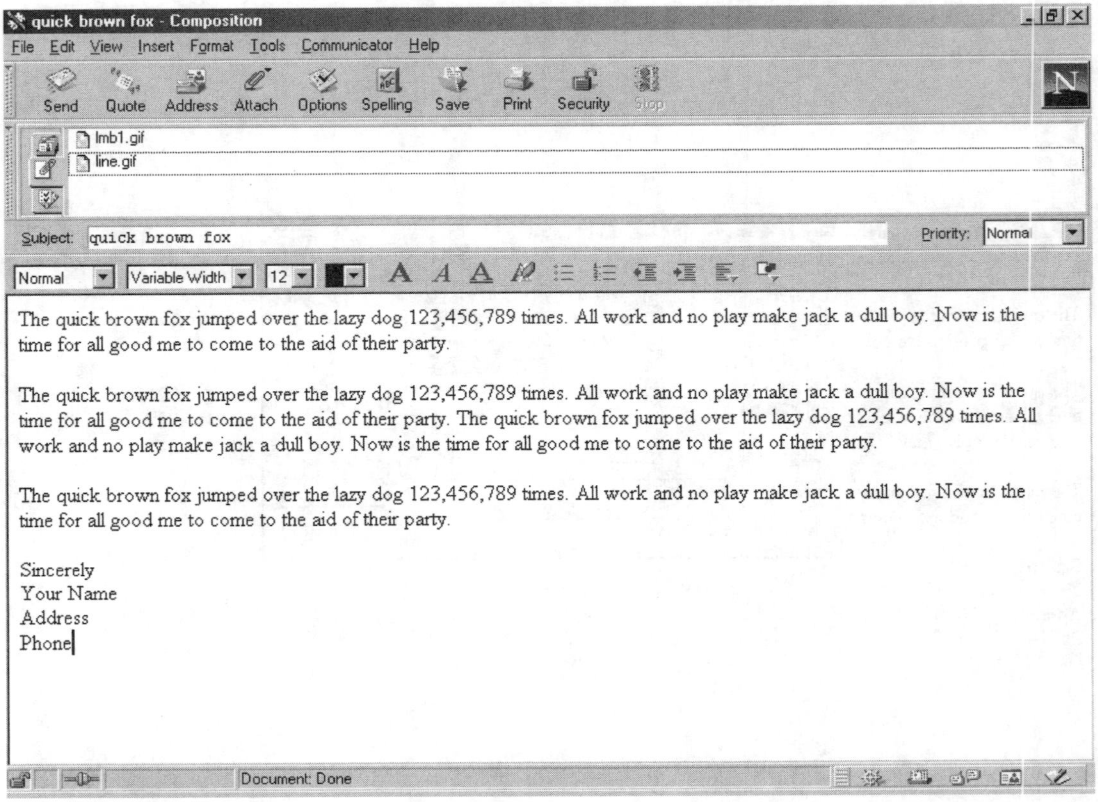

Figure 9.11 *The Netscape Composition window after attaching files to the message. In the upper left, above the Subject line, the space that previously displayed the recipient's e-mail address now lists the file attachments. The address can be redisplayed by clicking the "file card" icon.*

Stick to Business

E-mail is not a tool for building rapport. But it can be a tool for showing how serious you are and how much you respect the other person's time.

Use the Subject Line

Recipients get their new messages as a list of subject lines, so make sure your subject lines contain something of value for a busy person.

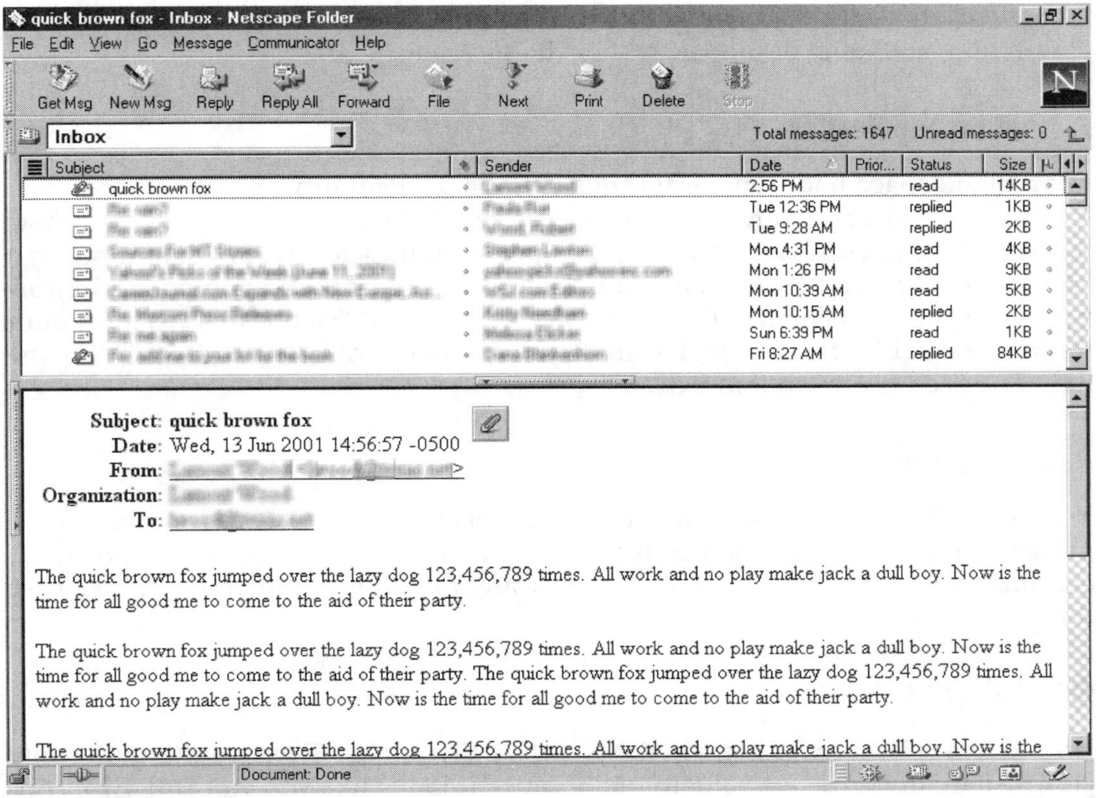

Fgure 9.12 *Netscape Messenger screen showing the messages in the inbox. The latest, concerning "quick brown fox" has been selected, and its contents appear in the lower window. File attachments can be reached by clicking the paperclip icon.*

Keep the Message Short

You're writing a message, not a novel. The recipient is sitting rigidly at a computer terminal, not curled up the couch. You're presenting information, not seeking to beat someone into submission with the weight of your words. Keep all that in mind.

And to the Point

Clearly identify yourself and your purpose at the start. If you are referring to a previous message, do so distinctly, rather than forcing the reader to guess what you are referring to. If you are quoting from a previous message, only include the text in question and cut out the rest of the message.

Format for the Reader

Put a blank space between paragraphs to enhance legibility.

Put a "signature" at the end of the message. You can't really sign it, of course, but you want to emphasize that this is a personal message from you. So put in a blank line, then add "Sincerely," and then put in your name and contact information. Some people have their software add canned "signatures" that amount to little textual billboards, including their personal motto and a thought for the day. You need not go to that extreme.

Don't Miss Pell

Your e-mail software may have a spell checker. Use it. Otherwise, write your message in a word processor that has a spell checker. After the text is polished, cut and paste it into the e-mail software. Your words represent you, so make sure they are presentable.

Avoid All Caps

USING CAPITAL LETTERS LOOKS LIKE YELLING. Even capitalizing only OCCASIONAL words is problematic because it looks like you can BARELY contain your urge to start RANTING.

Don't Be Cute

Those smiley-faced emoticons (see the Glossary) are nice in their place. Serious business correspondence is not that place.

Unable to use boldfacing and other textual enhancement, some people pour on exclamation points and other punctuation. Again, this is serious business correspondence, so avoid such frills. If you feel you absolutely * must * emphasize a word, frame it with asterisks as shown.

Abbreviate with Care

BTW, IMHO, before abbreviating you should RTFM lest the recipient be left LOL or worse ROTFL about you, IOW.

The Internet has proven to be fertile ground for the growth of abbreviations and acronyms. But business correspondence is not the place to show how with it you are. The acronyms from the previous paragraph are in the Glossary, and perhaps should be left there.

Don't Play with the Features

Your software may let you give a message "Priority" or "Urgent" status or to attach a "Receipt Requested" trigger. Rarely will these do anything other than annoy the recipient with your presumption. The recipient will decide how important your message is and whether it rates an answer.

With the latest e-mail software, it is possible to add HTML formatting tags to enhance the text just as it is done on a Web page, using headlines, centering, boldfacing, columns, and graphics. That is all nice, but if your recipient does not have compatible software, what he or she will see on the screen will be a mish-mash of HTML tags with your prose hidden somewhere inside. In addition, the use of such frills inflates the size of the message, which may not be a consideration at the recipient's broadband-connected office but could cause memorable problems when received through a wireless connection on the road. As with file attachments, you should only use HTML formatting after you have determined that it is okay with the recipient.

There is a facility called vCard that lets you attach an electronic business card to your messages in a format that can be imported by most personal information managers. Although this is a nice feature when you have a job, using it when looking for a job (when your data is subject to imminent change) does not seem wise.

Reply Wisely

If you are one of multiple recipients of an e-mail message, and the other recipients are listed in the To line, be careful if you send a reply or you might send your reply to everyone else who got the original message. Nothing generates flames faster.

Speaking of Flames

Don't send e-mail in anger. Once it is transmitted, there is no way to cancel it.

Meanwhile, everything in "The Verbal Minefield" section of Chapter 10 applies also to e-mail. Naked text communicates only words, and the sympathy, wit, and good feelings that underpin your words may not come across. The reader is ultimately alone with his or her thoughts. Conversely, at any random moment, you may find yourself reading something into an incoming message that the writer did not intend. Remember, the magic is powerful, but its results are not entirely predictable.

The one big thing you'll want to do, in terms of etiquette, is get a separate e-mail address for your job search. Fortunately, as explained in the next section, it's easy to do.

Free E-Mail

There are services—hundreds of them, in fact — that give away free e-mail accounts. You could probably set up a new one for every e-mail message you wanted to send. Although you need not go that far, you may want to get at least one for your job search, for good reasons:

- You'll have an e-mail account unconnected with your current employer, so there can be no objection to your using it for private purposes.
- You can be anonymous. In fact, not only will you not be johnsmith@ domain.com any more, but johnsmith is probably not available even if you wanted it. However, an address like xyz321.freemailservice.com will do fine as a temporary account during your job search.
- If you leave your job, you'll still have an e-mail account.
- If you are posting messages in Usenet, it is a good idea to use a "disposable" e-mail account on your messages because e-mail addresses in Usenet attract spam.

The downside is that free services typically depend on advertising for their daily bread, and at this writing the bottom has fallen out of Internet advertising rates. (Of course, some derive revenue from value-added services.) There has been turnover among free e-mail services since the beginning, but the rate will likely accelerate, especially among the lower-tier me-too rankings.

Another downside is that spammers have abused some services to the point that they have been blacklisted by other ISPs. If your recipient's ISP uses that blacklist, it will block all traffic from that service, meaning that the e-mail messages that you send from the service will go straight into limbo. Using name-brand services minimizes this danger.

Available services fall into three main categories: POP services, Web-based services, and mail-forwarding services.

POP Services

POP e-mail is the standard e-mail you get with an ISP account, and it uses standard e-mail software like Outlook Express or Netscape Communicator. Once retrieved, the messages are (typically) deleted from the server but live on in the inbox on your hard disk for future reference. The e-mail software has facilities intended for message composition, such as a spell checker and an address book. If you have had experience using e-mail, POP is what you're used to.

The downside is that the only way a free POP e-mail service can make money off you is to sell your address to advertisers. So you can expect a trickle of ads to appear in your free mailbox. But you can't really call it spam because you signed up for it.

Some free POP services have been so victimized by spammers that they no longer allow users to send e-mail. As a user, you can only receive e-mail. However, for job-search purposes, that may be fine.

POP services typically allow file attachments, but with size limitations (as everywhere).

Web-Based E-Mail

With Web-based e-mail, you go to the service's Web site, log in, and read your mail, which resides on the service's server. In other words, you don't download it to your hard disk. There will also be a limit to the amount of mail you can store on the server, although that may be several megabytes.

You don't need to configure a POP e-mail program when you are using Web-based e-mail. On the other hand, the message-composition functions that a Web-based e-mail service might be able to offer (spell checking, etc.) are unlikely to be as good as what you get from your desktop e-mail program. Also, you will typically have to put up with banner ads while you are at the site, and the service may add little ad blurbs to the bottom of your messages, alerting the world to the fact that you are using a free e-mail service. (Of course, while job searching you're almost expected to do so, so this may not be a big deal.)

There are usually special facilities for both uploading and downloading file attachments, with size limitations.

Mail-Forwarding Services

With an e-mail forward services, you receive an e-mail address that you can hand out to the people to whom you intend to correspond. Messages sent to that address will be forwarded to whatever e-mail address you specify.

Therefore, you need to have an e-mail address that you intend to keep, such as your home account. You would use the forwarding address when you don't want to hand out your permanent e-mail address, perhaps because it identifies you by name. (On the other hand, you may want to have a distinctive e-mail address, and it's easier to get one through the mail-forwarding service than through your ISP.)

Sites do spring up now and then that specialize in anonymous forwarding. But no one is immune to search warrants covering the contents of their servers. Therefore, anonymity cannot be guaranteed, even on the Internet. Of course, when you sign up for a free e-mail account, you can always give false information, stymieing any casual search. (A thorough search, based on the timing of the connections, can still trace a message back to you. Just what did you have in mind, anyway?)

Representative Services

As noted, hundreds of places offer free e-mail services. The following sites are a representative sample. They are also leading sites that should be around for a while. But remember that inclusion on the list does not constitute endorsement.

http://mail.yahoo.com

The Yahoo! Web-based service at mail.yahoo.com gives you 6 megabytes of storage or will sell you 25 megabytes for about $20 a year. You can also retrieve mail from other e-mail accounts to your Yahoo! mailbox. Not only are file attachments allowed (up to three files totaling 1.5 megabytes), but a file viewer lets you look at attachments before deciding if you want to download them. There is also a virus and spam filter.

http://www.hotmail.com

The Web-based service at www.hotmail.com is owned by a firm called Microsoft, so it may be around for a while. You get two megabytes of storage and can e-mail attachments with a total size of one megabyte. Your mailbox has virus protection and spam filtering. You can retrieve mail from up to four POP accounts to your Hotmail mailbox. The rules of use state that you can't use Hotmail as your mail business e-mail address, but you can use it for business purposes, such as when on the road. Your account becomes inactive (and refuses incoming mail) if you don't use it for 60 days. You can revive it if you use it within 90 days.

The Hotmail/Outlook Express Connection

Although Hotmail is a Web-based service, recent versions of Outlook Express (the e-mail software built into Microsoft Windows) includes a facility for using Hotmail as if it were a POP service. (In other words, you can download messages to your hard disk.)

After setting up a Hotmail account, you can click the "Tools" entry in the command menu in Outlook Express and then select the "Accounts" entry. The Internet Accounts window will appear. Click the "Add" button and let the "wizard" walk you through the process of configuring your Hotmail account. All you'll need is your user name and password.

Messages are composed and sent the normal way, but actual sending does not occur until you additionally use the software's Synchronize function (located under the "Tools" entry in the command menu). You can store messages on your hard disk by creating a new folder within the Local Folders section of the Outlook Express folders directory, usually presented on the left side of the screen. Then you can drag messages from the Hotmail inbox to the new folder.

http://www.amexmail.com

The advertising-supported Web-based site www.amexmail.com is owned by American Express. It's free to all comers, but American Express cardholders get extra services; for them, the site is a POP service.

http://www.postmark.net

The service at www.postmark.net gives you five megabytes of storage, and you can send and receive messages with attachments. The main service is Web-based, but there is an option for receiving (but not sending) mail via POP facilities so you can use your e-mail software.

http://www.netscape.net

Netscape's Web-based service, www.netscape.net, gives you five megabytes of storage. Attachments are allowed, up to three megabytes.

http://www.imailbox.com

The Internet Mailbox Company offers POP and/or mail forwarding at www.imailbox.com: You get either 20 megabytes or mail storage, or your mail will be forwarded to another address. The site has special facilities for consolidating mail from multiple addresses. However, the service is free only for the first 30 days. After that, it costs about $60 per year.

Other Sources

At this writing, the Free E-mail-Providers Guide lists about fourteen hundred free e-mail providers in about eighty-five countries. You can find their list at http://www.fepg.net.

Usenet is not as well known as e-mail but often uses the same software and can be an important resource for job searchers. The next chapter examines this medium.

CHAPTER 10

Using Usenet and Mailing Lists

The Internet is not just a publishing medium for Web sites—it is also a place where individuals can express themselves and exchange opinions, especially in Usenet newsgroups and mailing lists. These two media can also be valuable tools for job seekers. This chapter looks at them in detail, especially Usenet.

Usenet Basics

As mentioned in Chapter 1, you can think of Usenet as a bulletin board on the wall of some store or meeting hall, where people are free to pin messages. In this case, the board is called Usenet, and it exists only online. It is divided into thousands of sections, called newsgroups, each devoted (in theory) to a specific topic.

Many of these newsgroups are set aside specifically for the posting of job openings. Others are devoted to specific career fields or a specific technology, and job postings concerning that field or technology will appear there. The more popular jobs-related newsgroups (detailed in Chapter 11) accumulate hundreds of new job postings daily. Reading Usenet can be highly advantageous for a job seeker, especially one in a computer-literate field, where the people offering the jobs are likely to understand and use Usenet.

The main problem is that tens of thousands of newsgroups exist, and you can't possibly follow them all. (Estimates range from thirty thousand to a hundred thousand, but the higher estimates include unused, defunct, or duplicate newsgroups, as well as ones specific to various ISPs.) Most hold nothing more than chatter. Others harbor goldmines of information.

To use Usenet, you need "news-reader" software. (The term *news* is often used to refer to the message traffic on Usenet, stemming from its origins about 1979.) Fortunately, news-reader software is built into today's browser or e-mail software. Figures 10.1 and 10.2 show the same message in the same newsgroup, as displayed by (respectively) Netscape Communicator and Microsoft Outlook Express (which Microsoft Internet Explorer uses as its default news reader).

Both show the same information. To the left is the name of the newsgroup being used: alt.journalism.freelance. At the top of the screen is a list of available

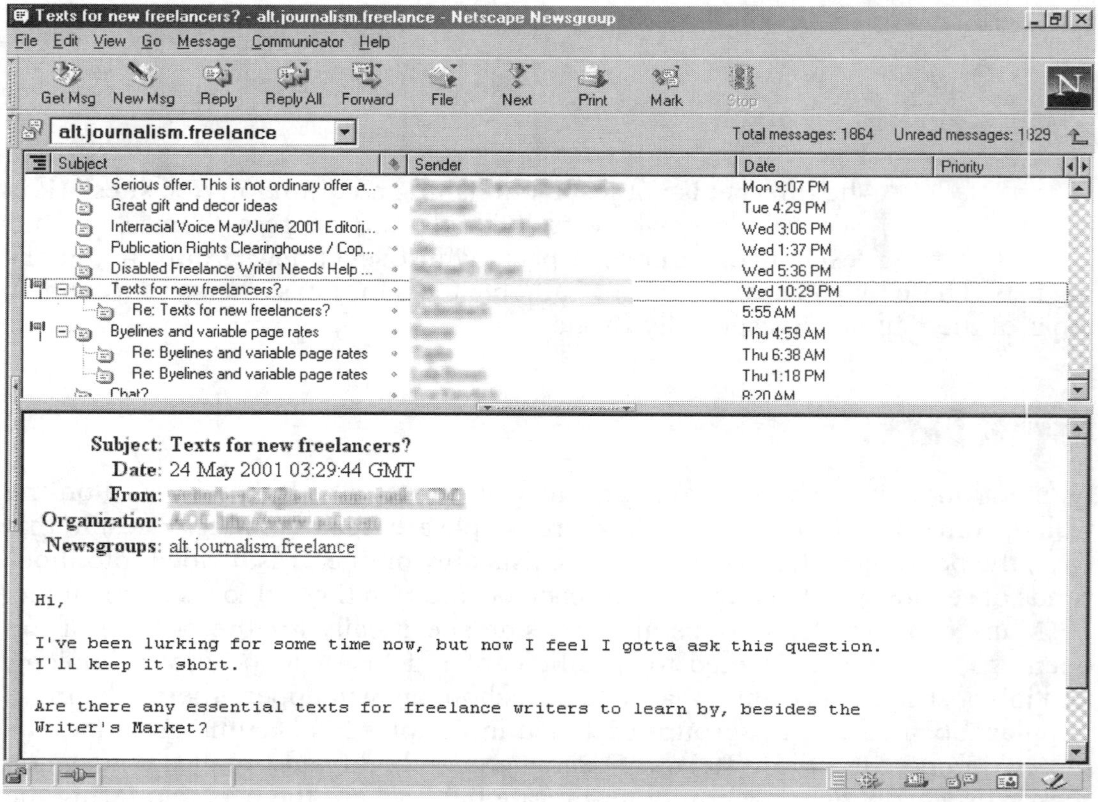

Figure 10.1 *Usenet newsgroup message displayed with Netscape Communicator.*

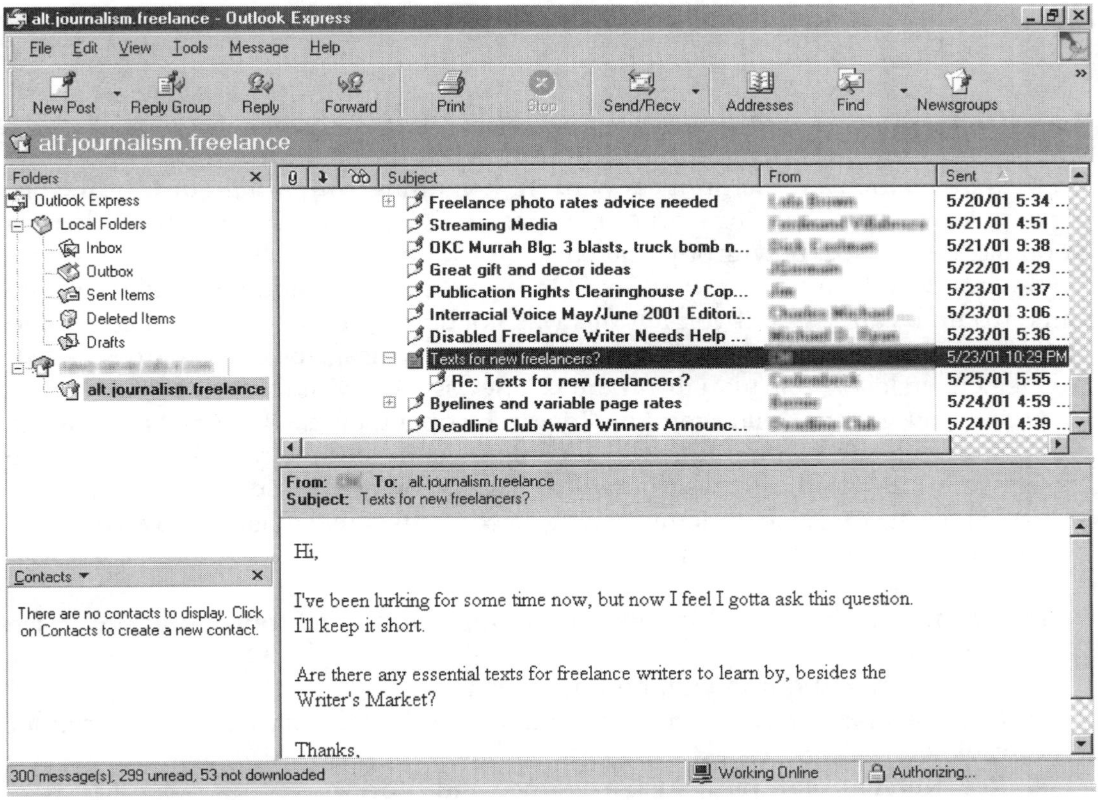

Figure 10.2 *The same Usenet newsgroup message shown in Figure 10.1, here displayed in Microsoft Outlook Express. (Screen shot reprinted by permission from Microsoft Corporation.)*

messages or postings. (The names have been blurred out.) The text of the highlighted message appears in a window at the bottom of the screen. (Outlook Express shows additional information, such as the name of the ISP's news server, which has also been blurred out.)

In both cases, the list of available messages includes some entries with a plus or minus sign to its immediate left. These signs indicate that the message includes at least one comment. A message and its comments form a "thread." All the messages that form a thread are listed together and can be seen by clicking the plus sign. If they are already displayed, you can get rid of them by clicking the minus sign. Messages that are not part of threads are listed in the order they were posted. Some threads can contain hundreds of contributions.

Messages are created with the "New Message" or "New Post" buttons, while comments are added to threads by using the "Reply" button.

The following sections discuss other aspects of Usenet that you'll need to understand.

Name Hierarchy

Usenet names follow a hierarchical pattern, beginning with a high-order category name followed by descriptor words, all separated by periods. For instance, there is a popular category of newsgroups called alt (for "alternative"). If you were to set up a newsgroup in the alt category devoted to breakfast preparation, called 2eggs, the name would be alt.2eggs. If you felt this was not descriptive enough, you could add further words to the name until you had alt.2eggs.sausage.beans.tomatoes.2toast.largetea.cheerslove. (Don't laugh—there is a newsgroup with that name.)

Other newsgroups build their own hierarchy on a theme. Of course, there is the ever-popular alt.sex newsgroup, whose contents can be imagined. Then there are about two hundred other newsgroups that expand on alt.sex, such as alt.sex.extra-terrestrial or alt.sex.fetish.agriculture, whose contents may be harder to envision.

The following are the main hierarchies:

- *Alt.* Alternative—anything under the sun, plus some topics that never see the sun.
- *News.* News about Usenet and newsgroups.
- *Biz.* Business news, announcement, products, services, and product reviews.
- *Rec.* Recreation topics, such as games and sports.
- *Comp.* Computer topics, including hardware, software, and consumer issues.
- *Sci.* Science topics, be it hard science or social science.
- *Humanities.* Fine art, literature, and philosophy.
- *Soc.* Social issues.
- *Misc.* Miscellaneous topics, including employment and health.
- *Talk.* Just that.

There are also regional newsgroup hierarchies, sometimes with hundreds of newsgroups. For instance, the Japan hierarchy has more than four hundred newsgroups, from japan.actress to japan.videogames.win95. Then there are newsgroups like jobs.offered that stand by themselves, with no hierarchy of expanded names.

Moderators versus Chaos

Some newsgroups have moderators. Because all contributions go through them, moderators can weed out off-topic digressions and settle feuds. Most groups are not moderated, however, and anyone can say anything at any time. The result can vary from an exquisitely polite tea party to a verbal riot—and it can vary between the two extremes over time within the same newsgroup. See the "The Verbal Minefield" section later in this chapter for details.

FAQ Files

The more active newsgroups often include FAQ (frequently asked questions) files that lay out the basic issues of the newsgroup's topic. They amount to an introduction to the topic and in technical groups carry technical specifications. They may be written by the moderator or by someone simply dubbed "the FAQ writer." FAQ files may be posted in the newsgroup at intervals, for example, every two weeks, so that a steady user is likely to see them. Archives of FAQ files can be found at http://www.faq-central.net and at http://www.faqs.org—and probably other places as well. If you are interested in seriously participating in a newsgroup, you should find and read its FAQ file, lest you annoy the other participants with ignorant comments and questions.

Binaries

Newsgroups with *binaries* in the name are usually devoted to posting graphics files. (Some are devoted to software.) Many binary postings consist of one message with one picture. Using a special format employed by some news-reader software, longer files are converted into text characters and broken into blocks small enough to fit into individual message postings without breaking the rules about message length. The blocks are put into consecutive messages, and video files can span hundreds of messages and take days to download with a dial-up modem. As you might have guessed, binary newsgroups typically have no place in the job search process, but you will see them every time you venture into Usenet.

Specialty Newsgroups

Newsgroups with the word *test* in their name exist for testing your news reader software. You should always try posting to a test newsgroup before posting to a real newsgroup. Names with *de* are newsgroups in the German language, and names with *announce* are for the posting of press releases.

Longevity

The length of time that a message stays available on Usenet depends on the storage policies of your ISP. It may keep the text-based newsgroups for a week or two and the binary-based newsgroups (which present heavy storage requirements) for two or three days. Your ISP may also host a set of newsgroups specific to that ISP. To excavate postings that have expired on your ISP's server, your only option is to go to Google.com, as explained later.

Spam

Although *spam* usually refers to unsolicited bulk e-mail, it can also refer to Usenet postings that have nothing to do with the stated topic of the newsgroup in which it appears. There are people who simultaneously post the same message in every last newsgroup, including the test newsgroups. The message may as well say, "I am a pathetic loser." (Responsible ISPs cancel the accounts of people who make a habit of Usenet spamming.) On quieter newsgroups, the bulk of the traffic can be spam.

Sex

Most of the spam that you'll run across concern porno Web sites. Most of the material in the binary newsgroups are naughty pictures. (You can just accept my word on this.) On Usenet, you get life in the raw.

Ranting

There are people out there who are desperate for an audience for their views and who spam as relentlessly as the pornographers. If you're looking for a conspiracy theory to explain any and every aspect of human existence, it's probably out there on Usenet.

Scams

Usenet is populated with perfect strangers who will make you rich if you send them typically about $35. At least, that's what they say.

Job Offers

Thousands of job offers appear on Usenet every day. For example on the newsgroup misc.jobs.offered, you can expect to find more than fifteen hundred per day. Which is why you'll want to read the next section.

Getting Online with Usenet

When you are connected with your browser and an ISP account, you can immediately start viewing Web pages. If you use e-mail, you in addition have to tell the browser (or e-mail software) your e-mail address and the name of your e-mail server, as explained in Chapter 9.

Similarly, to use Usenet, you have to tell your software the name of the "mail server" you will be using. Your ISP should supply this to you at the time you get your access account.

Armed with your news server name, you can get online with Usenet using a PC with either Microsoft Internet Explorer or Netscape Communicator. (There are other ways to do it, but this should get you online immediately.)

Microsoft Internet Explorer

Your Windows-based PC probably came equipped with Internet Explorer. Internet Explorer uses Outlook Express as its news reader—and your PC probably came with Outlook Express, also.

First, make sure that the two programs are configured to work together. Load Windows Explorer and invoke the "Tools" entry in the command menu at the top of the screen, and select the "Internet Options" entry from the pop-up list that will appear. The Internet Options screen should appear. Select the "Programs" tab, and you should see something similar to the screen shown in Figure 10.3. Set the Newsgroups line to show Outlook Express, and click "OK." That done, click the "Mail" icon in the toolbar line (in the second line of control near the top of the screen). Outlook Express will load.

The next step is to give Outlook Express the name of your mail server, which was supplied to you by your ISP. In Outlook Express, click the "Tools" entry in the command menu near the top of the screen. Click the "Accounts" entry in the pop-up screen that will appear. The Internet Accounts screen should appear. Select the "News" tab, and you should see something like that shown in Figure 10.4.

Click the "Add" button, and the "connection wizard" will walk you through the steps of inputting your screen name and e-mail address (to be added to the messages you post) and the news server name.

That done, click on the "Newsgroups" icon in the toolbar. Outlook Express will download a list of all the newsgroups carried by that news server. (This can amount to more than a megabyte of text and will require several minutes with dial-up access.) Select the ones you want to read using the "Subscribe" button, as

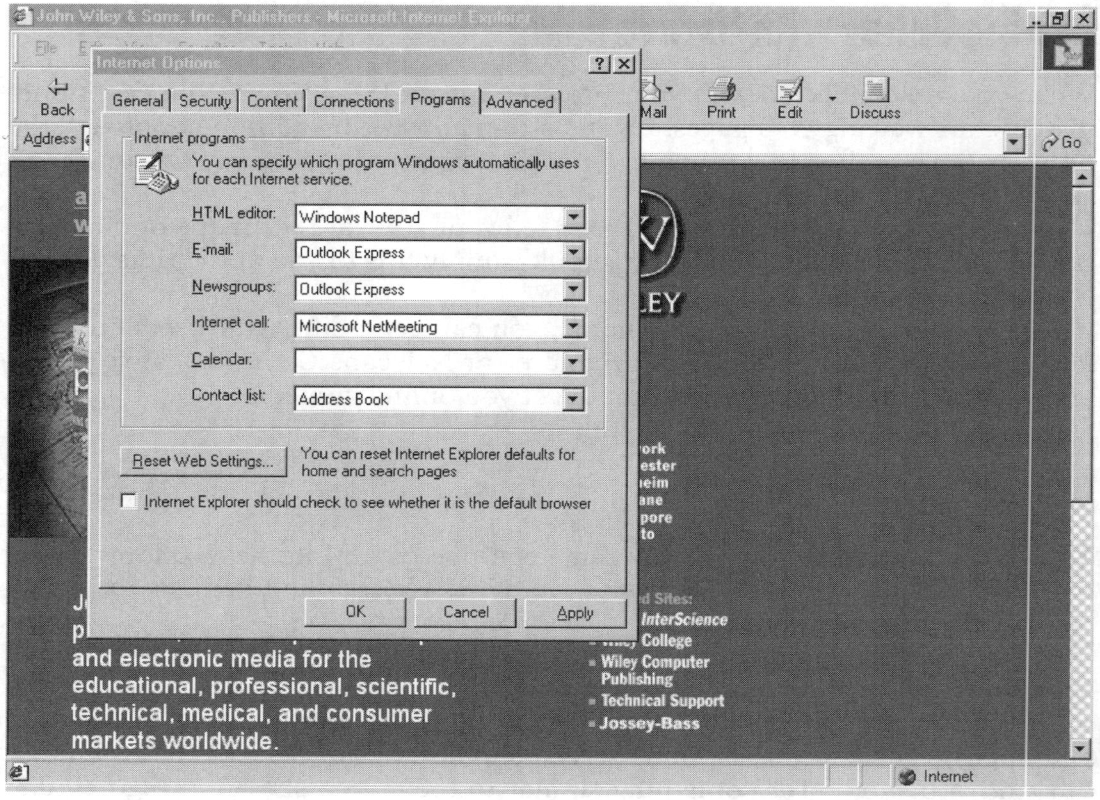

Figure 10.3 *Internet Options screen in Microsoft Internet Explorer, where you set the identity of your news reader software—in this case, Microsoft Outlook Express, which has been selected in the Newsgroups line. (Screen shot reprinted by permission from Microsoft Corporation.)*

shown in Figure 10.5. Then press the "OK" button. (You can read a newsgroup without subscribing to it by clicking the "Go To" button.)

You will then see a screen like that shown in Figure 10.2, with the subscribed newsgroups listed below the name of the news server in the frame on the left side of the screen. Click on the one you want, and the list of messages it contains will appear in the upper window of the screen. Select a message, and its contents will appear in the lower window.

Netscape

Netscape Communicator has a news reader system built into it. So just have Netscape on the screen and the name of the news server handy. Click the "Edit"

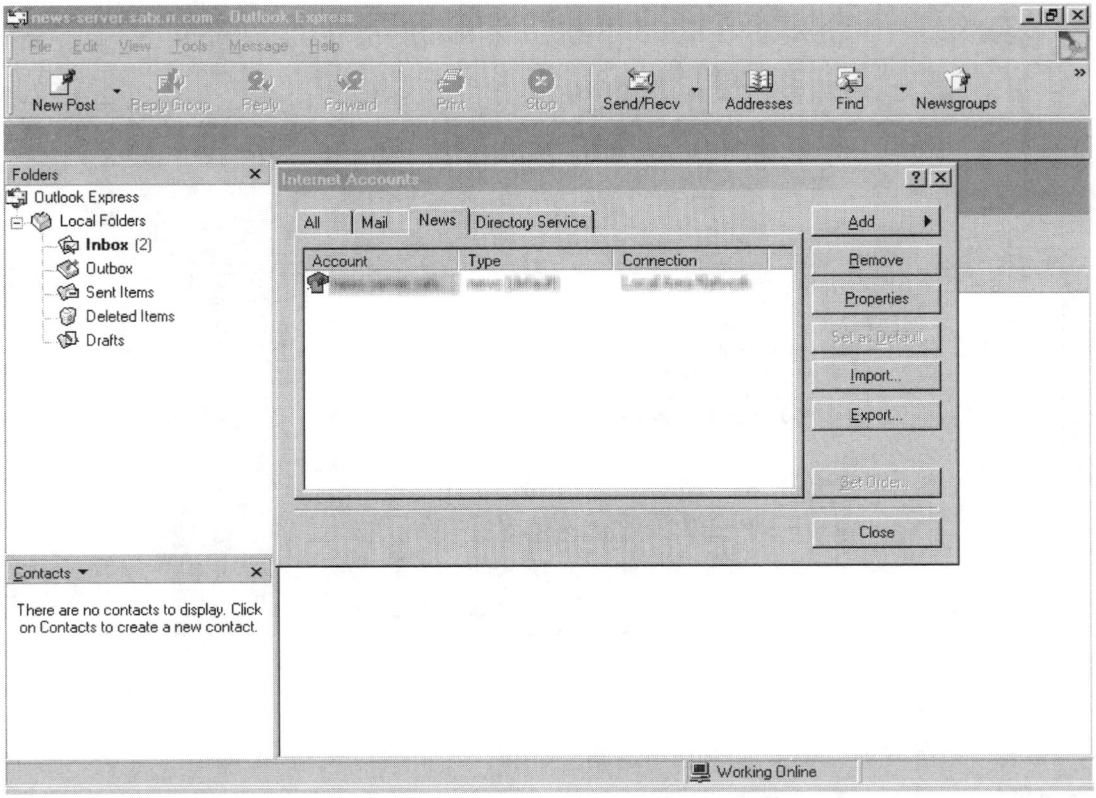

Figure 10.4 *The Internet Accounts screen in Outlook Express, where you can input the name of your ISP's news server, plus other necessary data, by using the "Add" button. (The name of the news server has been blurred out.) (Screen shot reprinted by permission from Microsoft Corporation.)*

entry in the command menu at the top, and then select the "Preferences" selection in the pop-up screen that will appear.

The Preferences screen will appear, as shown in Figure 10.6. If you click the plus sign for the "Mail & Newsgroups" entry, a list of options will appear below it. Select "Newsgroup Servers."

The Newsgroup Servers screen will appear. Add the name of your server to the list by using the "Add" button. Then click "OK." You should now be back at the main screen. Click the "Read Newsgroups" icon in the lower right of the screen. You will then get Netscape's news-reader screen.

Click the "File" entry in the command menu at the top of the screen. From the pop-up menu that should then appear, select the "Subscribe" option.

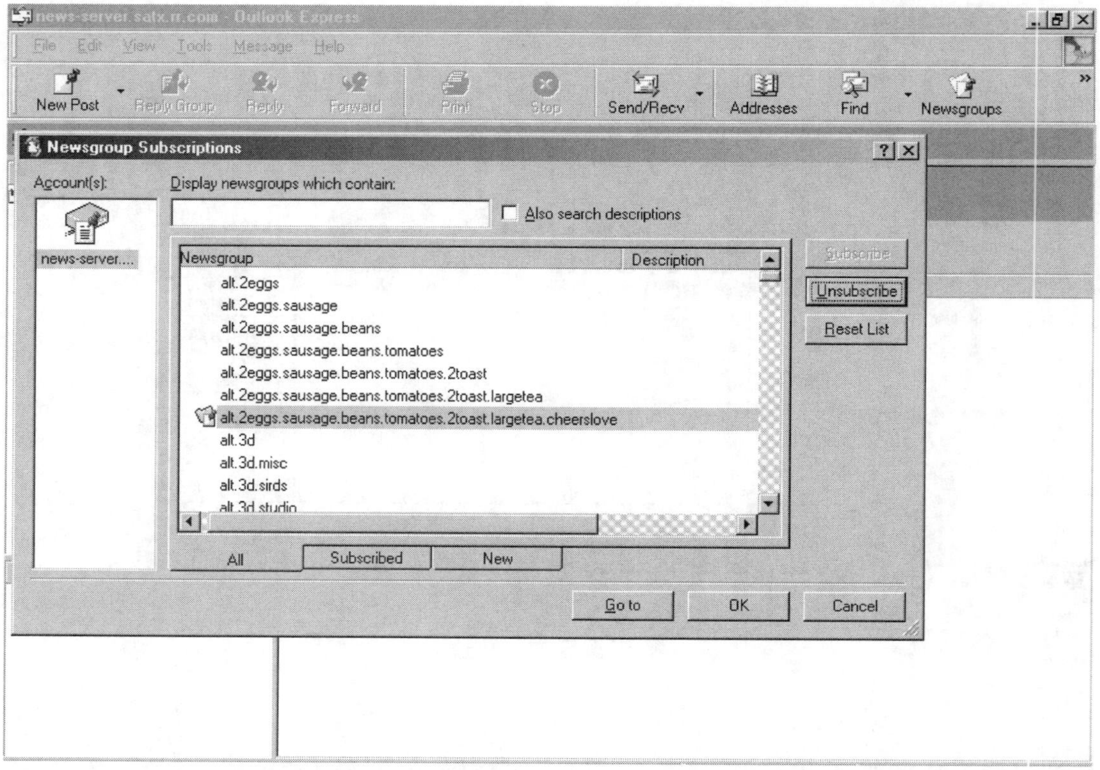

Figure 10.5 *The Subscription screen in Outlook Express, where you decide which newsgroups you want to read by scrolling through the downloaded list, selecting one, and clicking the "Subscribe" button. (Screen shot reprinted by permission from Microsoft Corporation.)*

The ISP should then download its list of newsgroups to Netscape, as shown in Figure 10.7. (This can amount to more than a megabyte of text and will take several minutes with dial-up access.) Names that represent the top of a hierarchy are shown with a plus sign, with a notation showing how many groups there are. Go through the list and use the "Subscribe" button to indicate which ones you are interested in. (Use the "Unsubscribe" button if you change your mind.) Then click "OK."

The address window in the third level of the controls should now show the name of your news server. Click on the down arrow at the right end of that window to see a list of the newsgroups that you have subscribed to (along with a list of your e-mail folders). If you click on the one you want to see, a list of messages

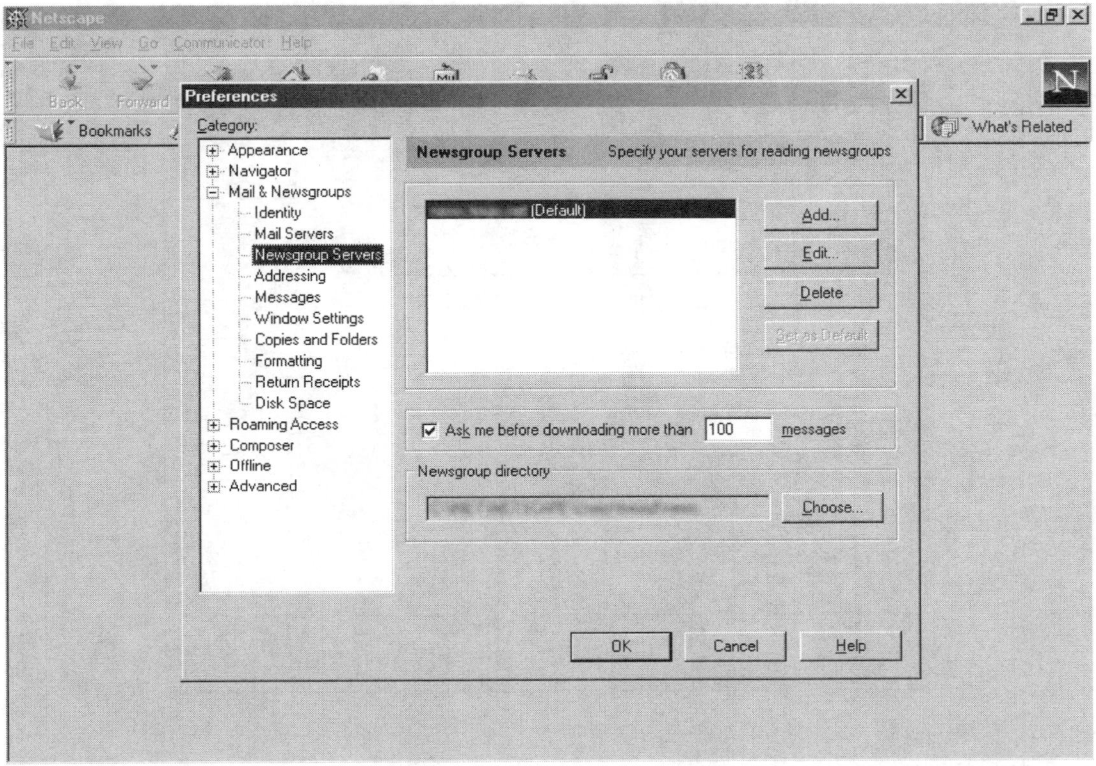

Figure 10.6 *The Preferences screen in Netscape Communicator, where you set the name of your ISP's news server, using the "Add" button. (The name of the news server has been blurred out.)*

should appear in the top of the screen. Click on one of the messages for its contents to appear in the lower window, as shown in Figure 10.1.

But . . .

No matter what software you use, the question of which newsgroup to subscribe to is still up in the air. You may already know which newsgroups serve your field, in which case you can simply subscribe to them and go on. (Chapter 11 includes a list of newsgroups devoted to carrying job openings.) On the other hand, you may not know the identity of any likely newsgroups. Or there may be so many candidates that following the traffic in all of them would be impractical. Or you

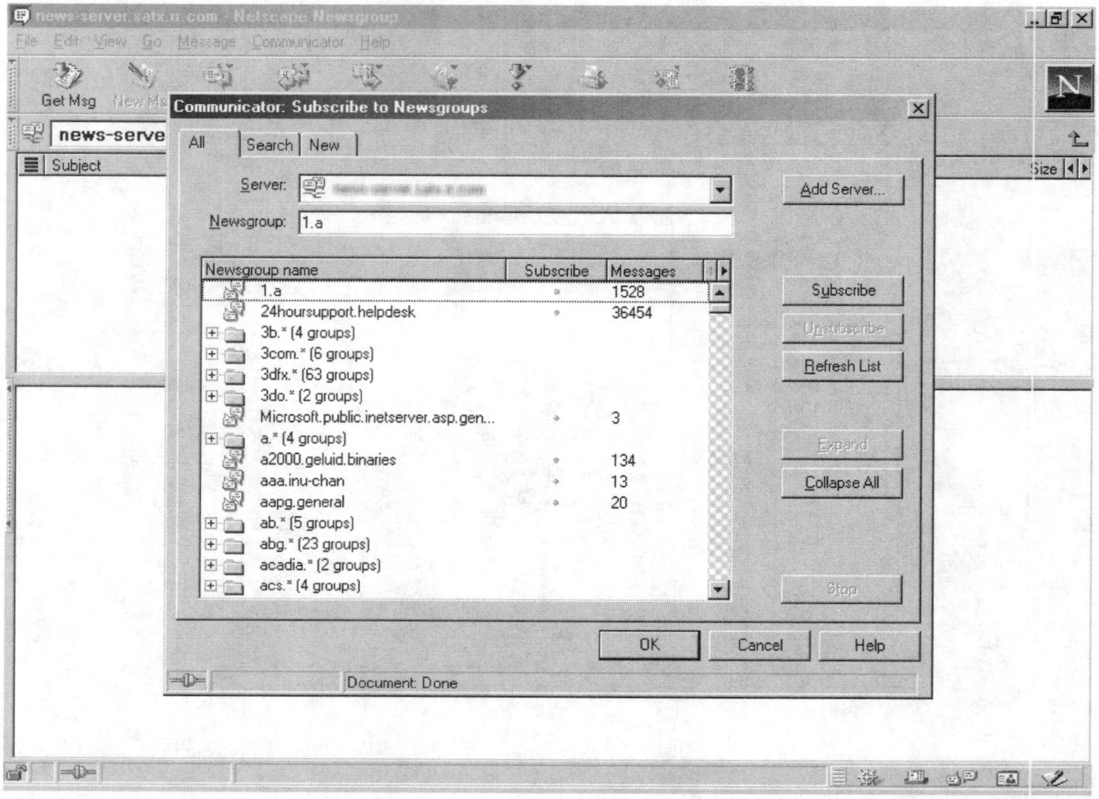

Figure 10.7 *The Subscription screen in Netscape Communicator, where you decide what newsgroups you want to read by scrolling through the list, selecting a newsgroup and clicking the "Subscribe" button. Members of a hierarchy can be seen by clicking its plus sign.*

have heard that an interesting job has been posted in a technology-related newsgroup, but you are not sure which one. At times like that you want to search Usenet, as described in the next section.

Searching Usenet

After you have subscribed to a newsgroup, your software will download the current traffic in the newsgroup, and you can search its messages with your newsreader software. For instance, with Netscape, you can click the "Edit" entry in the command menu, and then select "Search Messages." The Search Messages screen should then appear. Using the "Options" button, you can select whether the search command will search the messages that have been downloaded to your computer, or the messages in that newsgroup residing on the server. The search will run much faster if you use the "local system" option, and the software gives you more search options—you can search by the contents of the subject, the name of the sender, body text, date, status (i.e., whether it was read, replied to, or forwarded), or age in days. If you search the server, you can only search the contents of the subject line and the server.

In Outlook Express, you can only search the downloaded messages. Click "Edit" in the command menu, and then "Find." At that point you can either use "Message" or "Message in This Folder." The former will search the currently selected newsgroup by sender, subject line, body text, and date range. The latter will search the body text of the messages.

In either case, however, you are only searching the traffic in a single newsgroup. There's a whole sea of Usenet postings out there that you are not seeing and in practice cannot follow—there's just too much. Even if you did manage to subscribe to every likely newsgroup listed in Chapter 11 and took the time to search them, you still run into two limitations:

- You're lucky if your ISP carries more than a week of traffic for a given newsgroup. But there could be a great job, waiting to be filled by you, that was posted eight days ago.
- There is no law that says that all job postings must end up in job-related newsgroups.

So you must have a way to search the entirety of Usenet if you are going to make full use of Usenet. For that, you need a Usenet search engine.

The Usenet Search Engine

Offering a search engine for Usenet appears to be a thankless job. While entrepreneurs have rushed to set up Web search engines, there have been only a half-dozen attempts to set up Usenet search engines. At the end of the year 2000, all had faded away except Deja.com, and in early 2001 it too died—to be reborn as part of Google.com.

At this writing, the new entity could be found at http://groups.google.com, offering a database of postings going back to 1995, amounting to more than 650 million messages, occupying more than a terabyte (1 trillion characters) of data storage. (Maybe that explains why the job is so thankless.) Incidentally, the longevity of the database is popular in technical fields in situations when people suspect that a problem they are having was discussed and solved online years ago.

At this writing, then, using a Usenet search engine means using groups.google.com. Thus, you need to understand some basic facts about the site:

- The contents of binary newsgroups are not archived, and binary attachments are stripped from the messages of other newsgroups.
- Messages posted through an ISP can take up to 12 hours to appear in the database.
- You can post to Usenet through the Google database, using features offered at the site.
- Thanks to the facilities of Deja.com, much of the database has been purged of spam.

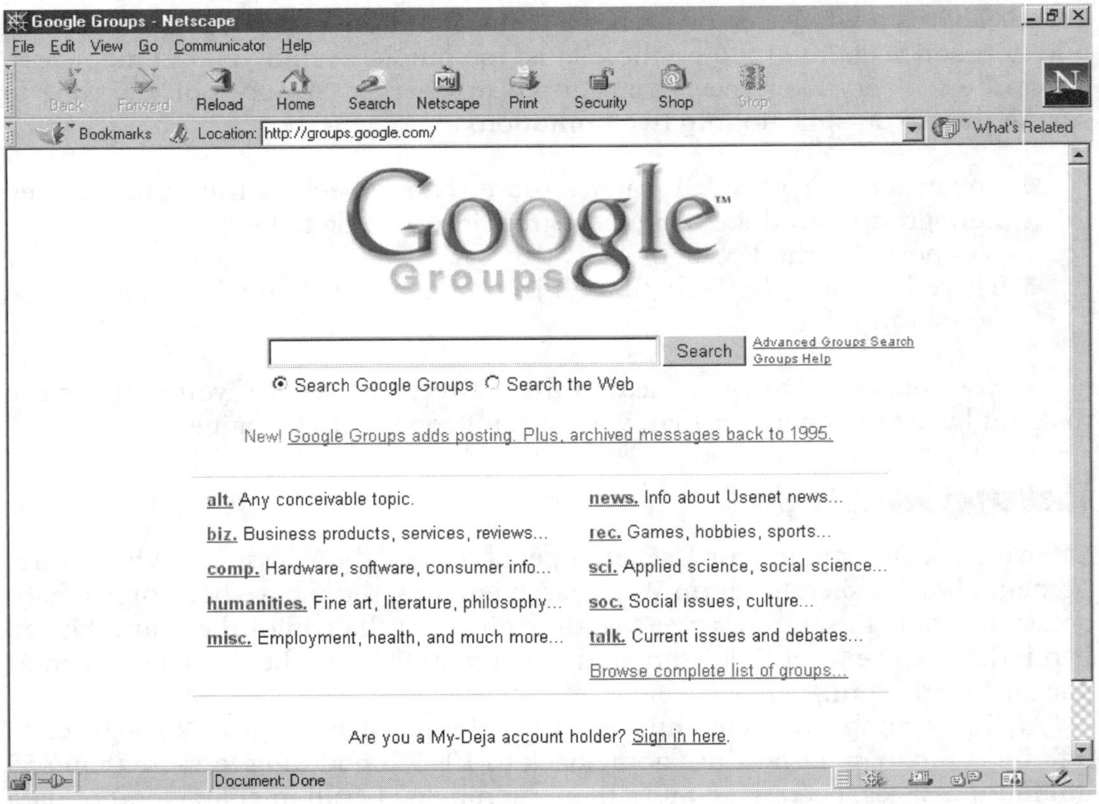

Figure 10.8 *Opening screen of the groups.google.com search engine for Usenet newsgroups. However, you should use the advanced search screen by clicking the Advanced Groups Search link. (Reprinted by permission of Google, Inc.)*

There are two ways to search groups.google.com: browsing and searching. Both can be reached from the main screen, shown in Figure 10.8. Both have their uses, as will be discussed.

Searching Groups.google.com

First, skip the opening screen shown in Figure 10.8 and go directly to the Advanced Groups Search screen, by clicking the link to the right of the opening page's search button. You should see a screen like that shown in Figure 10.9.

As you can see, the screen contains 10 different search parameters and 2 display parameters:

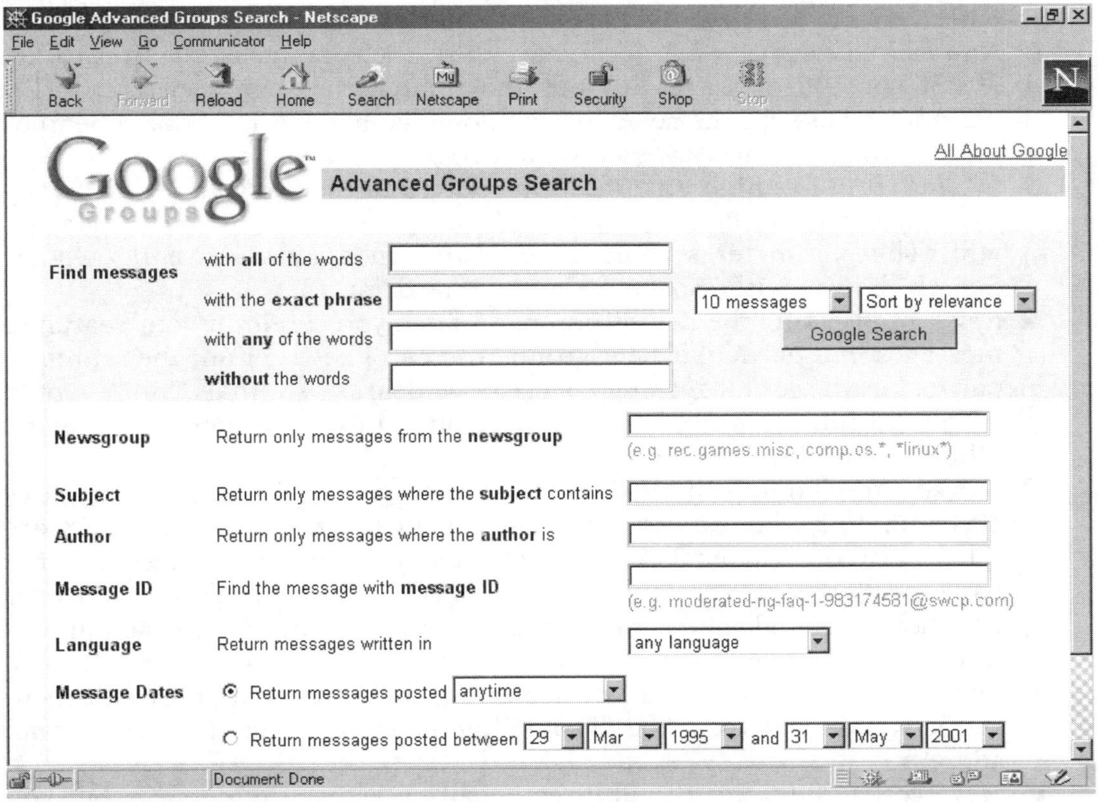

Figure 10.9 *Advanced Groups Search screen at groups.google.com, offering a more effective way to search the contents of Usenet than is possible using the opening screen. (Reprinted by permission of Google, Inc.)*

- *Find messages with all the words.* You can list the words to search in the body of the message, in any order. *Phoenix, accounting,* and *job* would find "accounting job available in Phoenix" and "Phoenix accounting job."
- *Find messages with the exact phrase.* You input the words you want to find in the order you want them found. Therefore, *accounting job* will find "accounting job opening" but not "job opening in accounting." (This option is best used when searching for names.)
- *Find messages with any of the words.* If you are not sure if the message is likely to use *job* or *opening* or *help-wanted* to denote an available position, you could go ahead and use all those words. This is equivalent to the Boolean "or" operator.
- *Find messages without the words.* This lets you cull out hits that you know you won't want, as when searching for *woods* without including anything with the word *forestry*.
- *Number to be displayed.* You can have the search engine list the first 10, 20, 30, 50, or 100 messages it finds that match the search criteria. (This parameter is set in the selection window just above the "Google Search" button, with "ten messages" as default.)
- *Sorting style.* The hits can appear on your screen sorted by relevancy or by date. Relevancy, of course, is a rules-based guess made by the Google system. (This parameter is set in the selection window just above the "Google Search" button with "Sort by relevance" as default.)
- *Newsgroup.* Using the newsgroup parameter, you can limit your search to messages in a particular newsgroup. You can likewise limit the search to particular hierarchies using asterisk wildcards, so that "alt.*" would search all nine thousand or so newsgroups in the alt hierarchy, but no other hierarchies.
- *Subject.* You'll notice in the display of a newsgroup message, as in Figures 10.1 and 10.2, the message includes a subject line, whose contents are filled in by the sender. This parameter lets you search for messages that have specified text in the subject line. (Of course, you have no control over whether the stated subject of a message has any relation to the actual subject of the message.)
- *Author.* This parameter lets you search for messages written by a particular person as shown in the "From" line of the message (i.e., the e-mail address.)
- *Message ID.* Message ID will directly call up a specific message, but you have to know its unique ID number. You can get this while reading the message. In Outlook Express, click the "Edit" entry in the command menu near the top of the screen, and then select the "Properties" entry. A win-

dow titled "Re:" will appear. There, select the "Details" tab, and you will see a screen that lists routing information for the message, including its ID number. In Netscape, click on the "View" entry in the command menu, and then select "Page Source." (The main use of the message ID is for those who have second thoughts about something they posted and want to ask Google to "nuke"—remove—it from the archive.)

- *Language*. The system lets you specify any of 25 languages, including English and "any language." This parameter can greatly cut down on the number of unwanted hits.
- *Message dates*. You can have Google search for messages posted any time, during the last week or the last month. Or you can set a date range, from the present day back to March 29, 1995.

Example

Suppose you want to check what jobs for accountants have been posted during the last week in the New York area. You would go to the groups.google.com advanced search page and do the following:

- Because you don't know if someone is going to use the word *accounting* or *accountant*, use them both, typing them into the "Find messages with any of these words" field.
- Then, in the newsgroup field, type "*jobs*" so that it will search only newsgroups with the word *jobs* in their name. (The asterisk is a wildcard character, telling the system to use anything.)
- As explained in Chapter 11, the generally accepted practice is to place an abbreviation concerning the job's location in the subject line (along with a lot other things). So you should type "NY" in the Subject field.
- In the Message Date field, select the "in the last week" option in the first radio button.

(Notice that the search fields that were not needed could be left blank.)

The search screen should now look something like that shown in Figure 10.10. Press the "Google Search" button and with any luck several dozen messages will be listed, as shown in Figure 10.11. (Some are likely to be duplicates, posted in multiple newsgroups.) Click the highlighted first line of any of them to bring up the actual message, such as the example shown in Figure 10.12.

At this point, you're not through. To be thorough, you'll want to run the search several different ways. For instance, you might want to search all the newsgroups with the word *accounting* for the word *job* or *opening*. Or you might

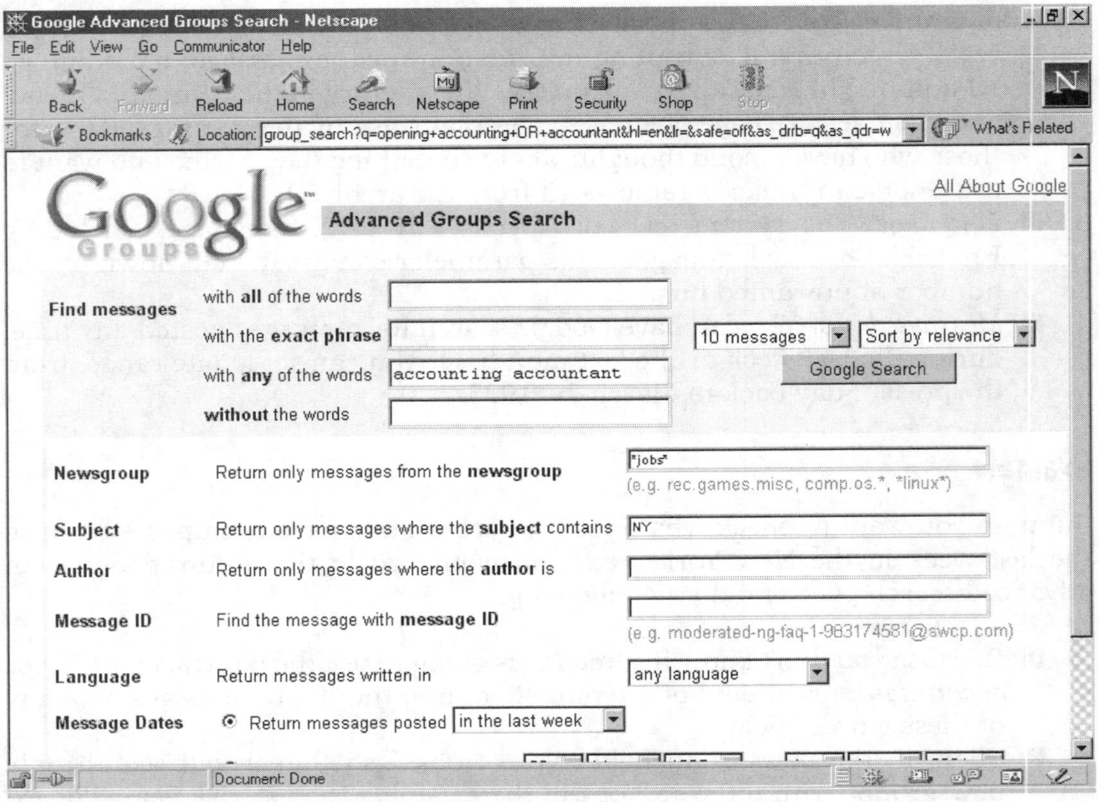

Figure 10.10 *The Advanced Groups Search screen with the input for the example search. (Reprinted from groups.google.com, by permission of Google, Inc.)*

want to search all of Usenet for the phrase *accounting job*. When you stop getting new results, you can rest assured that you have done a thorough job.

Responding

If you are interested in a job that you read about in a newsgroup message, you should get in touch with the author of the message via e-mail or by calling them. Presumably they will have included full contact information in the message. (If they didn't, you should not take them seriously.)

What you do not want to do is post a reply message. That is (almost invariably) not done in the jobs newsgroups. Although you will see message threads in the jobs newsgroups, the subsequent messages are typically announcements of

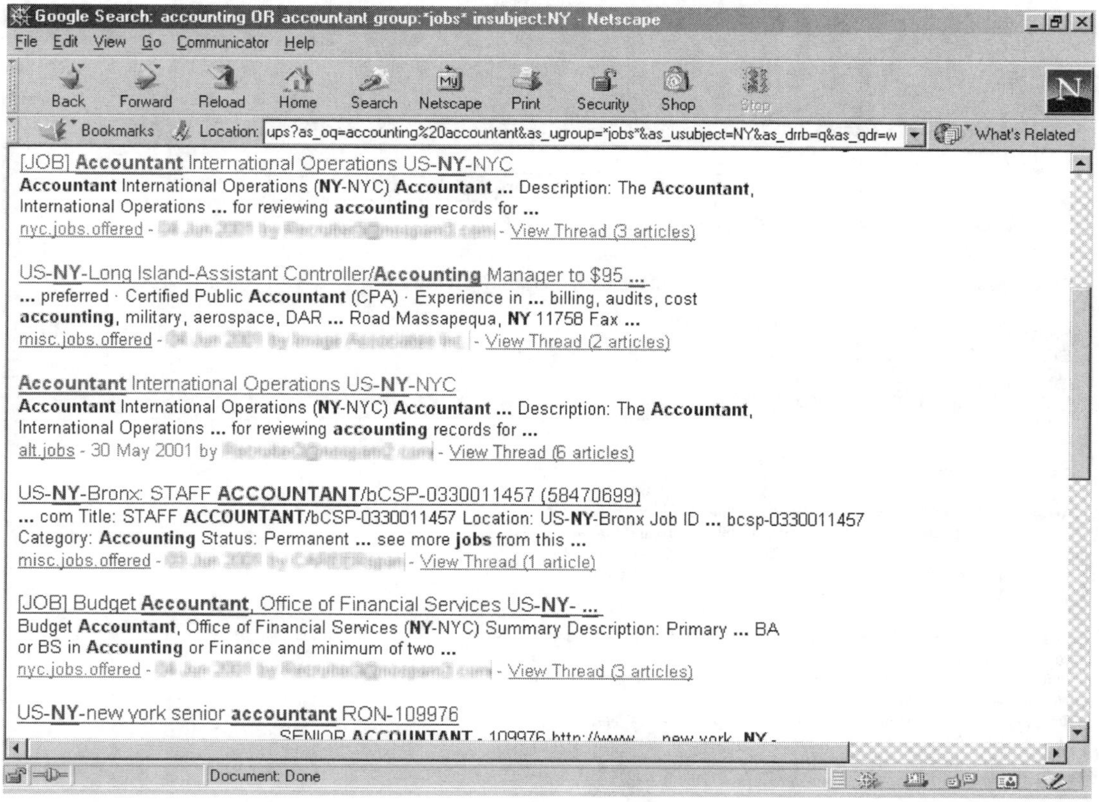

Figure 10.11 *Opening screen of the results found by the example search. Clicking on the first line will bring up the actual message. (The names of the senders have been blurred out.) (Reprinted from groups.google.com, by permission of Google, Inc.)*

additional openings from the same author, rather than third-party responses to the original job posting. Generally, when looking for a job, you should not post anything.

One exception is the newsgroups devoted to the posting of resumes. These newsgroups, and how to use them, are discussed in Chapter 11.

Meanwhile, you may find that you have wandered into one of the many general discussion newsgroups on Usenet and ache to comment on one or more of the postings that you have seen there. Don't let this book stop you. Participating in Usenet can open up a whole new world for you. But you may not like some of that world—read "The Verbal Minefield" section at the end of this chapter to see why.

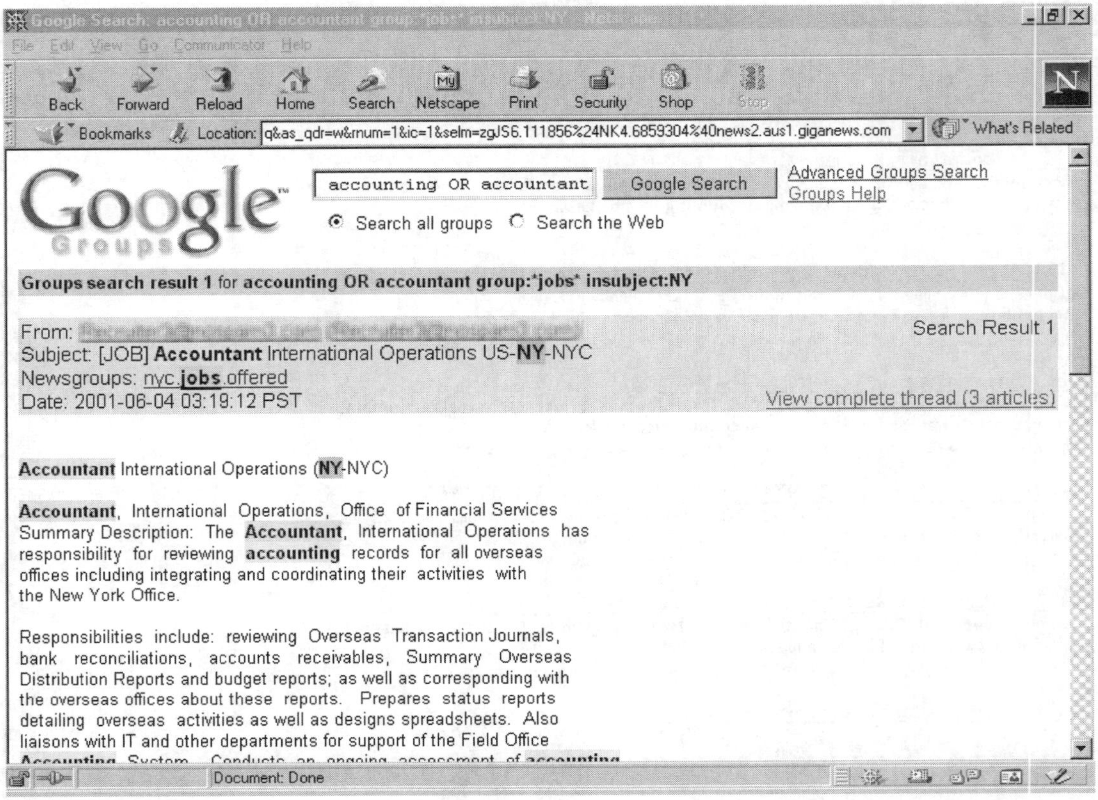

Figure 10.12 *Newsgroup message retrieved by the example search through groups.google.com. (Reprinted by permission of Google, Inc.)*

Mailing Lists

Mailing lists function much the same way as Usenet or old-style bulletin-board discussion forums—someone posts a message and other participants post a reply or comment. But there's a big difference: All the traffic here is in the form of e-mail. All postings and comments are sent to a specific e-mail address, from which they are rebroadcast to all members of the mailing list. Sometimes the traffic is moderated by someone who aggregates it, edits it, and broadcasts it at intervals, turning the forum into something closer to a newsletter.

The upshot is that a mailing list offers its users a private forum. A Usenet newsgroup in general circulation is available to anyone on Earth with Internet access, but to take part in a mailing list you have to know it exists and then subscribe to it. Some people say that the key to career, professional or business success in the future will be to find out where the online party is for your field and then join it. In other words, get on the best mailing list, participate, and become known in your field. Fortunately, the location of that list will probably not be a closely guarded secret—but you might have to demonstrate some credentials before they let you in.

To find the right mailing list, you can first simply ask around. Failing that, there are places online where you can search lists of publicly accessible mailing lists. But keep in mind that the mailing list that you need might have been formed initially because the participants did not want their forum to be publicly accessible. That means it might not be on any of these lists:

- *http://paml.net.* Publicly accessible mailing lists.
- *http://www.topica.com.* Publishing service for mailing lists (which it calls "e-mail discussion newsletters").
- *http://www.meta-list.net.* Lists almost two hundred thousand newsletters and mailing lists.
- *http://www.tile.net.* This service also lists newsgroups and file transfer protocol (FTP) sites.
- *http://www.lsoft.com/lists/listref.html.* List maintained by a mailing-list software vendor.

When you get the name of the mailing list that interests you, you also need to get the subscribe/unsubscribe information. Online, this will be stated with the mailing-list description. Off-line, you might need to ask that your informant send it to you by e-mail because you will need an exact e-mail address.

Typically, you send e-mail to the mailing list's address with the word *subscribe* in the subject line. Alternatively, *subscribe* may need to be the only word in the body of the message. Or you may need to also include the name of the mailing list, plus your name, in either the subject line or the text. The unsubscribe procedure is typically the same, replacing *subscribe* with *unsubscribe*. For other lists, you may need to go to a Web site. Most lists will send you an acknowledgment after subscribing that contains the unsubscribe information, which you should keep for reference.

Few mailing lists are devoted specifically to job hunting. However, job-related discussions frequently take place on mailing lists devoted to a particular field. Also keep in mind that mailing lists offer the same verbal dangers that lurk in Usenet newsgroups. Participate only after reading the next section.

The Verbal Minefield

Hang around Usenet for a while, or any other discussion forum or mailing list, and you will soon observe a sad phenomenon. At the drop of a participle, someone will lash out at some comment in another person's message. That person will lash back with an angry denial. Both will throw verbal tantrums as they insist on their own righteousness. Other participants will lash out at the combatants to try to get them to shut up and become combatants themselves. More and more of the forum's participants find something better to do, as do the combatants, eventually, and a tense silence falls over the forum. Noncombatants, perceiving safety, will emerge and pick up where they left off. Sweetness and light will prevail—until someone else gets offended and throws a tantrum, setting off a new round. The phenomenon is called *flame wars*. The trick is to not be shocked when you see one, and to avoid participation yourself.

That flame wars happen should be (at least in hindsight) no surprise. When conversing face to face, your demeanor indicates how you are comprehending what the other person is saying. The speaker's demeanor, tone, posture, and facial expression—conversational cues—likewise add considerably to what is being said. With this exchange of spoken and unspoken signals, the speaker and listener make adjustments as they go along. (Thanks to inflection and breathing patterns, it even works over the phone.) If offense is taken, the situation can be immediately addressed and probably rectified; raising an eyebrow, for example, can cause things to move in a new direction.

With naked text, on the other hand, you have a paltry surface manifestation of a complex process. In the absence of conversational cues, it appears that people tend to fill in the resulting void with noise from the environment or from inside their heads. Once they perceive a negative connotation, there is nothing to derail that perception, or at least nothing stronger than the original stimulus. Once motivated to flame, the motivation to stop flaming must also come from within. Because the flamer may think it is all the other person's fault, that motivation may be slow to emerge, and so you see adults acting like toddlers—even when their spelling, syntax, and formatting remains perfect. (The use of emoticons, explained in the Glossary, can partially make up for the absence of conversational cues.)

But looking askance at flamers is not enough; you must yourself avoid flaming. Congratulating yourself on your resolve never to flame is not enough either—in the next moment, you may feel tempted to post a comment that righteously points out someone else's flaming, and you're a goner. Instead, be proactive. You must consciously abide by the following rules.

Be Terse

Say what you mean, and mean what you say. Then shut up. The more you say, the more raw material someone else has to react to and take issue with. (Anyway, if you are long winded, few will even bother to read your contributions.)

Be Clear

If you say something that can be misinterpreted, it will be misinterpreted. If the misinterpretation involves negative connotations, you may be shocked to find that the other readers assume that the negative connotation represents your true meaning. (Why else would a clever person like you use that wording?) Simple misinterpretations are the cause of many flame wars.

Be Clean

Online, you are your words. Make sure they are words you feel comfortable being identified with. Swearing like a sailor is fine if you are a sailor. If you were hoping to get a job as a school counselor, there could be problems.

Be Literate

Use a spell checker. Format carefully, DON'T USE ALL CAPS BECAUSE IT LOOKS LIKE YOU ARE YELLING, and don't use control characters. Check what you write before you post it. Many people take their participation seriously and will be annoyed by evidence that you don't. These same people expect that anything posted to Usenet or a mailing list represents your heartfelt, carefully researched contribution, instead of steam you're letting off. If you make half-baked generalizations, they'll come out of the woodwork at you, armed with facts they dug up from the Internet in the intervening minutes.

Be Respectful

Say something negative about Person X by name on Usenet, and that person will know you said it in front of hundreds of thousands of people worldwide and is not going to forget it. Once you post it, it can be online, in some archive, forever—and you have made a permanent enemy.

Be Reasonable

If someone is not persuaded by your facts, logic, and clear presentation, that does not mean that you are supposed to escalate to personal attacks. People disagree without being disagreeable all the time. Join them. (Often, you will discover too late that the other person actually agreed with you but just wanted to make a separate point.)

Be Serious

Some readers will have no sense of humor. Others just don't share yours. And plenty of them read English as a second language and are mystified by your subtle wit. You can be funny and witty, but you should bluntly identify such attempts and explain yourself. Doing so demonstrates a respect for your audience that your readers will appreciate.

Be Sure

Second thoughts are expensive on Usenet. Once you have posted your message and your ISP's news server has forwarded it to the rest of the Internet, you have to live with what you have done. You can't undo it.

Your news-reader software probably has a Cancel Message feature that allows you to kill a message that you have written. But it probably only works on messages stored on your ISP's news server. Reacting to massive amounts of abuse (by people tweaking the feature to cancel the messages of personal enemies), ISPs usually won't forward cancel commands to the Internet any more. But if you cancel the message before it is circulated, you are safe.

In Netscape Communicator, you can cancel the current message by clicking the "Edit" entry in the command menu and then selecting the "Cancel Message" option. In Outlook Express, you can cancel the current message by clicking the "Message" entry in the command menu and selecting the "Cancel Message" option.

And, as previously noted, groups.google.com will "nuke" your message from its database if you contact them and follow certain procedures detailed at the site. (Basically, you have to avow that you were the author of the message.)

Ignore Domains

Many contributions come from corporate domains because the users made their posting from their desktop computers at work. This does not mean that they are speaking for their employer. You can assume that if they are, they will say so explicitly.

Use the Subject Line

The subject line should contain enough information so that someone who is not interested in what you have to say can simply skip it. Consider the difference between "cats" and "kittens to give way in Upper Metropolis." If your message is a response to a specific earlier message, say so in the subject line. If you are giving away the ending of a work of fiction that's under discussion, you should use the word *spoiler* in the subject line.

Respond by E-Mail

If you see a Usenet message with a job posting that you want to respond to, use e-mail. Don't just post a reply saying, "I'll take it."

Be Secure

As explained in Chapter 3, you should not post identifying information about yourself. (Although this is not strictly a flame war issue, you may be flamed if you do it.)

Quote Responsibly

There are people who copy long postings into their message and then add a one-line comment. Instead, copy only the relevant sentence. Whatever you do, don't reuse the contents of another message as if they were your own words.

Don't Spam

Although spamming usually refers to sending unsolicited bulk e-mail, it has the secondary meaning of posting the same message in multiple newsgroups. There are people who routinely post the same thing in every known newsgroup. Don't post until you have studied the newsgroup enough to know what its topic truly is (it may not be clear from the name) and what is acceptable to its participants. Basically, a newsgroup can be thought of as a private club, whose value to the participants is the ongoing creation of those participants. They will be offended by an outsider's attempt to use their creation. Their anger will be red-hot if they perceive a blatantly commercial attempt to use their creation. (Some technical newsgroups welcome commercial announcements from firms in that field, and some have special subnewsgroups for the posting of such announcements.) That you don't know about the customary practices of a particular newsgroup will demonstrate that you are an abusive outsider.

Summary: The Golden Rule

If it sounds like you should behave like a Boy Scout while walking a tightrope across a snake pit—yep, that about sums it up. But if the previous rules remain elusive, try to cling to this one: Never write anything that you would not want to appear in your local newspaper. For many people, Usenet is their newspaper. And reading a newspaper that they can also write in is, for some people, the same as being given enough rope to hang themselves.

Frankly, you should apply the rule to everything—Usenet, e-mail, paper mail, office memos, school homework, and so on. If you would not want it to come out in the newspaper, don't write it down. After it leaves your hands, you not only have no control over its circulation, you have no control over how people will react to it. In the spring of 2001, there was an incident in which a London financier newly transferred to South Korea sent out an e-mail filled with sophomoric boasts about how many women he had gotten to know there, in the biblical sense. The recipient forwarded it to others, who did the same, until it had global circulation. In a week, the sender was looking for a new job. Perhaps this book will help.

The next chapter examines some specific Usenet newsgroups that you might use for a job search.

CHAPTER 11

Jobs-Related Newsgroups

Chapter 10 dealt with the nature of Usenet, how to use its newsgroups, and how not to use them. That leaves the question of which newsgroups are best for a particular job seeker to subscribe to.

There is no simple answer. Fortunately, that's because there is such a substantial amount of material out there. There are hundreds of jobs-related newsgroups—the exact number is made meaningless by the multilingual nature of Usenet and the fact that not all newsgroups reach general circulation. As for what's carried in those newsgroups, during the spring of 2001, combined postings in all purely job-related newsgroups on Usenet amounted to a little under fourteen thousand messages per day. A little over half of those were in the English language.

However, that does not mean that an Anglophonic job-seeker has seven thousand jobs per day to choose from; many jobs are cross-posted (i.e., posted to multiple newsgroups) by employment agencies. An examination of the English-language traffic in misc.jobs.offered (which is often included in cross-posting) shows that the volume of unique messages there is a little over fifteen hundred per day. Taking in account unique postings in other hierarchies, two thousand jobs a day in English seems to be the average.

But that still amounts to a cornucopia of help-wanted notices, well worth tapping into by a serious job seeker. And although hundreds of newsgroups are devoted to job postings, the mother of them all appears to be misc. jobs.offered. Postings in the other job-related newsgroups by and large follow the guidelines used by misc.jobs.offered. The next section takes a look at those guidelines.

The Guidelines

All but a few jobs-related newsgroups are not moderated, meaning that anyone can post anything. The same spam that shows up everywhere else on Usenet also shows up in the jobs newsgroups. However, the misc.jobs hierarchy actually has a FAQ file that describes how postings are to be made. Messages that represent serious job offers typically follow those guidelines. (Even the many employment agencies that cross-post so relentlessly typically observe the guidelines.)

Basically, the rules are designed to let a job seeker intelligently scan or search the message traffic without having to read every message. To accomplish this, the message writers are supposed to use a specific format for the subject line:

COUNTRY-STATE/PROVINCE—City Job Description, Company

Therefore, if Acme Widgets was seeking a gimlet developer in Chicago, the subject line would look like this:

US-IL-Chicago Gimlet Developer, Acme Widgets

If the company was in Munich, the line might look like this:

DE-Munich Gimlet Developer, Acme Widgets

Dropping the company name (which should be in the body of the message anyway) is permissible in order to flesh out the job description:

US-IL-Chicago Entry-Level Bilingual Gimlet Developer

It is also permissible to expand the geographic designator with the name of a suburb or location descriptor:

US-IL-Chicago-Schaumburg Entry-Level Bilingual Gimlet Developer
US-NY-NYC-Midtown Entry-Level Bilingual Gimlet Developer

The use of the state/province is optional outside the United States and Canada but is important in those two countries to avoid confusion between California and Canada (both are abbreviated CA) and cities with similar names. Therefore, US-CA-Ontario is the city of Ontario in California in the United States, while CA-ON-Woodstock refers to city of Woodstock in Ontario, Canada.

Lately, job posters have also been adding the area code of the job to the geographic designator, at least for jobs in North America:

(312) US-IL-Chicago Entry-Level Bilingual Gimlet Developer

If the work can be done at home, then "Off-site" can be used for the geographic designator.

Here are the rest of the guidelines:

- The job must exist. (You can't post fake jobs to fish for resumes.)
- The job must represent legal employment in the place where it is offered.
- The name and phone number, or address, of the person responsible for the position must be given. The address must be complete, or the phone number must be more than an 800-number.
- A specific salary range in a specific currency should be given.
- The message should state if the job is full time, part time, or seasonal, how overtime (if any) is handled, and how much travel is involved, if any.
- Administrative or legal requirements for getting hired should be stated up front, such as citizenship, drug screening, adherence to a dress code, nondisclosure agreements, and so on.
- Two sets of background/experience/education requirements for the job should be given: the minimum and the desired.
- There should be a cutoff date for applications.
- A job-start date, if there is one, should be given.
- Unrelated jobs should not be combined in one message. Multiple, related jobs can be combined in one message, however.
- Discussions of job-related topics, or of the contents of misc.jobs.offered, should take place in misc.jobs.misc and only there. The rest of the misc.jobs hierarchy should not be used as a discussion forum.
- Individuals should post resumes in misc.jobs.resumes.

Implications of the Guidelines

Proper use of the guidelines should allow you to scan down a list of message headers and pick out the ones that involve your town and field of work. If even that is too daunting (and in some newsgroups it will be), then you can confidently use the local search command to search the current newsgroup, as described in Chapter 10. Likewise, you can use the search engine at groups.google.com, although its database may be a few hours less current than your ISPs.

Many of the newsgroups listed in the next section are actually part of deeper hierarchies, often with member newsgroups with endings like "offered," "contract," "resumes," and "misc" (or "discussion" or simply the letter d). Extrapolating from the misc.jobs guidelines, jobs should be listed in the "offered" newsgroup, contract positions (where you work on a project without being added to the full-time payroll) should be listed in the "contract" newsgroup, resumes should be posted only in the "resumes" newsgroup, and interactive discussion should be carried out only in the "misc" or "discussion" newsgroup.

The guidelines also apply to the content of resumes posted by individuals—which means that if you post a resume, you should try to configure the subject line as described for employers, with a place and job descriptor. For instance, if you are a Web site designer seeking work in Reno, Nevada, your subject line might read as follows:

US-NV-Reno Web designer seeks full-time position

Use plain text for the message contents (which should include your resume) rather than a file attachment.

Finally, keep in mind that the guidelines are unenforceable and that anybody can post anything, yourself included. When reading Usenet, remember that Usenet is like life—you're on your own. But you will want to put your best foot forward, and there are established norms for doing so.

Jobs-Related Newsgroups

Because the Usenet landscape is subject to constant change, there can be no definitive listing of newsgroups in any but the narrowest niche categories. In addition, there are local newsgroups that do not get global circulation. Even in the flagship misc.jobs hierarchy, there is no guarantee against major changes. (In the year 2000, there was an initiative to do away with misc.jobs.offered and replace it with a list of regional and occupational subgroups. However, there is no indication that it has or will be acted on.) The following list, and any list, should be taken as just representational of what's out there.

Nevertheless, the following newsgroups should get you started—and may be far more than you will ever need. Fortunately, there is a lot of cross-posting: If you miss one promising newsgroup, the same job is likely to show up in another.

In the following sections, the major English-language jobs-related newsgroups are organized by type, with commentary where appropriate, beginning with the flagship misc.jobs hierarchy and then covering U.S. regional newsgroups, Canadian newsgroups, overseas newsgroups with English content, AOL and alt newsgroups, and other categories of newsgroups.

Misc.jobs

The misc.jobs hierarchy is one of the busiest in Usenet.

- misc.jobs.
- misc.jobs.contract. For contract jobs; that is, the person hired will not be on the payroll.
- misc.jobs.offered. The mother lode.
- misc.jobs.offered.entry. For entry-level job offers.
- misc.jobs.fields.
- misc.jobs.fields.chemistry. For jobs in the chemical sciences.
- misc.jobs.misc. For job-related discussions and discussion of items in other misc.jobs newsgroups.
- misc.jobs.resumes. For posting resumes. (Use plain text with line breaks, as explained in Chapter 5, and an explanatory subject line.)
- misc.job. There are a lot of little-used misspelled newsgroups in Usenet. This is one of them, apparently a misspelling of misc.jobs.
- misc.jobs.offer. A misspelling of misc.jobs.offered.
- misc.jobd.offered. Another misspelling of misc.jobs.offered.
- misc.jobs.resume. Misspelling of misc.jobs.resumes.

U.S. Regional Newsgroups

The following newsgroups are in general circulation. (Other newsgroups specific to small regions can be found on local ISPs.) Each listed newsgroup is identified by region (it's not always obvious). When there is an extended hierarchy, usually only the first is identified.

- akr.jobs (Akron, Ohio).
- alabama.jobs (Alabama).
    - alabama.birmingham.jobs.

- atl.jobs (Atlanta, Georgia).
  - atl.resumes.
- austin.jobs (Austin, Texas).
  - austin.jobs.resumes.
- az.jobs (Arizona).
- ba.jobs (Bay Area [San Francisco, California region.]).
  - ba.jobs.offered.
  - ba.jobs.agency.
  - ba.jobs.contract.
  - ba.jobs.contract.agency.
  - ba.jobs.contract.direct.
  - ba.jobs.direct.
  - ba.jobs.discussion.
  - ba.jobs.resumes.
- balt.jobs (Baltimore, Maryland).
- blgtn.jobs (Bloomington, Indiana).
- ca.jobs (California).
- chi.jobs (Chicago, Illinois, area).
- cmh.jobs (Columbus, Ohio, area).
- co.jobs (Colorado).
- cmu.misc.jobs (Carnegie Mellon University).
- dc.jobs (District of Columbia).
- dfw.jobs (Dallas and Fort Worth, Texas).
- eug.jobs (Eugene, Oregon).
- fl.jobs (Florida).
  - fl.jobs.computers.
  - fl.jobs.computers.application.
  - fl.jobs.computers.misc.
  - fl.jobs.computers.programming.
  - fl.jobs.misc.
  - fl.jobs.resumes.
  - fl.jobs.telecommute.
  - fl.jobs.www.
- git.ohr.jobs (Georgia Institute of Technology).
  - git.ohr.jobs.digest.
- houston.jobs (Houston, Texas).
  - houston.jobs.offered.
  - houston.jobs.wanted.
- ithaca.jobs (Ithaca, New York).
- hsv.jobs (Huntsville, Alabama.)

- iijnet.jobs (Illinois and Wisconsin).
- in.jobs (Indiana).
- kc.jobs (Kansas City region).
- la.jobs (Used for both Los Angeles and Louisiana).
- li.jobs (Long Island, New York).
- lou.lft.jobs (Lafayette, Louisiana).
- md.jobs (Maryland).
- me.jobs (Maine).
- memphis.employment (Memphis, Tennessee).
- mi.jobs (Michigan).
- milw.jobs (Milwaukee, Wisconsin, region).
- nc.jobs (North Carolina).
- ne.jobs (New England).
  - ne.jobs.company (one of the few moderated jobs conferences).
  - ne.jobs.contract.
  - ne.wanted.
- nebr.jobs (Nebraska).
- neworleans.jobs (New Orleans, LA).
- niagara.jobs (Serves the Niagara Falls area on both sides of the border).
- nj.jobs (New Jersey).
  - nj.jobs.resumes.
- nm.jobs (New Mexico).
- nv.jobs (Nevada).
- nyc.jobs (New York City).
  - nyc.jobs.contract.
  - nyc.jobs.misc.
  - nyc.jobs.offered.
  - nyc.jobs.wanted.
- oh.jobs (Ohio).
- ok.jobs (Oklahoma).
- or.jobs (Oregon).
- osu.jobs (Ohio).
- pa.jobs (Pennsylvania).
  - pa.jobs.offered.
  - pa.jobs.wanted.
- pdaxs.jobs (Portland, Oregon, region).
  - pdaxs.jobs.clerical.
  - pdaxs.jobs.computers (this is by far the busiest newsgroup in the hierarchy).
  - pdaxs.jobs.construction.

- pdaxs.jobs.delivery.
- pdaxs.jobs.domestic.
- pdaxs.jobs.engineering.
- pdaxs.jobs.management.
- pdaxs.jobs.misc.
- pdaxs.jobs.restaurants.
- pdaxs.jobs.resumes.
- pdaxs.jobs.retail.
- pdaxs.jobs.sales.
- pdaxs.jobs.secretary.
- pdaxs.jobs.temporary.
- pdaxs.jobs.volunteers.
- pdaxs.jobs.wanted.

■ pgh.jobs (Pittsburgh, Pennsylvania).
- pgh.jobs.offered.
- pgh.jobs.wanted.

■ phl.jobs (Philadelphia, Pennsylvania).
- phl.jobs.offered.
- phl.jobs.wanted.

■ phx.jobs (Phoenix, Arizona, region).
- phx.jobs.wanted.

■ sac.jobs (Sacramento, California).

■ sat.jobs (San Antonio, Texas).

■ sdnet.jobs (San Diego, California, region).
- sdnet.jobs.discuss.
- sdnet.jobs.offered.
- sdnet.jobs.services.
- sdnet.jobs.wanted.

■ seattle.jobs (Seattle, Washington).
- seattle.jobs.offered.
- seattle.jobs.wanted.

■ stl.jobs (St. Louis, Missouri).

■ su.jobs (Stanford University).

■ tamu.jobs (Texas A&M University).

■ taos.jobs (Taos, New Mexico).

■ triangle.jobs (Research Triangle region in North Carolina).

■ tx.jobs (Texas).

■ uark.jobs (University of Arkansas).

■ ucb.jobs (University of California at Berkeley).
- ucb.cs.jobs (University of California at Berkeley, computer science).

- ucd.jobs (University of California at Davis).
  - ucd.cs.jobs (University of California at Davis computer science).
- ut.jobs (Utah).
- utcs.jobs (University of Texas Computer Sciences).
- utexas.jobs (University of Texas).
- uw.ece.jobs (University of Wisconsin).
- va.jobs (Virginia).
- vegas.jobs (Las Vegas, Nevada).
- wyo.jobs (Wyoming).

Canadian Jobs Newsgroups

- ab.jobs (Alberta).
- bc.jobs (British Columbia).
- can.jobs (Canada).
  - can.jobs.gov (Canadian government jobs).
- kw.jobs (Kitchener-Waterloo, Ontario).
- nb.jobs (New Brunswick).
- nf.jobs (Newfoundland).
- ns.jobs (Nova Scotia).
- ont.jobs (Ontario).
- ott.jobs (Ottawa).
- qc.jobs (Quebec).
- sk.jobs (Saskatchewan).
- tor.jobs (Toronto).
- van.jobs (Vancouver, British Columbia).

AOL

In addition to the regional jobs newsgroups already listed, America Online (AOL) sponsors a list of regional newsgroups for the United States and Canada that typically include a jobs newsgroup for each region covered. These are part of the aol.neighborhood hierarchy, which uses the format aol.neighborhood. state.city.subject. For instance, the AOL jobs newsgroup for Buffalo, New York, is aol.neighborhood.ny.buffalo.jobs. Because AOL is a rival ISP, your ISP may or may not carry the AOL newsgroups.

Overseas Jobs Newsgroups in English

There are far more overseas jobs newsgroups than the ones listed here. (Russia and Taiwan are particularly active.) But the contents of the following newsgroups passed the English-language filter at groups.google.com. That, however, does not mean that they are entirely in English—they may host occasional English-language jobs, or suffer from English-language spam. On the other hand, places like Israel and Singapore use English in business.

- at.jobs (Austria).
- aus.ads.jobs (Australia).
  - aus.ads.jobs.moderated.
  - aus.ads.jobs.resumes.
- be.jobs (Belgium).
- bln.jobs (Berlin, Germany).
- bremnet.jobs (Bremen, German).
- cz.jobs.offered (Czech Republic).
  - cz.jobs.wanted.
- ie.jobs (Ireland).
- israel.jobs (Israel).
  - israel.jobs.misc.
  - israel.jobs.offered.
  - israel.jobs.resumes.
- nz.jobs (New Zealand).
- scot.jobs (Scotland).
- sg.jobs (Singapore).
  - sg.jobs.offer.
- swnet.jobs (Sweden).
- tnn.jobs (The Network News in Japan [but used for Tennessee]).
- uk.jobs (United Kingdom).
  - uk.jobs.contract.
  - uk.jobs.d.
  - uk.jobs.offered (very busy newsgroup).
  - uk.jobs.wanted.
- za.ads.jobs (South Africa).

Alt Hierarchy

There is no shortage of jobs-related newsgroups in the alt hierarchy. As with the other lists, this list should be taken as representational. Keep in mind that the alt hierarchy is intended to have global circulation, with no attempt to limit content to appropriate regions. Therefore, pundits advise that anyone who wants to post a job opening should use the regional Usenet newsgroups listed previously. (Anyway, some of these duplicate the regional newsgroups in the alt hierarchy.) But the alt jobs newsgroups exist, and have traffic in them, so even if you don't actively follow them you should at least include them in any searches you run. Other jobs-related alt newsgroups, such as alt.building.jobs, have no equivalent outside the alt hierarchy.

- alt.bestjobsusa.boston.jobs (alt.bestjobsusa appears to be related to a jobs site on the Web called www.bestjobsusa.com).
- alt.bestjobsusa.california.jobs.
- alt.bestjobsusa.career.jobs.
- alt.bestjobsusa.chicago.jobs.
- alt.bestjobsusa.cleveland.jobs.
- alt.bestjobsusa.colorado.jobs.
- alt.bestjobsusa.computers.jobs (by far the busiest in the alt.bestjobsusa hierarchy).
- alt.bestjobsusa.dallas.jobs.
- alt.bestjobsusa.engineering.jobs.
- alt.bestjobsusa.florida.jobs.
- alt.bestjobsusa.healthcare.jobs.
- alt.bestjobsusa.kansas.jobs.
- alt.bestjobsusa.kentucky.jobs.
- alt.bestjobsusa.management.jobs.
- alt.bestjobsusa.manufacturing.jobs.
- alt.bestjobsusa.portland.jobs.
- alt.bestjobsusa.sales.jobs.
- alt.bestjobsusa.seattle.jobs.
- alt.bestjobsusa.tennesee.jobs.
- alt.building.jobs.
- alt.building.resumes.
- alt.business.career.
- alt.business.career.opportunities.
- alt.business.career-opportunities.
- alt.business.career-opportunities.executive.
- alt.business.career-opportunities.executives.
- alt.jobs (use misc.jobs instead, pundits say).
- alt.jobs.as400.
- alt.jobs.gis.offered.
- alt.jobs.houston.
- alt.jobs.jobsearch.
- alt.jobs.nw-arkansas.
- alt.jobs.offered.

- alt.jobs.overseas.
- alt.jobs.resumes.
- alt.jobs.uk-jobsearch.
- alt.medical.sales.jobs.
- alt.medical.sales.jobs.offered.
- alt.medical.sales.jobs.resumes.
- alt.resumes.

Field-Specific Jobs Newsgroups

There are thousands of newsgroups dealing with specific fields of interest or endeavors, and any of them may end up being host to a job listing. The following appear to have been specifically intended for jobs.

- bionet.jobs (biosciences).
  - bionet.jobs.offered.
  - bionet.jobs.wanted.
- borland.public.cpp.jobs.
  - borland.public.cppbuilder.jobs.
- borland.public.delphi.jobs.
- borland.public.intrabuilder.jobs.
- borland.public.jbuilder.jobs.
- borland.public.vdbase.jobs.
- dod.jobs (U.S. Department of Defense).
- hr.misc.jobs (used to post miscellaneous white-collar jobs).
- microsoft.public.fox.helpwanted.
- microsoft.public.ph.phillippines.certified.jobs.
- muc.lists.freebsd.jobs.
- netcom.uk.jobs.
- sol.lists.freebsd.jobs.
- vmsnet.employment.

The Troubled Comp Hierarchy

Comp stands for computers, and the comp hierarchy is naturally a busy place on the computer-based and computer-oriented Usenet. So busy, in fact, that there has been an effort to delete all comp.job neswsgroups because they do nothing but draw spam and agency postings. Your ISP may still be offering them. If not, you might be better off following the rest of the comp hierarchy for job postings.

There are more than thirty other comp hierarchies, including comp.ai, comp.databases, comp.games, and especially, comp.lang (for languages). If available, the comp.jobs newsgroups include the following:

- comp.job.
- comp.jobs.
- comp.jobs.computer.
- comp.jobs.computers.
- comp.jobs.contract.
- comp.jobs.misc.
- comp.jobs.offered.
- comp.jobs.offred (misspelled newsgroup).
- comp.jobs.programming.

Other Marginal Newsgroups

The following either are not widely accepted as legitimate newsgroups, are little used, or appear to have little purpose.

- gov.us.topic.gov-jobs. It may say something about government jobs, but this hierarchy has very little traffic.
  - gov.us.topic.gov-jobs.employee.
  - gov.us.topic.gov-jobs.employee.issues.
  - gov.us.topic.gov-jobs.employee.news.
  - gov.us.topic.gov-jobs.hr-admin.
  - gov.us.topic.gov-jobs.offered.
  - gov.us.topic.gov-jobs.offered.admin.
  - gov.us.topic.gov-jobs.offered.admin.finance.
  - gov.us.topic.gov-jobs.offered.admin.ses.
  - gov.us.topic.gov-jobs.offered.announce.
  - gov.us.topic.gov-jobs.offered.clerical.
  - gov.us.topic.gov-jobs.offered.engineering.
  - gov.us.topic.gov-jobs.offered.foreign.
  - gov.us.topic.gov-jobs.offered.health.
  - gov.us.topic.gov-jobs.offered.law-enforce.
  - gov.us.topic.gov-jobs.offered.math-comp.
  - gov.us.topic.gov-jobs.offered.misc.
  - gov.us.topic.gov-jobs.offered.questions.
  - gov.us.topic.gov-jobs.offered.science.
  - gov.us.topic.gov-jobs.offered.technical.

- computer.jobs. The computer hierarchy is not universally recognized.
    - computer.jobs.contract.
- jobs.offered. The jobs hierarchy is not universally recognized. It appears to be a mirror of misc.jobs.offered.
- prg.jobs. Programming jobs (not universally accepted).
- us.jobs. Full U.S. geographic coverage (not universally accepted).
    - us.jobs.offered.
    - us.jobs.contract.
    - us.jobs.misc.

If and when your search leads to a job posting that interests you, you should then check out the employer behind it. The next chapter should supply the tools you will need.

CHAPTER 12

Corporate-Information Sites

Getting a job typically involves approaching a corporation. But if you are sitting at home thinking it might be nice to work for a particular firm, you need to figure out how to reach that firm. Having done that, you may begin wondering if the company is going to be around next year or if there is a healthier company in the same field that you might feel more confident working for. Or maybe you want to work in some other industry. Or maybe you've found an employer you want to work for but are confused about its location. Or maybe you're totally mystified about where to start.

The Web has answers. This chapter will look at the following:

- Sources of corporate information.
- Big-picture sources.
- Map services.
- When all else fails.

What you'll find there is data. Turning data into information, refining the information into knowledge, and distilling knowledge into wisdom is up to you.

Sources of Corporate Information

You're in luck—there are plenty of sources of corporate information on the Web. You can find numbers, names, and addresses in moments. With a little digging, you can cut straight to the dirt on a company. If its auditors have reservations about its practices or future, you can read their actual words (see Figure 12.1). If it's been the laughingstock of the business press, you can gauge the currents of vituperation yourself.

But remember two things: First, don't rely solely on what you see on the Web. It's yesterday's news, or worse. Let's just say that if you could read it in the library, some of it would smell pretty musty. For critical points of information,

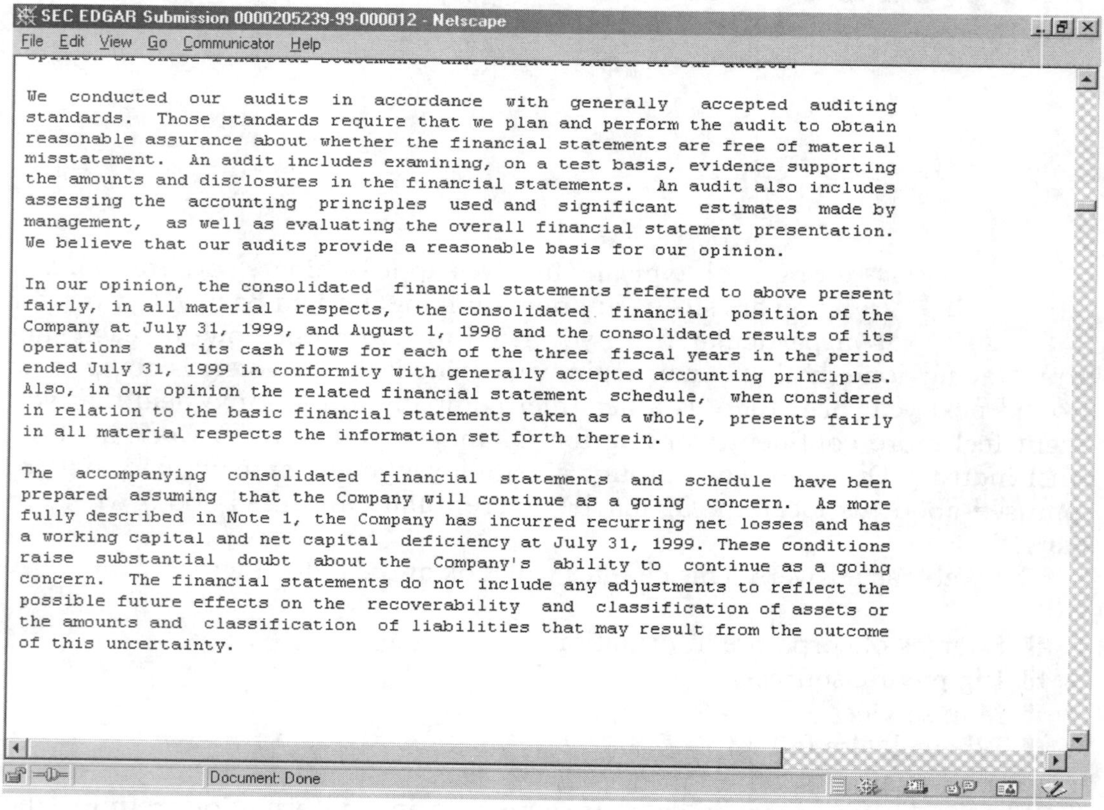
SEC EDGAR Submission 0000205239-99-000012 - Netscape

We conducted our audits in accordance with generally accepted auditing standards. Those standards require that we plan and perform the audit to obtain reasonable assurance about whether the financial statements are free of material misstatement. An audit includes examining, on a test basis, evidence supporting the amounts and disclosures in the financial statements. An audit also includes assessing the accounting principles used and significant estimates made by management, as well as evaluating the overall financial statement presentation. We believe that our audits provide a reasonable basis for our opinion.

In our opinion, the consolidated financial statements referred to above present fairly, in all material respects, the consolidated financial position of the Company at July 31, 1999, and August 1, 1998 and the consolidated results of its operations and its cash flows for each of the three fiscal years in the period ended July 31, 1999 in conformity with generally accepted accounting principles. Also, in our opinion the related financial statement schedule, when considered in relation to the basic financial statements taken as a whole, presents fairly in all material respects the information set forth therein.

The accompanying consolidated financial statements and schedule have been prepared assuming that the Company will continue as a going concern. As more fully described in Note 1, the Company has incurred recurring net losses and has a working capital and net capital deficiency at July 31, 1999. These conditions raise substantial doubt about the Company's ability to continue as a going concern. The financial statements do not include any adjustments to reflect the possible future effects on the recoverability and classification of assets or the amounts and classification of liabilities that may result from the outcome of this uncertainty.

Document: Done

Figure 12.1 *Actual text of an unfavorable auditor's report, from a 10-K report (annual report) on the Web site of the U.S. Securities and Exchange Commission (SEC) at www.sec.gov/edgar/searchedgar/formpick.htm.*

such as the name of an executive you wish to contact, always call in and get confirmation. People come and go. Offices relocate. Firms are divested and spun off. Data entry clerks write "Lloyd" when the guy's name is really "Floyd." And so on.

Second, don't assume that you can get what you need from corporate Web sites. If you want information about X Corporation, you may think that you can just go to www.x-corporation.com and find every piece of information you could ever think of needing about the firm from to its extensive, richly detailed, and constantly updated Web site. Think again. What you often find is a glorified billboard, with pictures of smiling models flanked by columns of textual pabulum that leave you wondering what the company actually does for a living. Sometimes, you're lucky to find an address and phone number. Even if the site does make an effort to be informative and complete, you're not going to find the straight dope about its prospects or its situation in its market niche. All you'll see is party-line blather. (However, the use of the word *challenges* is often a euphemism for *impending disaster*.)

Fortunately, plenty of third-party sites are eager to fill the vacuum with real information. The following sites are available for nothing (although they may offer fee-based services as well), and their inclusion does not constitute an endorsement. Even if they offer only a single paragraph of nitty-gritty, that's better than reams of puff.

http://www.yahoo.com

Running a search for a corporate name from the opening page of Yahoo! will often locate the URL of the firm's Web site for you. But not always; a company has to register with Yahoo! to be on Yahoo!, and there are always people who don't bother. If you do find the site of the corporation in question, keep in mind the warnings previously given.

But you may not need to. For larger corporations, Yahoo! also has its own corporate profiles. When you call up the company name, you get a link to its corporate Web site and the sites of its subsidiaries, but this page also contains a description of the corporation, a stock-price chart, and links to recent news stories about it. And, if you click the Company Profile link, you'll get a page with its address and other contact and ownership information, a business summary, a financial summary, and (if you scroll down) a list of officers and a chart of financial statistics.

Clicking the Research link will get you a list chart of its stock-price history and a score of how many brokers are recommending buy, hold, or sell. Clicking the Chart link will bring up stock-price history charts that you can customize. The News link will bring up recent news stories concerning the company, and the Quote link will get you the stock price current to within 15 minutes. There's also a message board, to discuss the company or anything else with anyone else who wanders in, under the Msgs link.

http://www.hoovers.com

"'Hoover's Online: The Business Network' was built to serve the needs of people behind desks," says hoovers.com of itself. The business-information site (operating out of Austin, Texas) offers a pithy one-sentence blurb (comparable to the one just quoted) for about sixteen thousand companies, usually followed by a couple of paragraphs of description. Also included are columns of data, including contact information, officers, stock-price information, financial history, links to news items, links to press releases of the company in question, links to the firm's home page and U.S. Securities and Exchange (SEC) filings, links to sources of industry newsletters, and even links to the entries of major competitors.

And that's just what's available gratis. For a subscription of $199.95 per year, you can get more detailed information, a longer list of officers, more competitors, downloaded financial charts, and more. All that is probably great if you want to try your hand at day trading, but a job seeker will probably be satisfied with the free material, especially the capsule descriptions and contact information.

Hoovers stands out by making an effort to follow both private and public companies. The financial figures for private companies may be educated guesses, but at least the contact information is readily available.

It also has a Career Development section, which has links to a Job Bank, a Training Center, a Salary Calculator, trade-show listings, and industry snapshots.

The Job Bank searches more than three hundred job sites, by industry, state, and keyword. The Training Center includes links to training material you can buy on various topics, from the use of specific office software to management-related topics. There is also a list of the top employers in the 14 largest cities in the United States.

The Industry Snapshots section is also of interest to job seekers because it lists the companies in a particular industry (at least it lists the companies that Hoovers follows) and a profile of the industry itself. It may include links to glossaries of the terms used in that industry and lists of things like the latest initial public stock offerings (IPOs), magazines that follow that industry, trade shows, and other industry events.

Job seekers in the information technology field who wish to avoid dead ends will not want to miss Hoovers' "Dot-Com Death Watch List," with two separate charts of troubled Internet companies, one listing dot coms that have announced layoffs and the other listing dot coms who have entered eternal repose. (Click on the News Center tab to reach it.)

http://www.fuckedcompany.com

What's an epithet or two when you need to keep up with who's who (and who's doing what to whom) in the hubris-ridden dot-com world? The moderator of www.fuckedcompany.com, "pud," tracks news and, especially, gossip about which firms are about to fall victim to their own intoxication with business buzzwords and their ignorance of practical business knowledge. (At least, that was the case at this writing. Surely, at some point, time will have swept away the debris left by the dot-com gold rush of the late 1990s, and the people who congregate at this site will have to return to their families and/or loved ones.) As for the nature of the contents of this site, let's just say that if you use "nanny" software to protect your children from certain aspects of the Internet, make sure it filters out this site, too.

http://www.sec.gov/edgar/searchedgar/formpick.htm

The only site that approaches the previous site in terms of brutal honesty is www.sec.gov/edgar/searchedgar/formpick.htm, the search engine of EDGAR (the Electronic Data Gathering, Analysis, and Retrieval service) of the SEC. The epithets are absent, however, because the material is written by corporate lawyers and accountants.

Of interest to job seekers here are the annual reports, called 10-K forms. (There are also shorter quarterly reports called 10-Q, as well as forms for things like stock offers that will be of interest mostly to investors.) Publicly owned firms with more than $10 million in assets and more than five hundred investors are required to file 10-K forms. These are not the same as the slick, printed annual reports you get in the mail, with their charts and smiling models. The 10-K lists specific information, including financial histories and operating results, which are mandated by the SEC. The annual report may have much the same information, but it's in fine print in the back. The rest is devoted to trumpeting the wonders of the company and the wisdom and farsightedness of its management.

The 10-K, however, will include information like the executives' salaries and other perks they are getting, any special deals they have been offered, and any family or nonobvious relationships between them and their suppliers and contractors. Not only is there the usual financial results, but you can find a discussion of those results with realistic appraisal of future expectations. If the auditors think the company is doomed, their words are right there. All this honesty is mandated by the SEC, and enforced by the constant threat of stockholder lawsuits. Plus, the usual contact information is included.

The 10-K is usually offered in either ASCII or HTML versions. If a PDF version is also offered, it may actually be an electronic version of the firm's slick annual report. Because using the ASCII or HTML version is fast and reliable, it is probably best to avoid the PDF version.

Basically, all you have to do is load the ASCII or HTML version and then use your browser search-in-page facility to find what you need on the page, such as "address" or "compensation."

To use the site, just go to EDGAR's search engine URL. Go to the middle of the page where it says "Enter a company," and don't worry about anything else. Type the name and click on "Submit Choices." You'll then get a screen listing all the SEC forms on file from companies whose name contains the text you input, sorted by form type and data. Find the correct company and click on the most recent 10-K.

http://www.annualreportservice.com

If annual reports are what you crave, www.annualreportservice.com collects and lists links to online corporate annual reports. Remember, these are annual reports, not 10-K forms, and are usually found somewhere deep in each corporation's Web site. In some cases, it is also possible to order a hard copy of the report.

http://www.prnewswire.com

For the polar opposite of the previous two sites, there's the PR Newswire site at www.prnewswire.com, containing press releases put out by corporations that use it. Using the search facility, you can find an archive of every press release they have put out since they began using the service. Yes, it's mostly self-congratulatory blather, but you can determine in advance whatever it is that they consider a big deal by noting the press releases they bothered to put out. The announcement themselves often include contact information in the text, albeit mostly for their PR and investor relations departments.

The same press releases are often posted on the corporation's Web sites as well, but at this site you can flip over to another company's press releases and compare them. Some companies also post financial information, annual reports, stock charts, and similar information here.

http://www.businesswire.com

The Business Wire site at www.businesswire.com also carries press releases from corporations. On the opening page, you can find a link to a Company News Archive and then search by name. You get a listing of all the firm's announcements (if it uses Business Wire) by category, such as earnings reports, management changes, and product announcements. There may also be links to its Web site, its SEC filings, its Hoovers listing, stock quotes, and stock-price history chart.

http://www.individual.com

The site at www.individual.com lets you categorize the news you want to review, by topic (1,500 topics are predefined) or by company name. The resulting news stories, culled from about forty different news services, can be sent to you by e-mail. The service is free. This could be a good tool for following developments in a particular niche. As a tool to stay generally informed, it has a flaw: You're only looking at whatever you're already looking at.

http://www.companysleuth.com

The site at www.companysleuth.com is similar to the previous one but concentrates on corporate and financial news. Free, customized information on companies you select is sent to you as daily e-mail. It combs not only SEC filings but also patent and trademark filings, message boards, and other niches on the Web. Of course, it has the same drawback—you are only seeing what you have chosen to look at.

http://www.superpages.gte.net

This "phonebook" site at www.superpages.gte.net lets you search for businesses nationwide, by name and by phone number. You can also do the same for residential numbers, nationwide.

http://www.thomasregister.com

You may have seen the 14-volume Thomas Register in the library. Well, now you can access its contents at www.thomasregister.com for free. You can search by corporate name, brand name, or product description and get the company's headquarters address and phone number.

http://www.corporateinformation.com

The Corporate Information site at www.corporateinformation.com boasts links to more than three hundred fifty thousand company profiles, but a search will produce links to corporate profiles and research reports from about two dozen different sources. Some are purely stock-price charts, but others include contact information.

http://www.zdnet.com/companyfinder

The ZDNet company finder does just that—find companies. But they have to be technology companies. You can also search for companies by product category or browse alphabetically. When you find a firm, you are given a page with the contact information, as well as links to that corporation's Web sites and possibly to product reviews and sources of corporate news.

http://www.wsrn.com

The Wall Street Research Net site at www/wsrn.com lets you search for a company name and then presents a full page of material, including financial history, recent announcements, earnings estimates, links to its Web page, and SEC filings. The last two items should have that contact information that you're looking for.

The Big Picture

Instead of moiling around in detail, maybe you think you should stand back and examine the big picture. That's what executives do, anyway—get the big picture and then "do the vision thing." Having the big picture, plus about twenty-five years of successful business experience, will make you attractive to headhunters. I can't help you with the twenty-five years of experience, but below are some Web sites that would be good jumping-off spots for the big picture.

http://www.hoovers.com/company/lists_best

Who are the *Fortune* 500? What's the best place to work? The worst? Who are the richest people? Which were the greatest pop songs? Who has been laying off recently? How does a particular college rate? Who has the most patents? Who gives the most to charity?

You can find that and much, much more in this List of Lists maintained by Hoovers, at www.hoovers.com/company/lists_best. It links you to lists maintained by various magazines and organizations. There are three sections: The Best, The Biggest, and The Emerging (the latter covers fastest-growing companies and industries, etc.).

http://www.ceoexpress.com

CEO Express's opening page at www.ceoexpress.com contains no news itself, but it offers a dense list of news sources, especially corporate and business news. There are also links to online newspapers, business magazines, lifestyle magazine, financial reports, and more. Don't miss the airport delay reports and the business travel advisories. And who could forget the National Buoy Data Center?

Map Services

Why worry about getting lost on the way to an interview when you can get a detailed map of the location of nearly any street address in the country? As long as the interview is not being held at a post office box number, one of these services can get you a map of the locale, and perhaps even verbal driving instructions. (If none of these services can find the address, perhaps warning bells ought to chime in your head.)

http://www.mapquest.com

At www.mapquest you can even download the maps to a Palm. There are also driving directions and a road-trip planner.

http://www.mapblast.com

The service at www.mapblast.com is similar to www.mapquest.com, except it will also add fast-food restaurants to your map.

http://maps.yahoo.com

The map section of the Yahoo! service, at maps.yahoo.com, will not only give you driving directions but will find a local business, such as hotels and restaurants, in the vicinity of the address (with straight-line distances, in miles) and give you a map of that place, too.

When All Else Fails

There are major corporations that think that their Web site should be a sort of static billboard to be displayed to passive Web surfers, offering a distillation of the firm's media imagery and messages. In other words, when you dig into it, you find no useful information—certainly nothing as mundane as an address and phone number. Perhaps being on the Web means that you must pretend to have severed all ties with bodily reality, especially the kind where real people gather in an office.

The Web's powers that be suffer no such delusion and require that Web sites be registered by a real person. Sitting at your desk, you can get right to the resulting registration data, at a registrar site like the following ones. (There are others.)

http://www.networksolutions.com/cgi-bin/whois/whois

Network Solutions offers a "whois" site at www.networksolutions.com/cgi-bin/whois/whois. You can input a domain name and see who it was registered to—as well as the registrant's address and phone number. You can also put in a name and see all the registrations that use that name. And you can put in a person's name and see all the commercial e-mail accounts that are in his or her name.

Remember, when the site asks for a domain name, you should drop the "www," if present. In other words, www.wiley.com becomes wiley.com. You could also just put in (as shown by the pages direction) "name wiley" to see all the other registered domains with "wiley" in it.

http://www.allwhois.com

The Web site www.allwhois.com specializes in international domain "whois" data.

CHAPTER 13

What Comes Next?

You did everything—self-assessed, wrote a riveting resume, mastered job sites and newsgroups, exchanged e-mail, and so on. And then it happened: someone expressed interest in you.

But they didn't offer you a job. They offered you an interview.

Suddenly, the online world must give way to the off-line world. Forget how good your resume looks. What matters now is how good you look. Essentially, there are more ways to blow things off-line than online. To reduce the likelihood of that happening, this chapter addresses the following:

- *First contact.* Good first impressions are vital.
- *Types of interviews.* After first contact, the situation should develop into an interview. There are several patterns you can expect.
- *Questions to expect.* There will be chitchat, but there will also be make-or-break questions for which you must have ready answers.
- *Illegal questions.* There are things they can't ask about, but lightning will not strike them if they do, especially because the issue is fraught with gray areas.
- *Interview no-nos.* Too bad there's no *Funniest Interview Video*s television program.

- *The morning after.* Proper follow-up can separate the employed from the unemployed.
- *The second interview.* No, you don't have it made yet.
- *Establishing rapport.* You can't hypnotize them into giving you a job, but there are subtle techniques you can use to make it more likely that they'll accept you.
- *The corporate zoo.* While establishing rapport, you also have to be mindful of whom you're dealing with—and reading their ID badges is not enough.
- *Salary negotiations.* Don't seem too eager—or too passive.

Okay, you've downloaded a map to the interview site. You've got everything planned. Now it's time to turn off the computer and do some real work.

First Contact

How you speak is more important than what you say. And your demeanor and posture can be more important than how you speak. After all, if the interviewer decides at a glance that you're a unwashed slacker and thus unfit for the job, any sparkling wit and vast knowledge you display in the following minutes may be too little, too late.

The "Establishing Rapport" section gets into a detailed description of how to make the interviewer comfortable by building rapport. But the techniques presented there have to build on a good first impression. For a good first impression, display the following:

- *Good posture.* Act like you are happy to be there.
- *Firm handshake.* Don't extend a limp hand that communicates an inner cringe. Don't pump like an oil derrick, either.
- *Conservative dress.* You want them to remember you, not your outfit.
- *Calm demeanor.* Don't avoid eye contact. Don't fidget or slouch, do untoward things with your hands, gesture wildly, or compulsively jingle the keys in your pocket, and so on.
- *Appropriate hygiene.* Everything your mother said is true.
- *Looking alive.* There was a headhunter in the 1960s who said he deliberately interviewed clients with them facing his window overlooking New York City's skyscraper canyons. He wanted to see if the candidates at least acknowledged the view. But there were always some who acted like the window did not exist. Those he struck from the list.

Types of Interviews

This section describes the main types of interviews you can expect to encounter. But in all of these, remember that the interview is not the place for salary negotiation. Avoid talking directly about how much the job pays. They are supposed to offer you money; you are not supposed to ask for money. If someone does ask you about your "salary requirements," say something about how you are confident that you are worth as much as any top candidate in the field.

As for what salary you might reasonably expect, you should have researched that topic before agreeing to the interview (see Chapter 4). If you were not able to do that research, so be it—but don't try to do it during the course of the interview.

In a screening interview, however, the interviewer may be required to fill in the answer with a number. Here you must be careful, since if you ask for too much you may be cut from further consideration. Instead, give a broad range. Of course, to do that you have to have some range of salary expectations.

That said, here are the various kinds of interviews in common use.

Screening Interview

The screening interview is a simple interview to determine if you should go on to the next step in the hiring process. It may be done over the phone, or it may be done at a table in a large room with other prospects lined up behind you. Interviewers in this type are probably just going through a checklist. In fact, they may know less about the job than you do and may be stumbling through terminology that they don't understand. There is no point in establishing rapport, but you do want to respond in a clear, confident manner that assures them that you meet the job requirements. But having answered a question, do not volunteer additional information because you risk confusing them. Anyway, they are looking for excuses to weed you out, and the sad truth is that anything you say could be used against you.

If you anticipate a telephone screening interview, keep your resume by the phone so you can answer immediately and precisely. But if you are caught unprepared or busy, it is legitimate to ask them to call back at another time. At that time, be sitting down in a quiet place, with the materials you need. In other words, treat it like a serious task.

Standard One-on-One Interview

After it has been established that you look hirable on paper, you may have a one-on-one interview with a middle manager to see what you are like in person, what you might be like to work with, if your skills really match what the organization does, and if you would fit in with the rest of the employees. You need to establish rapport (see the "Establishing Rapport" section) and be ready with answers to common interview questions (see the "Questions to Expect" section).

The Stress Interview

The stress interview is a variant on the one-on-one interview, with twists designed to see how you function under pressure. They may mock you, argue with you, respond sarcastically, or make dismissive comments. The interviewer may suddenly break off and just look at you silently, waiting for you to say something. Do not take any of this personally and do not act offended. Continue answering thoughtfully. Worse than breaking down, however, would be to continue droning on without noticing the interviewer's performance.

Lunch Interview

You may be taken to lunch if the organization has decided to take you seriously or simply because the interviewer is hungry. Either way, it is still an interview and all the rules still apply. Do not let your guard down.

Do not set out to feast on the interviewer's expense account. In fact, you should probably eat lightly, consuming only enough to demonstrate that you are not anorexic. Establish what the interviewer plans to order, and then order something in the same price range. Likewise, follow the interviewer's lead in terms of etiquette. But it is hard to say what to do if the interviewer orders alcohol. If you don't drink, you should just say that: it's pretty certain that you would not be the first person to ever say that to the interviewer. Otherwise, you might want to consider a famous clause in an old IBM sales manual: The customer must not be forced to drink alone.

There's an old legend about Thomas Edison and how he would take applicants to lunch and then watch to see if they salted their food before tasting it. He would not hire anyone who did, assuming that they would not make good researchers. The story is probably just a myth—but do keep it in mind. It may help you to remember to watch your behavior. Eating is a very primal activity, and you are quite likely to forget yourself while doing it.

The Case Interview

You may be asked about how you would handle a certain situation. This could happen in any type of interview, but the interviewers may also give you actual material to work on at a desk. If it is part of an interview, they will be more interested in your thought processes than in the answer. In the latter case, they will want to see actual professional output.

Video Interview

For a video interview, you will be asked to stand in front of a video camera and talk for a few minutes on a topic they gave you moments before, such as "the hardest thing I ever did." Tapes will be compared later by the hiring committee. If you are disorganized, inarticulate or rattled, it will show. Be confident, friendly, and organized, and don't be rattled if you stumble—just press on. If you are too shy to allow yourself to be videoed, then you have self-selected out.

The Group Presentation

You may be asked to speak to a group, usually of potential fellow employees. (They may also meet you in a series of one-on-one meetings.) They will later compare notes. With the group meeting, it is best to just appear relaxed and friendly. With the one-on-one meetings, rapport takes precedence because the questions could be about anything.

The Group Interview

Candidates may be asked to attend a meeting and discuss a topic. The interviewer will be looking for the candidates with the most effective interpersonal style—leadership, in other words. Even if you were never head of the football team, don't despair; leadership is actually a situational thing. Just don't be a wallflower and hope for the best. (If you are a wallflower, and the job calls for a politician, you probably don't want the job anyway.)

The Committee Interview

The committee interview is a formal version of the peer group interview. Instead of meeting with whatever employees happen to be available, you meet with an appointed hiring committee. You can establish rapport mostly by being relaxed and friendly. However, when answering a question, speak directly to the person who asked it. Do not try to declaim to the entire committee, like a lawyer addressing a jury. Each person of the committee will probably have pet questions. If the committee members appear friendly to each other, you can be open with your answers. If you see that they are disagreeing with each other, do not volunteer extra information. That way, your answers to one member's questions are less likely to tread on the toes of another member.

Questions to Expect

You can expect certain questions to recur, and you'll do better if you have an answer in mind. Certainly, you don't want to be reduced to stammering amazement by a question you haven't thought of before. Some of these questions require a serious decision on your part, which is best made in advance.

What Do You Think Your Weaknesses Are?

When interviewers ask you about your weaknesses, they want to hear about something related to the skills needed for the job, not something your enemies would say about your character flaws. Mention an area where you reasonably feel you need more training and experience but for which you are either on track to get the training or getting this job would supply the experience. But make it an area that is somewhat peripheral to the job in question—don't fault your "basic people skills" if it's a sales job. Instead, talk about your "prospecting skills."

Tell Me About Yourself

The "tell me about yourself" question can be surprisingly tough. But remember, they don't want to hear a rambling version of *War and Peace*. Come up with a one-minute spiel (or two pages, double-space, maximum) about who you are, how you got here, and how that makes you a good job candidate. Don't memorize it—the act of preparing it ought to be enough for you to remember the main points. The basic subject matter is, after all, well known to you.

Give Me an Example of . . .

Questions that begin with "Give me an example of" come up in "behavior-based interviews," which are all the rage these days. The idea is to ask questions that bring to the surface patterns of accomplishment in the prospect's background that are relevant to the job in question. After all, the reasoning goes, how the candidate responded to a situation in the past is the best predictor of how that person will respond to that same situation in the future. Unfortunately, there are infinite possible situations, both in the prospect's past and in the prospective job's future, so such questions can be both unpredictable and vague. But the vagueness also means that you should be able to fit the answer around some achievement that you'd like to point to.

Why Should We Hire You?

Why should they hire you? Because you can do the job, as indicated by your knowledge, experience, and skills. Don't bring anything monetary into it, like "minimal relocation expenses." That's probably not their concern.

Why Are You Leaving Your Present Job?

When you are asked why you are leaving your current job, the best answer is "I no longer see any future there." If the news has been filled with coverage of your present employer's financial problems, the interviewers may be satisfied. Otherwise, they may want to hear why you see no future there, and you will need a ready answer that you are comfortable with. Just don't go on at length about how the deep personality flaws of your coworkers and bosses made it impossible to be productive. If there actually are any emotional tinges to your reasons for departure, you may want to rehearse your answer with uninterested third parties until you arrive at something they think is businesslike, straightforward, and concise.

If interviewers ask deeper questions about your old firm, just say it "afforded many fine growth experiences." The subtext is that you won't gossip or bad-mouth your old job—and that you won't gossip about or bad-mouth this job, either, after you move on.

(I was once visiting my alma mater and got into a deep discussion with a former teacher about my then-job. He asked detailed questions, so I named names and told exactly what I thought about everyone there. Two weeks later, my company announced the hiring of a new boss—him. I about swallowed my eyeteeth. There's a moral there, somewhere.)

What Do You Hope for in This Job?

When the interviewer asks what you want from this job, mention personal and professional satisfaction and growth, wider experience, excitement, fulfillment, recognition, the pride that would come from being associated with this employer—anything but money. (Remember, the interviewer probably has no control over how much the job pays.)

How Long Do You Think It Would Take You to Be Productive?

Don't pretend that you will have no learning curve. When they ask how long it will be before you can get up to speed, give an answer that shows you have an intelligent appreciation of the situation. And that appreciation may involve the realization that these people have no internal training resources, or they would not be asking the question.

How Long Do You Plan to Stay with This Firm?

How long will you stay? For as long as you continuing to feel that you are making a meaningful contribution. Don't let on that this is just a stepping stone or resume stuffer. (If it is the kind of job that no one keeps for more than two years, you don't have to bring it up—they already know it.)

What Can You Do for Us (That Someone Else Can't)?

When they ask how you would be better for them than someone else, mention how your experience has involved solving problems similar to those likely to be encountered with the job in question. Don't pretend to be unique: just talk about how you yourself are fitted for the job.

What About This Gap in Your Resume?

You doubtless have something in your past that you don't want them to ask about. But whatever it is, it is probably not as bad as what they might imagine. (For all they know, you were in jail.) It is up to you to figure out what you don't want them to ask about—and then to compose an answer. Be as truthful as you feel you can, don't whine or blame others, but most especially, keep it brief. It's in the past, and you want to focus on the present. In the end, you may find that they really aren't very interested, assuming it's not something that would automatically disqualify you.

What Do You See Yourself Doing in This Job?

"Doing what I'm told," is not the right answer when they ask what you see yourself doing at this job. Instead, talk about the problems you will likely face and how you expect to solve them.

How Much Money Did You Make in Your Old Job?

Yes, how much you are making comes up. It's best to give the figure—but then qualify it. You must explain that this figure does not represent your true worth at the moment. Instead, it reflects the pay scale in force when you were hired, with the level of experience you had when you started the job. It does not reflect your level of experience today.

If that answer does not sound like it's on target with your situation, try these qualifiers for size:

- You were only recently officially promoted to this position. Of course, before the official promotion, you had performed many of the same job functions.
- The dire financial condition of your previous employer forced them to cap salaries and raises or prevented performance reviews from taking place or being acted on.
- It was a small company.
- For family reasons, you had accepted a job with fewer responsibilities.
- The cash salary you received did not reflect the numerous job benefits, such as stock options, telecommuting, a car, subsidized housing, shares of a beach house, wine-and-cheese lunches, and so on.
- The job was in a labor-intensive and therefore low-paying industry. But you feel you have gained enough experience to move on.
- It was a starter job in this industry, but you feel that you have gained enough experience to move on.

Can You Relocate?

If you live in one city and are applying for a job in another, the subtext to the question "Can you relocate?" is whether you are willing to relocate to another city if they ever want to transfer you but your spouse already has a job in this one.

You really do need to talk about this issue with your working spouse, should you have one. Going on the road to promote the career of one partner while the other plays second fiddle can tear marriages apart. But if you feel any anxiety about this issue, a job interview is not the place to confront it for the first time. Just say that you and your significant other are aware of this issue and can deal with it. Outside the interview, however, make sure that you do deal with it.

Tell Me About a Project You Worked on That Failed

It's assumed that you have already touted your successes. When they ask you for an example of a failure, be honest, but remember that what they want to hear about is what you learned from it. So don't dredge up any total defeats. Instead, talk about roadblocks that you managed to get around.

Why Do You Want to Work for This Company?

"You have a job and I need one," doesn't cut it as an answer to "Why do you want to work here?" Nor should it—there are doubtless other places with openings out there. So why did you apply to this one? You did have a reason, didn't you? This is your chance to show that you know something about the company, but you don't have to get carried away. "I've always been fascinated by the injection molding industry" is fine—if it's true. Something like, "I want to live in the mountains" is fine, too—they know what the view is like outside the window.

Is There Some Reason You Could Not Work Overtime on a Regular Basis?

When interviewers ask about your willingness to work regular overtime, what they really want to ask is, "Are you going to put your family life ahead of your job?" But they don't dare. The trick is not to react with dismay. Shrug, and say that it was never an issue at your old job. But if you are seeking a profamily environment, you now know that these people are manifestly antifamily.

Where Do You See Yourself in Five Years?

You don't have to say that you intend to stay with the company forever when the interviewer asks the "Where do you see yourself in five years" question. Give an answer that shows you have put some thought into your career goals.

What Are the Major Trends You See in Our Industry?

When they ask you to name the major trends in their industry, they just want to see that you are in touch with the situation. So just mention some trends without going into detailed narratives.

What Do You Do in Your Spare Time?

Interviewers may ask you how you spend your free time. They may also ask what books you have read recently, what magazines you subscribe to, what sports you follow or play, what kind of hobbies you have, and so on. Usually, they are not looking for a particular book, magazine, sport, or hobby that is a prerequisite for the job. Instead, they want some indication that you have a balanced life. But there are exceptions—for instance, if the job involves promoting a basketball team, you probably want to be able to point to some interest in that sport.

Are You Physically Able to Perform the Job's Essential Functions? Can You Perform Them with Reasonable Accommodations?

If they ask you whether you are physically able to perform the job, they need to have a written list of the physical demands of the job's functions.

Have You Ever Been Convicted of a Crime?

If they ask whether you have ever been convicted of a crime, remember that being arrested is not enough—you have to have been convicted. If you have been convicted, you need to be able to talk calmly about the irrelevance of the incident in terms of the job in question. Emphasize that the past is the past. Don't dwell on the actual incident; doing so might tell them that you are still obsessed with whatever got you in trouble. And if you don't go into it, there is a chance they won't go into it either.

Can You Show Proof of Eligibility to Work in the United States?

You probably won't have to display the papers showing elegibility to work in the United States until you are signed up.

Is There Anything You'd Like to Ask?

When they ask if you have any questions, don't just shrug or indicate a desire to bolt from the room. Ask particulars about the job in question, any associated career-path questions, whether there is a probationary period, and any suggestions for preparation. In other words, ask what you think you would need to know if you were actually going to get the job—just don't ask about money.

Be sure and ask, "What is the hardest thing that new hires encounter?" They'll hear it as an intelligent question, rather than an admission of fear. But if they can't answer the question, you might want to reconsider what you're getting into.

Illegal Questions

Interviewers cannot ask any personal questions that are not directly related to the demands of the job. Because such questions open the door to discrimination, an employer cannot (under federal regulations) ask about your race, color, national origin, religion, sex, age, or disability. Certain states add other topics, such as weight, height, and gender preference.

But you quickly get into gray areas. They can't ask if you are married or if that is your maiden name you are using, but they can ask if that is your full name or if you have used other names in the past. They cannot ask your age, but they can ask if you are of legal age. They cannot ask directly if you are disabled, but they can require a postoffer medical exam. They cannot ask if you take medication, but they can ask if you are taking illegal drugs. They cannot ask about your race, but they can ask you to fill out voluntary affirmative-action questionnaires. And so on. (Note that questions that are proscribed in preemployment interviews are standard on post-hiring insurance forms.)

Keep in mind that if you bring up a proscribed topic during an interview, the interviewer is then free to pursue the matter and discuss it with you.

Reacting negatively to a question that you feel is illegal will likely not win you any points, however, or get you the job as a sort of consolation prize. The trick, therefore, is to address the concern behind the question. If they ask if you plan to get pregnant soon, assure them that you are not there just to get health benefits and then quit after your paid maternity leave runs out. If they ask about your religion, respond that it won't get in the way of doing the job. If they ask about national origin, say that you have strong roots in this community. And so forth. Remember that they are asking questions to assure themselves that you will not be an additional headache.

Or they should be, anyway. If you decide that they are asking personal questions in pursuit of some social agenda, walk.

And yes, people have successfully sued employers who asked them illegal question and then did not hire them.

Interview No-Nos

Don't Show Up Late

Of course, you don't want to start off on the wrong foot by showing up late. But arriving grossly early is a problem as well because they will wonder if you don't have anything better to do and will feel uncomfortable with you sitting around. When in doubt, you should arrive in enough time to, yes, go to the restroom. This will give you a chance to make small talk with the receptionist. When you ask for the location of the facilities, you can also ask something like, "Lot of interviewing going on today?" The response you get might be worth hearing:

"Yeah, and whoever they hire will have a real mess to clean up." In the restroom, whatever else you do, wash your hands with warm water. That will counteract (long enough for a handshake, you hope) whatever off-putting physiological effects your nervousness has had on your extremities.

If you *are* late, don't mumble something about the confusing directions you got from the company, even if that is actually the case. Apologize profusely for wasting the interviewers' time. (Don't get carried away, though—they doubtless had something else to do in the meantime.) Blame yourself—say you misjudged the traffic, and then make a joke about it at your expense. That can lead into some chitchat and rapport building.

Don't Look Like You Just Got Out of Jail

Do look like you're a self-respecting person who pays some attention to your appearance. The interview should be important enough that you put some thought into what to wear, your hair, and so on. At least, the interviewer thinks so, so play along.

Don't Act Like You're About to Go to Jail

You are there because you want to be there. (Aren't you?) So act like it. Sit up. Pay attention. Maintain eye contact with the interviewer. Act like what is being said is important. (It is, if you want the job. If not, stay home.) The simple act of being attentive may cause the interviewer to go away with a positive impression of you.

Don't Show Up Stoned

Your responses should be organized, focused, and articulate. Don't ramble, natter, break off because you suddenly thought of something important about the world situation, or slur your words. They don't want to hire druggies, so don't give the impression that you are one. If you are one, there is something more important that you need to do before looking for a job—get clean.

Of course, nerves can tie the tongue of the most sober person. If stress has eroded your ability to sparkle, just look attentive and show that you are thinking carefully before answering. In response, they'll be sympathetic to any verbal gaffes. But remember—being too low-key can make it seem that you have no enthusiasm for the job. And if you just answer "yes" or "no" to every question, interviewers will get impression you are being evasive. Worse, they will learn nothing about you and will go away with a negative impression — assuming they even remember you.

You will also give the impression that your mind is elsewhere if you launch into a memorized speech. Certainly, the interviewers' mind will be elsewhere, wondering if the next candidate will be someone that they can actually talk to.

Don't Sound Like an Idiot

Show up with some background knowledge of the company and what it does, so you won't make bizarre comments: "You make movie trailers? I thought they were small enough to be sent by UPS." Remember, leaving a positive impression is not the same as causing them to collapse into laughter as soon as they get behind a closed door.

Also, don't address interviewers by first names. Keep things formal unless you see that doing so rubs them the wrong way. But whatever name you use, get it right.

Don't Boast

You may be totally convinced that you are the greatest thing on Earth in terms of this company's HR needs. But if you come out and tell them that, they won't believe it and will resent you for being an annoying boor. If later, they decide you were indeed perfect, they'll resent you even more for having obscured the issue with boorishness. Instead, you must lead them to an inner realization of your attributes by modestly describing your accomplishments and experiences until the picture is complete.

Even if they come out and ask, "Are you good at this?" you should not answer in kind. Instead, say, "Well, I was able to do this, that, and the other thing."

Having established your competence (however you do it), do not neglect to tie that competence to the company's needs. Having convinced them that you are an accomplished heavy-equipment salesperson, you then need to show how that indicates that you can handle the job of selling construction cranes.

Don't Take Constant Notes

In some settings, such as business-to-business sales calls, it is considered good practice to take notes. Doing so implies respect for the speaker's words and enhances the general atmosphere of acceptance that the salespeople are seeking. But such settings usually involve a group, one of whom takes notes while someone else does the talking. In a job interview setting, taking notes will make it impossible to maintain eye contact and remain attentive. There's no reason to get down every word, anyway.

Don't Beg

You may be desperate for a job, but that's not the interviewers' problem, and they will resent it if you try to make their problem. Like everyone else, interviewers already have their own problems, which take precedence over rescuing you from yours. Anyway, this is business, not social work. If they are going to give you a job, it will be because they need you to do something, not because you need work, or because they sympathize with you, or because they are somehow socially obligated to empower your need for self-validation.

Along the same lines, don't blurt out things like, "So, how am I doing?" or "You think you'll hire me?" This is not like figure skating in the Olympics, where each performance is immediately scored. And the interviewer will feel uncomfortable for being put on the spot.

Don't Make Salary Demands

(See "Salary Negotiations" later in this chapter.) The words "If you can't match $70,000, there's no sense going through with the interview" may be ringing in your head, but don't actually say them. If things fall through later because of an inadequate offer, at least you did not annoy them to their faces. And you might meet them again down the road, after they have switched jobs for a better salary, and you want things to be cordial then. For now, remember that the interviewer likely has no control over the salary offer—and probably also wants a raise. In addition, no one else may feel inclined to match your demands, leaving you painted into a corner.

Don't Bad-Mouth Anyone

Sure, your old boss was a posturing buffoon who fired you in a fit of rage when you would not go along with his plan to cut costs by canceling all trade magazine subscriptions, when they are free anyway. But a job interview is not a forum for you to vent. The job interview is about the next job, so don't poison it with rantings about the previous one. Certainly, you don't want to leave the impression that you are a whiner who thinks that throwing a tantrum is more important than getting a job. If the job is between you and one other applicant, who doesn't rant, guess who gets the job?

Of course, it may be that the unpleasantness at your previous job is unavoidable. You should consider adopting the Hollywood practice of icy euphemisms: "There were creative differences." If they press for specifics, give them sparingly, with obvious reluctance. Being adults, they'll get the picture. And they won't take away a picture of you whining.

Things You Should Never Do

The following represent real complaints from interviewers:

- Answer your cell phone.
- Make a call on your cell phone.
- Take off your shoes and socks and start medicating your feet.
- Bring a pet.
- Bring your children.
- Ask, "Are you married?"
- Leave suddenly while the interview is still in progress.
- Use profanity.
- Ask for a cigarette break.
- Apply makeup.
- Disappear into the bathroom.

The Morning After

During the course of the interview, you should have gotten the business card of the person leading the interviewing effort. If one was not offered, ask for it. (Never be shy in any setting about asking for a business card; they exist to be handed out.)

Armed with the business card, the next day sit down and write a thank-you note to that person.

Right now, of course, you are perhaps reacting with shock to the idea embodied in the previous sentence. If you are like most people these days, you've never done such a thing in your life. For occasions when you do want to observe social niceties, such as sending Christmas cards, sympathy cards, or thank-you cards for wedding presents, you buy a box of printed cards. If you are moved to action beyond that, you pick up the phone.

But even if the store does sell "thank you for a great interview" cards, don't buy any. Instead, get out a piece of paper and write "thank you for a great interview" on it, and express the hopes that you can work together some day.

This simple act will cause you to stand out like a lightbulb in a dark room. Just because no one does it does not mean there is some law against it or that they will see you as a throwback to the seventeenth century. Instead, they will see you as:

- Someone who is uniquely considerate and thoughtful.

- Someone who understands the importance of follow-through.
- Someone who possesses all-important written communication skills.
- Someone who has more to say.

Returning to that last point, doubtless, by the time you got home, you had turned the events of the interview over in your mind and were screaming to add something to what you said, or say something differently, or add emphasis to something, or take something back.

So, having spent paragraph one thanking the interviewer, you then go on to paragraph two and say something like, "I also wanted to add to what I said concerning my experience as a hacker in BASIC. By 'hacker,' of course I meant . . ." Then end the letter with another expression of thanks.

Your letter, like your demeanor during the interview, should be calm and friendly. If the interview convinced you that it would be a sunny day in the netherworld before they hire you, don't let on. Write a nice note anyway. You still want the interviewer to remember you in a good light because it is likely that your paths will cross again.

The Second Interview

If you are called back for a second interview, that means that the company has decided you are indeed qualified for the job. But that does not mean you can relax and just slide on through. During the second interview, you must be doubly careful about your demeanor because the intent of the second interview is to size you up as a person. They want to get an idea about how you will fit in the organization and perhaps compare you more closely to the other candidates who made the first cut.

Although establishing rapport is always a good idea, in the second interview it may be the deciding factor. Which brings up the next topic.

Establishing Rapport

Rapport is a fancy French word that means "a relation marked by harmony." In this setting, it means making the other person comfortable with your presence during the course of the interview. The interviewer *must* be comfortable in your presence. If he or she ends up feeling uneasy about you, you're likely to be dropped from the list with a thud. The interviewer will rationalize a reason for it later.

Trouble is, there is no sure way to make interviewers (or anyone else) comfortable in your presence—you can't reach into their heads and adjust the controls. What you can do, however, is make sure that you are not making them uncomfortable. Then you use some subtle techniques to build on that neutral setting to enhance their comfort level. The interviewer is probably not overtly hostile to you to begin with. Actually, you have many things in common, such as a desire to make a career in your particular industry. Therefore, you have every hope of being able to establish rapport with this person. Having felt rapport with you, the interviewer will be less likely to remember anything you said or did with unease. (But you can still blow it—rapport does not give you hypnotic control over the interviewer.)

Industrial sales reps face this problem every day—they must establish rapport before anyone will sit through a meeting with them, and it takes a bunch of meetings to make a sale. So they put serious study in establishing rapport. One of them told me that you can establish rapport with anyone in 60 seconds. I had felt well-disposed toward him initially, and there was some subtle thing about him that made him comfortable to talk to. So I believed him.

If, incidentally, you do encounter open hostility, remain cool and professional but wrap things up as quickly as you can and get out, taking solace from the fact that you have learned something important about that person. That happened to me one time—the interviewer would not even look at my resume. But the receptionist asked for it on the way out. Three days later, I had a job offer from them. I had passed the test. I hadn't wilted. But I found that the work atmosphere to be the same as the interview atmosphere.

The following are some techniques used by high-power sales reps. You, privileged reader, won't have to attend a seminar to learn them. On the other hand, an expert won't be at your side you coach you through intense, lengthy practice sessions.

Rapport techniques flow from your attitude toward people generally and will work better if you are basically a nice person who likes other people and is interested in talking to them. That's not to say that you need to remake your soul into the image of Dale Carnegie—but you probably won't go far wrong if you heed the following advice.

Match Them

People (healthy ones, anyway) love themselves. Become like them—enter their personal little world—and part of that self-love will rub off on you. (If they don't love themselves, then you don't want to work for them.)

Entering their personal world is as simple as realizing it exists, looking for it, defining it, and then paying respect to it. There is nothing diabolical about doing so—you're really just being consciously polite. Just note the various dimensions through which their world is expressed, the key elements of that expression, and adopt some of it yourself. (Or at least, do not exhibit discomfort at their expression.) These dimensions include the following:

Grooming. If even the vice presidents are wearing T-shirts and you show up dressed as if for the Academy Awards, rapport is not going to happen. If you are dressed in rags and they appear to be waiting for the photographer from *GQ* to show up, you may have trouble getting past the receptionist. Things are usually not so extreme, but if you have any doubt, you might call ahead and ask the receptionist about office attire standards there. Don't be shy—the receptionist will understand.

Speech patterns. As the interview gets underway, note the words, phrases, and intonations that mark the interviewer's speech. Try to weave some of them into your responses. A little of this goes a long way, so don't overdo it. If he or she is from Atlanta and you are from Boston, don't try to use "y'all" for the first time in your life—the strain will show.

Posture. As the interviewer talks, he or she will adopt one body position for a while and then shift to another. Note the initial posture. When the interviewer shifts position, wait for a few moments and then shift position, too—adopting his or her initial posture. During the course of the interview, continue mimicking the interviewer's posture, retaining a time delay so that what you are doing is not obvious.

Emotions. Show sympathy for the interviewer's opinions, although you don't have to pretend to adopt them.

Lifestyle. If there is a gym bag in the corner, mention your own love of exercise—or at least your desire to get some exercise, someday. If there are pictures of a family, mention your own family. Likewise if there are pictures of horses or cats, and so on. But don't put the interviewer on the spot by asking probing questions. That gym bag could have been gathering dust in the corner for two years, those family pictures could be from happier predivorce years, and the interviewer might be defensive about people making fun of the animal pictures. It is sufficient to make a passing reference that shows respect for the observable lifestyle. (One executive once mentioned to me that he rose every morning at three A.M. for iron-man triathlon training. I believe that my response was incoherent.)

Appetite. If you go to lunch, show interest in the interviewer's choice of food, even if you ordered something else.

Body form. Small people often unconsciously flinch at the approach of large people. If you are a large person and find yourself being interviewed by a small one, you need to shake hands from a distance by leaning forward to the point where you are looking at rather than down on the interviewer, and sit down immediately. Large men often end up adopting mannerisms intended to minimize the impact of their physical presence. For instance, they might make a point of tripping and dropping their things and then joke about themselves as they get on the floor to gather them up. Then they slide into the chair rather than standing all the way up.

Compliment Them without Unsettling Them

Saying complimentary things is a way to be remembered later in a positive light—but you have to do it so it won't fall flat or lead to an awkward moment while the interviewer sits there trying to figure out what you meant by that. Male business executives and male and female technical personnel are more geared to exchanging facts and figures than social graces. After groping for a moment to assign meaning to your words, they will find they have no easy, habitual, gracious response, and an awkward moment of embarrassment ensues. And later, they will remember feeling uneasy around you. If they are used to receiving compliments, the danger is that you will simply trigger their respond-to-sycophant behavior, and they will be dismissive when they remember you.

So you have to give the compliment in three steps:

1. State your compliment.
2. Explain why you are saying that.
3. Ask a question derived from the subject.

Instead of saying, "Golly, your science fiction show is great and I watch it all the time," you should say, "It's a great show. I like its faithful depiction of orbital mechanics. Do you have an astrophysicist on staff?"

By giving an explanation, you don't force the complimented person to grope for meaning. By asking the question, you are providing an easy way to respond, inviting them to talk about themselves. And people generally feel comfortable talking about themselves. And presumably, you have asked an intelligent question, which always puts you in a good light.

In addition, you should always have something gracious to say whenever you are complimented, even if the compliment is done awkwardly, without the three-step process.

Redirect Them without Confronting Them

There will be times when things are rolling out of control and the interviewer is talking about something tangential and seems to have forgotten you. People sometimes respond to familiar questions by launching canned spiels. Or you might bring up a topic that annoys the interviewer.

In these situations, you have to derail their playback mechanisms. You don't have to start taking your clothes off—a slight derailment will do. Once playback is interrupted, focus can return to you.

The trick is to interrupt by saying something that is not objectionable but that has nothing to do what was being talked about. Preferably, it should be from out of left field, so that the other person has no canned response. "Great tie tack. Did you get it overseas?"

Be Congruent

What you say must be congruent (match, align with, totally agree with) what you are thinking. How many times have you been watching the news and seen politicians saying something like, "Yes, I totally agree with the need for campaign fund-raising reform." Meanwhile, they're wincing, or shaking their heads, or avoiding eye contact with the reporter, or suddenly remembering an appointment, or angrily kicking someone out of the way, or doing something else that indicated that their words did not reflect their feelings at that moment.

You, meanwhile, are going to be in front of the interviewer for a lot longer than the duration of a network news sound bite. There will be something about your tone, your eyes, your posture that will tell them not to trust you. And they won't.

Life is short. Don't live a lie.

The Corporate Zoo

Establishing rapport is fine, but it amounts to unspoken communication. At some point, you will have to say something. At that moment, you should, like any performance artist, be aware of the makeup of your audience.

Basically, the corporate world is populated by line managers, staff managers, and worker bees. Line managers are responsible for a line in the organization's budget. Staff managers report to line managers and are responsible for projects and departments. Line managers spend the money (and approve hirings), usually on the recommendation of staff managers. Worker bees do as they are told.

But their behavior is more a result of their personality type than their functional position, although the personality type and the position often go together. (In a small or family business, however, they can be totally mismatched, sometimes horrifyingly so.) These personality types fall into several widely recognized subpopulations, and each requires special treatment.

Fire Breathers

People at the line manager or Chief Officer position (called "CXO level") are typically fire breathers. They value their time and are wary of being taken advantage of—which in your case means having their time wasted by dithering. They are numbers oriented rather than people oriented, although they won't admit that. They are also highly competitive. The best way to establish rapport is by not trying to establish any: Just state your business and get out. They will see you as appropriately businesslike rather than curt. They will interrupt you if they think you are getting too detailed or are digressing.

Anyone who reaches this position typically has an ego that is perceptible out in the hall. That makes them direct and to the point—but also, thankfully, decisive. Sound prepared. Don't ask questions whose answers are available someplace else. Don't ask questions or make statements in any way implying there is something at fault with the department's budget or policies—the fire breather probably established them.

If you find yourself in front of a fire breather, you were probably sent there by a staff manager who wants you hired and who wants basically to show that you don't have two heads. Keep the desk between you and the fire breather (remember, they really aren't people oriented) and look intelligent and honest. Never offer a resume—fire breathers will not admit that they have time to read it. That's what the staff is for.

Middle Managers

Middle managers are the staff managers and are much more people oriented than are the fire breathers. Rather than quantifiable results, they want to know how well you worked with so-and-so. And they want to hear you talk about it at length, not because they are probing you but because they crave social interaction. They're nice people. Just don't expect high levels of organization or assume that they remember what you just told them. In fact, it may be up to you to keep the interview focused. Basically, they have used their people skills to get comfortable staff jobs where they are not burdened by having any authority.

One result of their people orientation is that they need to trust you. You can satisfy this need by being open and friendly and remembering what they have to say. But because they are excitable, you need to watch out for misunderstandings.

Whereas you should be subdued with a fire breather, with a middle manager it helps to be colorful and lively. You can sit anywhere.

Occasionally, middle managers end up at the CXO level by accident. They may see the interview with you as a welcome relief from burdensome duties, so try to be entertaining.

Good Sams

Now you've reached the worker bees. Good Sams have probably been working hard and conscientiously at their jobs for at least 15 years, and the organization is not going to wreck everything by promoting them. But half the people you come across, of either gender, will be Good Sams—or should be, if the organization has any future.

Good Sams are team oriented at work and family oriented at home, so try to make some positive reference about your family or about how you enjoyed the team you worked with at your old job. They are also wary of change, and your presence indicates a pending change in the organization. So put the rapport building into high gear.

Stress the importance of reliability and loyalty, because Good Sams believe in those things. Also stress your past achievements. They will appreciate a well-done resume and will not be put off if it is thick. But (unlike the middle managers) they will warm to you slowly, so don't get personable too fast, and keep the desk between you and them. But if you feel nervous, also remember that Good Sams tend to be patient.

Quant Jocks

Quant jocks are the kind of people who go to great lengths to find out what the rules are so they can follow them. They are numbers oriented, wary of people, and highly critical. Because they are also critical of themselves, and fear making a mistake, they are slow to make decisions.

They will demand information and ask increasingly detailed questions to the point of weariness. No resume is too thick or too detailed. They may go through and edit it.

Stress your technical competence and training certificates. Keep the desk between you and a quant jock. But if you are being interviewed by a quant jock, it is probably because you are a quant jock as well, so the minimal necessary rapport should come naturally. If you are not, try not to be put off by their lack of social skills.

The Recalcitrants

The lower strata of worker bees is composed of people who resent having to be employed, resent having to come to work that morning, and certainly resent being pulled away from their reverie to participate in an interview with you. They may see your willing participation in the process as an act of collaboration with the boss's arbitrary, tyrannical regime. Their aspiration is to skate through to quitting time, and their career goal is to surround themselves with fellow members of a conspiracy of mutual inefficiency. Their input in the interview process will be pure lip service. (In fairness to them, there is a doubtless a role or job somewhere in which they would shine. They just don't happen to be in it.)

Even if you identify with them (you don't, do you?), there is no point in demonstrating the fact at this time; doing so won't change their behavior toward you and could alienate the other personality types (or at least endanger any rapport you've established). But you must not alienate them either; that could trigger unpredictable future problems if you do get the job. So remain polite and friendly, talk about sports, and tell jokes that have nothing to do with the job.

But if all the people you are put in front of look mostly at the floor, roll their eyes when you talk about the job, or exchange glances and smirks, and what they say about the job sounds clipped and listless, then you may be in trouble. You are not being seen by anyone with authority. You need to find who is in charge and get in front of that person. Don't worry about the recalcitrants—you won't alienate them by cutting short the meeting.

Salary Negotiations

Remember, discussion of salary should be avoided during the interview process. You are there to convince them that they want to hire you. Talk of money is a dangerous distraction.

Now, however, assume that you have made it through the interview process and that someone in HR has called you with a job offer, and mentions a specific salary or wage. You must respond.

Remember, that, you don't have to settle everything with the next breath you take. You can ask for time to study the issue and other offers, ask how to get back to them, and ask how soon they are hoping for an answer.

On the other hand, you should not keep going back asking for something else that you just thought of. You need to decide what the issues are and get everything on the table. Issues to be considered include the following:

More Money

Of course you want more money. But to robotically respond to an offer by asking for 15 percent more is not a tactic that will get you anything. Your response needs to be based on a belief that you are worth X. And your conviction that you are worth X is best fortified with research conducted in the real world—you'll have something to prop up your resolve, as well as something to point out to the HR department.

Salary research resources were covered in Chapter 4. Use them. Then, knowing what the range is in your industry and region for someone of your experience, you can go forth and ask for that. As for the intrinsic worth of the unique, wonderful human being that you are, forget it. Only market value counts, even when they are talking about you.

You'll hear some pundits say that if the company loves you, they will find a way to meet your demands. And you'll hear tales of negotiations collapsing over a surprisingly small gap between the bid and ask price. Both are true—but in the latter case, the participants remained fixated on money. That's a mistake because there are other issues on which you might get them to move, making the lower salary more attractive.

Stock Options

If there is a lesson from the dot-com gold rush of the late 1990s, it is that you should not accept stock options in place of salary. Taking a job at a minimal salary in exchange for a piece of paper saying you can buy the stock at $8 when it was climbing past $35 seemed like a great idea. But six months later, when the option can be exercised, the stock price may be at 25 cents.

Stock options as a way to sweeten a basically acceptable offer are another thing. But remember: It's a gamble. You can't see into the future, and neither can the company. Think—if a company was to offer you a bushel of lottery tickets, would you be interested? Actually, you might. But you would not confuse it with salary.

Start Time

They probably want you to start now, or at least in two weeks. You probably have other business to wrap up. Relocating also takes time. So decide what you want, and put that on the table.

Vacation

Maybe you want immediate vacation time so that you can move your family and help your children adjust. Maybe you want more vacation time, period. An alternative is something called sabbaticals—unpaid but sanctioned vacation time that can extend for months, with the stipulation that you don't spend it working for a competitor.

Benefits

You may want immediate health insurance coverage while asking for a delayed start time. Or there may be benefits that you don't want (perhaps because your spouse has better coverage) and would rather see the difference added to your salary. But in a large corporation the difference may be, in the corporation's view, not worth the trouble to make the changes.

Negotiating Tips

Once you decide what you want, it's time to go get it. But you need to circle the prey a few times before striking, as the following tactics indicate.

Silence Is Your Friend

Make your counteroffer and then fall silent. Let them respond. If you can't think of anything to say when hearing the initial offer, then say nothing until you have made a decision (or decided to ask for time to think about it). If they feel a little guilty knowing this is a lowball offer, they may hear your silence as polite disapproval and may scurry to sweeten the offer. (I once received an offer on a day that I had a cold. When the interviewer stated the amount, I responded by clearing my throat—I had to anyway. "Oh, well, let me look at the spreadsheet," the guy said—and then raised the amount by 15 percent.)

Aim High

An engineer once relayed this advice he got from a fellow engineer who was an Asian immigrant. "You go. You ask for moon. They give moon? You take."

Generally, you don't get what you don't ask for. But before you open your mouth, you have to understand the difference between "high" and "ridiculous." Do the research.

Be Realistic

They may not be able to match your demands. Or your demands may make them philosophical about hiring someone else. But, as already mentioned, there may be things other than money they can offer.

Be Professional

The amount of the offer (in fact, the existence of the job itself) is a manifestation of the market process, and you should not take it personally. This is business. Your behavior during negotiations should reflect the businesslike way they can expect you to perform on the job—rather than giving them a peek at the kind of tantrums you can throw when you feel slighted. Meanwhile, remember that the HR person is just doing his or her job.

Be Clear, but Flexible

Get all your concerns listed. Do not keep any secrets about how you feel about each. If the HR person manages to get together a meaningful response, do not counter with a new list. Be willing to sacrifice money for something else.

Counteroffers

One final word: If you are looking for a job simply to get an offer so that you will have leverage to ask for a raise at your present job, the effort could backfire. While your employer may indeed come back with a counteroffer acceptable enough to make you stay, the company may also fear that you will pull this stunt again. Also, your actions have put out the message that you are ready to leave at the first good offer. So your current employer may plan on you doing so and may even begin looking for a replacement. As you feel the ice of distrust forming around you, you will realize that you also snubbed the people who offered you the other job, effectively burning a bridge that you may later decide you should have taken.

People take job searching seriously, and if you don't, you may wish you had. So take the advice given here to heart.

And whatever your reasons for job hunting, good luck.

Glossary

Alphanumeric Refers to data that can be represented by keys on the keyboard, transmitted as a character code, such as ASCII. Numeric data, while represented on the screen in alphanumeric fashion, is stored using a format that recognizes the value of the number.

Animation The GIF file format—one of the formats used for graphics files on the Web—allows multiple images to be, basically, stacked on atop another in the file. If multiple images are present, the browser will automatically display one after another, allowing a small (and silent) animation to be added to the page without any programming.

AOL (America Online) This commercial online service, which seems intent on paving the Earth with promotional discs, amounts to a subset of the Internet with commercial features and a centrally managed network, plus a flashy proprietary interface.

Applet A small program, usually in a language called Java, which can be embedded in the HTML code of a Web page and run by the user's browser when the page loads. They are not supposed to be full-fledged programs that can take over the computer.

Archive A compressed file that, when decompressed, forms a collection of files. Or an online storage area used by a particular conference, forum, or newsgroup.

ASCII text A message whose content is restricted to the ASCII character set, without enhancements such as boldfacing, italics, underlining, and tab settings.

ASCII American Standard Code for Information Interchange. The computer character code in common use except in IBM mainframes. Similar versions exist for various European languages.

Async Asynchronous, the start-stop style of data communications used in the PC world.

Asynchronous In data communications, signals that are not synchronized to any timing signal but instead consist of discrete bytes whose spacing may be random.

Attachments Files that accompany an e-mail message. Although the e-mail message is limited to ASCII text or, at best, HTML text, the file can be anything.

Audio streaming The process of broadcasting audio clips from a Web page.

B2B Business to business.

B2C Business to consumer.

Bandwidth In the computer arena, bandwidth is the volume of material that you can move through a connection.

BBS Computer bulletin-board system, often offering e-mail, discussion conferences, and file libraries, maintained as a hobby or for business purposes, often running on a PC. BBSs used to be a flourishing subculture, but today the Web has supplanted them.

Binary A base-2 system number system, using only the integers 1 and 0.

Bit A single binary integer—a single 1 or a single 0.

Bits per second The speed rating of a data communications connection, referring to how many bits that can be moved in a second. Today's modems can achieve speeds of close to fifty thousand bits per second, depending on line conditions. Typical DSL lines can achieve at most about nine megabits per second downstream and three hundred thousand upstream, but the maximum falls off rapidly as the user gets farther away from the telephone company's central office. Cable modem speeds vary from network to network but usually run about two megabits downstream and maybe three hundred thousand bits per second upstream. However, the bandwidth may be shared by a neighborhood. Ethernet connections can offer either 10 or 100 million bits (megabits) per second, and optical fiber can carry multiple channels each running at 10 (sometimes 40) billion bits (gigabits) per second.

Blue screen of death A condition sometimes encountered when upgrading from one version of Windows to another, where the installation software has erased the previous operating system but has encountered a problem that prevents it from installing the new operating system. This leaves the system unusable.

Bluetooth Short-range (10-meter) radio technology to connect computers and peripherals at about seven hundred thousand bits per second, as a replacement for wiring, especially in mobile devices.

Bogus Not real. A bogus Usenet newsgroup is one that is not carried by all ISPs or one in worldwide circulation that has no content.

Broadband Any connection to the Internet that is faster than a dial-up modem, especially DSL and cable modems. (That's the current usage. Old-timers remember when broadband implied that you had enough bandwidth to run full-motion full-screen video.)

Browser wars The struggle for market share between Microsoft (with Internet Explorer) and Netscape (with Navigator, later Communicator) by giving away the product. Netscape has faded after an early lead and was acquired by AOL.

Browser The software on a user's machine that interprets the HTML formatting codes in a Web file and displays the material on the screen. It also executes the hypertext links, thus giving the user access to the World Wide Web when connected to a Web host.

BTW By the way. "BTW, we missed you yesterday."

Byte Eight binary integers, which gives 256 possible code permutations (two raised to the power of 8).

C Programming language commonly used by professionals for commercial projects. The latest version is C++.

Cable modem A method of getting broadband access to the Internet through an existing cable television network. Cable modems are more popular than DSL for home users because many homes in the United States and Canada already have access to a cable network. However, each home shares it bandwidth with other homes in the neighborhood. Speeds vary but can reach two megabits per second.

Call waiting A special service offered to telephone subscribers whereby someone talking on the phone can answer a second incoming call and switch between the two conversations. Unfortunately, the call waiting tone can knock a modem off-line. SOHO users therefore often get a second phone line without call waiting and use it for modem and fax connection.

Central office The phone company facility in which individual lines from nearby homes or businesses are combined onto a trunk line. The term is archaic—the central office is neither central (there are scads of them in any city) nor even an office (being automated).

Chat A conversational connection with one or more members of a network, whereby the messages of each can be seen and responded to immediately, in real time. Web sites and online services often host "chat rooms," whereas IRC (Internet relay chat) is an Internet service entirely devoted to chatting.

CLEC Competitive local exchange carrier, an upstart phone company offering either voice (usually to business customers) or data (usually DSL) in competition with the local phone company or ILEC. The ILEC owns the phone facilities and lines, but under U.S. law it must be willing to rent them to the CLECs.

Co-location Typically, the term refers to the practice of installing a server you own on the premises of a host provider in order to enjoy its high-speed backbone line, maintenance, and security.

Compatibility Refers to the ability of hardware and software to work together, regardless of their origins.

Compression Method of making files consume fewer bytes for easier storage or faster transmission.

Conference Online discussion forum devoted to a specific topic.

Cookie A line of identifying data that the server gives to a browser upon its first visit, which the browser is expected to store and give back to the server when it visits again or asks for another page. No browser currently in circulation will identify the user by name to a server, but cookies let the server recognize a user as someone, for example, who has been there before or someone whose shopping cart contains.

Counter A number, often placed on the bottom of the page, showing how many times the page has been viewed. This feature is not automatic and must be rigged through HTML applet coding.

Cyberspace Everything that happens online.

Database A collection of data configured for easy access and analysis by specialized software.

Dial-up access To access the Internet or other online service using a modem and a standard phone line, as opposed to using a broadband connection.

Digital Communication method whereby data is encoded in binary form.

Dittoheads. People who quote excessively from conference messages they are replying to.

Domain name The identifying portion of a URL. At www.wiley.com, the domain name is wiley.com. The .com means "commercial." There is also .net (net enterprises), .gov (government sites), .mil (military sites), .edu (colleges and universities), and .org (for nonprofit organizations). A new generation of suffixes is being promoted, but with mixed results. Overseas, a suffix is added to identify the country. For example, www.ourplace.com.ca would be a Canadian (not Californian) site.

DSL Digital subscriber line, a broadband Internet connection that can be offered over standard copper phone lines—as long as you are close enough to the phone company's central office. If you are, you can get nine megabits per second from the Internet and 300 kilobits per second to the Internet. If you are not, speed falls with distance, until at about 20,000 feet it is no better than a dial-up modem. (Older phone lines also cannot be used at all.) The phone company often limits access to 12,000 feet. DSL is more popular with businesses than cable modems because the connection is not shared and because businesses are more likely to be close to a central office. DSL is often referred to as xDSL because there are various flavors.

Emoticons Alphanumeric creations that substitute for the writer's facial expressions in otherwise sterile text files. (AOL has them built into its e-mail system.) Some examples:

->	tongue in cheek
(o.-)	wink
(O.O)	wide-eyed amazement

(@.@) total shock
:-) smile face (sideways)
:-(frown face (sideways)
!@#$% &* expletive

Encryption The process of turning text or other data into what appears to be random gibberish to anyone who does not have the decryption key.

ERP Enterprise resource planning. Corporate system that plans what is needed tomorrow on the basis of what is being manufactured today and what was sold yesterday.

FAQ Frequently asked questions. An informational file concerning a specific Web site or Usenet newsgroup, explaining its purpose and answering basic questions that newcomers would be expected to ask.

Fax Facsimile transmission, involving sending the image on a page to be reproduced by a distant facsimile (fax) machine. Most data modems can also (with appropriate software) send and receive fax images, so that you can print out your word-processing file on anyone's fax machine.

File uploading To transmit a file, of any description, so that a copy of it ends up on the receiving machine.

Flamers Online users engaged in flaming. Lacking the visual cues that give extra meaning to face-to-face conversation, people can drift into and out of flaming without understanding what is going on.

Flames Online messages, usually in newsgroups, discussion forums, and chat rooms, that constitute a heated exchange, quarrel, or feud between two or more users.

Frames An HTML feature whereby a Web page can display contents from multiple HTML files, allowing for more sophisticated presentation. Typically, they will have the site contents in a narrow column on the left side of the screen, and the file being read in a wide column on the right. Older browsers cannot display frames, and not all search engines can follow links from a frame-based index page. Therefore, sites based on frames often include a link to a no-frames version of the site.

Freeware Software that is given away free, although the originator may still retain copyright.

FTP File transfer protocol. The most common method of moving files between two Internet sites. In a practice predating the advent of HTTP and the Web, many sites "publish" files by placing them in subdirectory that can be reached using "anonymous" as the password. These are called "anonymous ftp servers" but in fact have names and remain in contact with their families.

FUBAR Fouled (ahem) up beyond all redemption. Test or demo files are often named foo.bar, indicating a schism between the fields of computer science and etymology.

FUD Fear, uncertainty, doubt. The ruling emotions of corporate computer buyers, traditionally dispelled by writing a check to IBM.

FWIW For what it's worth. "He's just running his mouth, FWIW."

Graphics Refers to a computer's ability to plot individual pixels on the screen, rather than simply displaying alphanumeric text as if it were a glass typewriter, as was the case with original PC and other early examples.

Hacker (1) Programmer who uses intuitive, seat-of-the pants methods—"hacking" at a problem until it's solved. (2) Online intruder who gains unauthorized entry into a computer system or network. (Voice-mail systems have also been subject to hack attacks.)

Headers In e-mail, the date, sender's name, subject, recipient's name, and routing details. To see full details, you need to find a View Full Header or Page Source command.

Hit The act of a server sending a file from a site to a browser. Some Web entities use hits to boast of their site's popularity. But any given page may contain multiple files, and the sending of each file will be counted as a hit, inflating the count. Therefore, the hits that count are "page impressions" or "page views"—the hits on the page's underlying HTML file.

Home page, Homepage The opening page of a site, the first one a visitor normally sees, also called the index page.

Host A computer that performs an ongoing service, such as running a Web site.

Hosting provider An enterprise that provides Web space to third parties, usually for money. Typically it does not provide dial-in Web access, such as an ISP does.

HTML Hypertext markup language. The formatting language used to create Web pages. HTML controls the layout of the material, using control codes placed inside angle brackets (<>) called "tags" that a Web browser is programmed to respond to. Tags unknown to a browser are ignored, making it easy to create new generations or flavors of HTML or to add programming commands that affect the server.

HTTP Hypertext transport protocol. The protocol for moving Web files across the Internet. The servers that use HTTP comprise the subset of the Internet called the World Wide Web.

Hypertext A system akin to automated footnoting. Invoking material with a hypertext link will cause the display of the material it is linked to. The World Wide Web is based on hypertext, allowing users to navigate the Internet without knowing anything about Internet protocols.

IC Integrated circuit—a "chip."

ILEC Incumbent local exchange carrier, the local phone company that owns the lines, central offices, and other PSTN components in a region.

Image map An image that has been mapped into hypertext links, so that clicking on different parts of it will trigger links to different files. A national map may have a different link for each state, for instance.

IMHO In my humble (or honest) opinion. "IMHO, you're mistaken."

Internet A network of networks, all sharing the same addressing scheme and transmission protocol. The World Wide Web is the subset of the Internet that relies on HTTP.

IOW In other words. "IOW, you don't agree?"

IP Internet protocol. The addressing and data handling scheme used internally by the Internet.

IRC Internet relay chat, the Internet version of a chat room.

ISDN Integrated services digital networks, digital phones lines that run at about 128 thousand bits per second. For 20 years ISDN was seen as the future of the phone network. Today, DSL and cable modems have passed it by, but you can get ISDN even if DSL or cable is not available. Also, you need it for industrial-grade videoconferencing connections.

ISP Internet service provider. An enterprise that provides third parties with access to the Internet, usually for a fee. Typically, an ISP also provides hosting.

Java Programming language used for applets—small programs downloaded with a Web page and run by the browser.

JavaScript Programming language similar to intent to Java, but much simpler.

K As a telecommunications term, K means thousand, so that 28.8k bits per second means 28,800 bits per second. In computer science, it more properly means 2 raised to the 10th power, or 1,024. Therefore, in any discussion of storage, there are more bytes available than the figure indicates.

Keyword A word input by a user to a Web search engine (or other database system) to get a list of the Web sites (or database entries) that contain that keyword.

Kill file A list kept by news-reader software, so that a particular posting will not be downloaded if it was written by someone on the list or if the posting's subject line includes a particular name or word.

Kilobits Transmitted bits measured in increments of one thousand.

Kilobytes Stored bytes measured in increments of 1,024.

LAN Local area network, an arrangement whereby computers can share each other's disk files and other peripherals, usually through coaxial cable or some other method of direct connection. Ethernet is the most common LAN protocol seen in offices.

Linux Committee-written operating system often used for servers, although Windows emulation is available for desktop use. Officially freeware, it is often bought on "distribution disks" from vendors whom the buyers hope will provide technical support.

Log off To issue the necessary commands to end a connection with a remote computer.

Log on To complete the necessary steps to connect with and use a remote computer.

LOL Laugh (or laughing) out loud. "Your message left me LOL."

M In computer science, M means million, not thousand.

Macro A simple program that (usually) plays back a series of keystrokes and thus automates a chore or task, such as setting up a word-processing document or printing an envelope. Some macro languages include elaborate programming functions.

Mail bomb Vast quantities of e-mail sent to a particular address in order to crash the account, sometimes done to take revenge on spammers.

Mailing list A sort of inverted newsgroup, contributions sent to the list's e-mail address are automatically forwarded to everyone on its subscriber list. Some lists are moderated. Like newsgroups, mailing lists can be rife with flaming.

Megabit One million transmitted bits.

Megabyte 1,048,576 (2 raised to the power of 20) stored bytes.

Megahertz One million cycles per second. In references to radio, it refers to transmission frequency, but in computer science it refers to the speed of the computer's internal clock—the original PC ran slightly under 5 million cycles per second, and the latest processors run faster than a thousand megahertz. In the first microcomputers, it took multiple cycles to accomplish any meaningful operation, but the latest machines are down to one cycle or so per operation.

Message base All the messages posted in a particular conference.

Modem The interface device between a computer and the phone line.

Moderator Someone who monitors the traffic in a particular conference or newsgroup, settling quarrels and keeping discussion on track.

Multitasking The ability to run multiple programs at the same time, as opposed to loading multiple programs but running only one.

News The traffic of messages in Usenet newsgroups. Also, that stuff about world events that is read to you by talking heads on television.

Newsgroup Individual discussion conference on Usenet.

News Reader Software that lets you download unread messages in newsgroups you belong to, read them off-line, write comments off-line and then upload the comments.

Online The act of communicating with a remote computer of any kind.

OTOH On the other hand. "OTOH, we may both be wrong."

Page impression/view A hit involving a Web page, without regard to the number of files it may contain.

Parallel Data connection where each bit in a byte has its own line. Parallel connections were the mainstay of printers and similar peripherals, but USB is supplanting them.

PC Personal Computer. A microcomputer that uses the Wintel architecture, meaning that Windows (or DOS) software for the Intel line of processors (8088 through the Pentium dynasty, plus processors from Advanced Micro Devices and other clone-makers) will run on it. A PC running Linux or other operating system is usually not referred to as a PC.

Phone phreak A phone-system hacker who takes control of phone company switching equipment in order to make free long-distance phone calls or prevent his or her calls from being traced while computer hacking.

PIN Personal identification number, the form of password protection used primarily by automatic teller machines, security "tokens," and smart cards.

Pixel One dot on the display screen.

Platform The combination of hardware and operating system that defines a particular, standardized, computing environment.

Plain Text Text that is composed of ASCII characters, with no software-dependent enhancements, such as underlining or boldfacing. "With line breaks" means that the text is saved with an end-of-line character at the end of each line, turning each line into a separate short paragraph. (In ASCII, the end-of-line character is also used as the end-of-paragraph character.) Otherwise, each paragraph is saved as one long line. Without word wrapping, such lines may extend off the right edge of the screen.

Ponzi scheme Named after Charles Ponzi, who ran a pyramid scheme in Boston in 1920. Investors are promised high rates of return, and initial payments are made that reflect those rates. The payees are merely getting the money of later investors, but word of the apparently juicy investment draws more investors, whose money fuels further payouts, until the stream of new investors dries up, the scheme collapses, and the perpetrator absconds—or the authorities intervene.

POP (1) Post office protocol. The protocol that your e-mail software uses to fetch e-mail from your host's mail system. It lets anyone get e-mail from any host anywhere, as long as they have the e-mail address and password. (2) Point of presence. The place (usually downtown) where you can get a connection to your carrier's network.

Portal A Web site listing other Web sites and online services, sources of information, and chat rooms, offered by itself or other sites, of interest to a particular population.

PSTN Public switched telephone network. If you can pick up a phone and dial another phone that is outside your organization, then your phone is attached to the PSTN.

Pyramid scheme A scam (also called a Ponzi scheme), constantly rediscovered by get-rich-quick spammers, in which returns on an investment are actually derived from the input of later investors rather than any commercial activity.

ROTFL Rolling on the floor, laughing.

RTFM Read the friendly (ahem) manual.

RYFM Read your friendly (ahem) manual. Variant of RTFM.

Script file A record of the commands necessary to (usually) log on to a remote system, used with a modem software package to automate the procedure.

Script kiddies Juvenile hackers who use script files they find on the Internet to try to hack into Internet servers. Usually they can only get into a computer that has already been compromised by another hacker.

Search engine A Web site tied to a database that catalogs or searches the Web. Because the Web changes faster than it can be searched or cataloged, no search engine can offer comprehensive, real-time coverage.

Serial port Input/output connection on a computer designed to be used with a modem or modemlike device (such as certain printers or scanners).

Serial Data connection in which all the bits of every byte are sent sequentially and serially down the same line. Used for modem connections and for certain peripherals.

Server Strictly speaking, a server is just a computer that provides a specific service to another computer, called the client. On the Internet, a server is a computer that transmits files to clients who request them or that runs certain programs. On the Web, the "clients" are users at their desktops running browsers. The computer that hosts your site, the computer that forwards your e-mail, and the computer that runs the multiuser game you're addicted to are all servers.

Shareware Software that is distributed without charge, but the originator expects to be paid if the person who acquires it makes serious use of it. Payment may also bring an expanded version, with vendor support.

Signature Personalized billboardlike presentation at the end of a message or posting, to add personality and authenticity.

Site A set of linked Web pages accessible through a single address, typically devoted to one purpose and maintained by one party.

SOHO Small office/home office, not (in this case) south of Houston.

Spam Bulk, unsolicited promotional e-mail of an annoying nature. Typically, the less targeted the e-mail is, the more moronic (and persistent) the come-on, with the crowded nadir belonging to pyramid schemes and get-rich-quick chain letters. The term *spam* is said to come not directly from a brand name for canned spiced ham, but from a Monty Python sketch.

Spoof In reference to e-mail, to send a message with a false return address in order to cover the source of spam.

SSL Secure sockets layer. An Internet protocol designed to encrypt online credit card transactions.

Store and forward The mode that most e-mail uses, whereby messages are stored until forwarded to the receiver, usually when the receiver eventually logs in.

Surfing The act of casually looking around on the Internet.

T-1 A digital phone line that can carry 1.544 megabits per second, sometimes licensed by business users not satisfied with DSL and by ISPs to link to an Internet backbone.

T-3 A digital phone line that runs at 44.736 megabits per second, used for trunk lines between cities.

Thread Messages within a conference that address the same theme. Usually, they are comments on the same original posting. Some software allows you to read a particular thread in a conference to the exclusion of other messages.

TINAR This is not a review/recommendation.

TLA Three-letter acronym/abbreviation.

Toolbar An on-screen arrangement of icons that will call up functions pertinent to the task at hand.

Unix Also rendered as UNIX. An operating system, originated by AT&T, designed for multiuser systems, with built-in telecommunications functions.

URL Uniform resource locator. Addressing protocol for files on the World Wide Web.

USB Universal serial bus, a connection type that is expected to replace both serial and parallel ports, as well as mouse and keyboard connectors. USB offers a connection speed of 12 million bits per second. USB devices support Plug and Play and can be hot-plugged, meaning that you can connect them while the computer is on and the computer will notice them and configure itself to support them. A USB port can support 127 devices, although you have to use special hubs.

Usenet A semiformal network of discussion conferences associated with the Internet, although also carried by other networks. Individual conferences are called newsgroups.

Video streaming The process of broadcasting video from a Web server.

Virus In the computer world, a self-replicating program that attaches itself to a legitimate program (such as an operating system utility) and seeks to attach copies of itself to other programs. May also cause damage to the system, intentionally or otherwise.

Web page What you see on the screen when you go to a specific Web address, being the sum total of the contents of the HTML file at that address and any graphic files that it links to, as formatted on the screen by your browser.

Windows A graphical user interface for the PC from Microsoft.

Wintel Windows-Intel, the architecture of the PC.

World Wide Web That part of the Internet using the HTTP protocol and HTML files, whose users depend on graphical browsers. It is officially rendered as three words, not two.

Index